THOMAS AND THE GOSPELS

Thomas and the Gospels

The Making of an Apocryphal Text

Mark Goodacre

Published in the United States of America in 2012 as
Thomas *and the Gospels: The Case for* Thomas's *Familiarity with the Synoptics* by
Wm. B. Eerdmans Publishing Company, 2140 Oak Industrial Dr. N.E.,
Grand Rapids, Michigan 49505

First published in Great Britain in 2012

Society for Promoting Christian Knowledge
36 Causton Street
London SW1P 4ST
www.spckpublishing.co.uk

British Library Cataloguing-in-Publication Data
A catalogue record for this book is available from the British Library

ISBN 978–0–281–06776–3
eBook ISBN 978–0–281–06777–0

First printed in Great Britain by MPG Books
Subsequently digitally printed in Great Britain

eBook by Graphicraft Limited, Hong Kong

Produced on paper from sustainable forests

Contents

Preface

This is a book about *Thomas* and the Gospels. That "and" is worth under-lining. The book is not just about the *Gospel of Thomas*, but also about the Synoptic Gospels. It explores the relationship between *Thomas* and the Synoptic Gospels, an exploration that will at times require some detailed discussion of the Synoptics Gospels themselves. This makes the book unusual. In spite of the fact that it remains one of the most vexed questions in the study of Christian origins, not a single monograph in English explores the case that *Thomas* knew the Synoptic Gospels.

Many studies of the *Gospel of Thomas* work hard to try to understand the evolution of this enigmatic text, but they remain ambivalent about the idea that *Thomas* was familiar with the Synoptic Gospels. It may be the case, though, that *Thomas*'s relationship with the Synoptics provides a gateway to the study of the Gospel. Once one has considered the evidence for *Thomas*'s knowledge of the Synoptic Gospels, questions about how, when, and why the author used the Synoptics naturally follow.

Although many readers will, quite understandably, wish to dip into selected chapters, this book attempts to construct an argument in order along the following lines. In chapter 1 ("First Impressions"), I explore the way that the issue appears on early acquaintance with it, looking at some of the general arguments offered for an independent *Thomas*, and drawing attention to the telling argument from *Thomas*'s parallels to every strand of Synoptic data. In chapter 2 ("Verbatim Agreement between *Thomas* and the Synoptics"), I argue that there has been a missing step in many discussions of *Thomas*'s relationship to the Synoptics and that the verbatim agreements suggest a direct relationship between *Thomas* and the Synoptic Gospels. In chapters 3 to 6 I argue that this relationship is one of *Thomas*'s familiarity with the Synoptics, established by "Diagnostic Shards" (chapter 3) of Matthean redaction (chapter 4) and Lukan redaction (chapter 5) appearing in *Thomas*, with a special case saved for its own chapter, *Thomas* 79 and Luke (chapter 6). One of the characteristics of *Thomas*'s appropriation of the Synoptics is the phenomenon of "The Missing Middle" (chapter 7), where the middle section of Synoptic sayings and parables goes missing in the Thomasine parallel, sometimes leaving an inconcinnity. Phenomena like this lead to questions about the manner of *Thomas*'s knowledge of the Synoptics, which raises questions about orality and literacy in the early Christian movement. In chapter 8 ("Orality, Literacy, and *Thomas*") I explore the renewed stress on orality in recent scholarship and suggest that the role played by literacy should not be underestimated, and that there are difficulties with the search for primitive oral traditions in *Thomas*. In chapter 9 ("Dating *Thomas* and the Gospels") I argue that the Synoptic Gospels postdate 70 CE and that *Thomas* postdates 135 CE. In chapter 10 ("Secrecy, Authority, and Legitimation: How and Why *Thomas* used the Synoptics") I contend that *Thomas* reworked material from the Synoptic Gospels in order to lend legitimacy to his sayings, to provide an authentic-sounding Synoptic voice for its secret, living Jesus.

This book is ambitious in only one respect, the attempt to argue the case for *Thomas*'s familiarity with the Synoptic Gospels, a case that I think is stronger than it is usually perceived to be. I have not attempted to solve all the problems faced by scholars of the *Gospel of Thomas*, and I have tried to keep the discussion focused on this key issue, an issue that as a student of the Synoptic Problem I find to be one of particular interest.

Since my previous book was an attack on a well-beloved and time-honored element in New Testament studies, the Q hypothesis, I have faced a dilemma in writing this book that is like Elizabeth Bennett's predicament as she ponders Mr. Collins's proposal. "An unhappy alternative is before you, Elizabeth. From this day you must be a stranger to one of your parents. Your mother will never see you again if you do not marry Mr. Collins, and I will never see you again if you do." I think that the case against Q helps one to see the case for *Thomas*'s familiarity with the Synoptics, but I am aware that this is a view that will alienate some of my readers, who remain attached to Q. But I risk alienating others if I pretend to ownership of a hypothesis against which I am a public opponent. My solution has been to proceed by working on the basis of the generally held common ground of Markan priority, for which I have been an enthusiastic advocate, and to point to possible difficulties with the use of the Q hypothesis to bolster the case for *Thomas*'s independence, but at the same time to relegate discussion of Luke's familiarity with Matthew to the footnotes. I hope that the case has not been expounded with pride, and that it will not be received with prejudice.

Except where otherwise stated, English translations are my own.

I would like to thank my colleagues in the Religion Department at Duke University, as well as in the Graduate Program in Religion, for their encouragement and interest while I have been writing this book. I would like to offer special thanks to those who have read all or parts of the manuscript, and have offered many helpful comments and criticisms, especially Loren Rosson, Stephen Carlson, Ken Olson, Michael Grondin, Jeffrey Peterson, and Andrew Bernhard. And the biggest thank-you is to Viola, Emily, and Lauren for their love, support, and patience.

I wish I had managed to finish this book before Michael Goulder's death in January 2010. Although he was not a scholar of the *Gospel of Thomas* his brilliant contributions to the study of Christian origins, still underestimated or ignored by too many, have influenced my own thinking in many ways. He would always ask about the progress of the book and would love to discuss it. I cannot now present him with a copy, but I can at least dedicate it to his memory, with gratitude and great affection.

Abbreviations

AB	Anchor Bible
ABD	*Anchor Bible Dictionary*
AJT	*American Journal of Theology*
Ant.	Josephus, *Antiquities of the Jews*
BA	*Biblical Archaeologist*
BBR	*Bulletin for Biblical Research*
BETL	Bibliotheca ephemeridum theologicarum lovaniensium
BTB	*Biblical Theology Bulletin*
BZ	*Biblische Zeitschrift*
BZNW	Beiheft zur *ZNW*
CBQ	*Catholic Biblical Quarterly*
ET	English Translation
ETL	*Ephemerides theologicae lovanienses*
ExpT	*Expository Times*
HE	Eusebius, *Historia ecclesiastica*
HTR	*Harvard Theological Review*
HTS	Harvard Theological Studies
ICC	International Critical Commentary
IQP	International Q Project
JBL	*Journal of Biblical Literature*
JSHJ	*Journal for the Study of the Historical Jesus*
JSNT	*Journal for the Study of the New Testament*
JSNTSup	Journal for the Study of the New Testament Supplement Series
JSP	*Journal for the Study of the Pseudepigrapha*
JTS	*Journal of Theological Studies*
J.W.	Josephus, *Jewish War*

Abbreviations

KJV	King James Version
L	Special Lukan material
LD	Lectio divina
LNTS	Library of New Testament Studies
LXX	Septuagint
M	Special Matthean material
NA²⁷	Nestle-Aland, *Novum Testamentum Graece*, 27th ed., 1993
NH	Nag Hammadi
NHS	Nag Hammadi Studies
NIV	New International Version
NovT	*Novum Testamentum*
NovTSup	Supplements to Novum Testamentum
NRSV	New Revised Standard Version
NTS	*New Testament Studies*
PIBA	Proceedings of the Irish Biblical Association
P.Oxy.	Oxyrhynchus Papyri
QC	words in double tradition passages common to Matthew and Luke
QD	words in double tradition passages differing in Matthew and Luke
R	redaction (with Gospel references)
RBL	*Review of Biblical Literature*
RHR	*Revue de l'histoire des religions*
RRT	*Reviews in Religion and Theology*
RSV	Revised Standard Version
SBL	Society of Biblical Literature
SBLDS	SBL Dissertation Series
SBLSymS	SBL Symposium Series
TU	Texte und Untersuchungen zur Geschichte der altchristlichen Literatur
SJT	*Scottish Journal of Theology*
VC	*Vigiliae christianae*
WMANT	Wissenschaftliche Monographien zum Alten und Neuen Testament
WUNT	Wissenschaftliche Untersuchungen zum Neuen Testament
ZNW	*Zeitschrift für die neutestamentliche Wissenschaft*

First Impressions

The Gospel of Thomas is the noncanonical gospel par excellence. It has been studied more than all the other noncanonical gospels put together, and for good reason.[1] Among all of the extant gospels that did not make it into the New Testament canon, this is the one that has the best claim to antiquity, the only one that provides the potential for extended reflection on the sayings of the historical Jesus.[2] However much we may wish to draw attention to the importance of understanding the development of Christianity in the second century, reaching back into the first century is still far more attractive to most historians of Christian origins. There is romance in the idea that this text, so recently discovered, could provide a special witness to the earliest phase of Christianity.[3]

For many, the text takes its place in a dynamic early Christian world in which variety and diversity are the chief characteristics. Words like "orthodoxy" are firmly out of favor. Talk of "Christianities" is in. Indeed, the discovery of the *Gospel of Thomas* provided a catalyst for the development of this perspective in which it now plays such a major role. The impetus for

---

1. Bart D. Ehrman, *Jesus: Apocalyptic Prophet of the New Millennium* (Oxford: Oxford University Press, 1999), 71, describes it as "without question the most significant Christian book discovered in modern times."

2. Its main competitors for attention in historical Jesus studies do not feature sayings from Jesus' ministry. Our only major extant fragment of the *Gospel of Peter*, for example, deals with the passion and resurrection.

3. See Stevan L. Davies, "Thomas: The Fourth Synoptic Gospel," *BA* 46/1 (1983): 6-9, 12-14, for an illustration of this kind of enthusiasm: "The Gospel of Thomas was buried away for 1600 years and has been wished away for another 30. It should now be taken very seriously. Not only is it a fourth synoptic gospel — it is a Q, too" (14).

this new approach, in some senses its manifesto, was *Trajectories through Early Christianity* by James Robinson and Helmut Koester, first published in 1971.[4] The book was in part a development of and in part a reaction to Rudolf Bultmann's views, now packaged for a new era. Early Christian diversity looms large, and newly discovered early Christian texts take their place in a world of competing trajectories. *The Gospel of Thomas*, unavailable in full to Bultmann when he was writing his seminal *History of the Synoptic Tradition*,[5] now rises to new prominence alongside the hypothetical source Q, as two early witnesses to a passion-free, sayings-based trajectory in early Christianity, which contrasted with the passion-centered, Pauline-influenced versions of Christianity that later won the day.

Trajectories has influenced a generation of scholarship on Christian origins, and its legacy is perhaps most pronounced in the key contributions of scholars like Robert Funk[6] and John Dominic Crossan,[7] most famous for their prominence in the Jesus Seminar,[8] who have applied a model that prioritizes Q and *Thomas* in historical Jesus research. The responsible historical Jesus scholar now works outside canonical boundaries, and those who ignore texts like *Thomas* are chastised for their canonical bias. They are seen as engaging in a kind of stubborn, confessional attempt to skew the field by ignoring much of the best evidence.

Many of the major books published on *Thomas* in the last generation are indebted to a model of Christian origins that is inspired by *Trajectories*. Perhaps most importantly, Stephen Patterson's influential *Gospel of Thomas and Jesus* argues the case for an early, autonomous *Thomas* that enables us to reassess its witness to the historical Jesus and the movement he inspired.[9]

4. James M. Robinson and Helmut Koester, *Trajectories through Early Christianity* (Philadelphia: Fortress, 1971).

5. Rudolf Bultmann, *History of the Synoptic Tradition* (ET; 2nd ed.; Oxford: Blackwell, 1968). It is worth noting that Bultmann already took full advantage of the P.Oxy. fragments that were later discovered to be early Greek fragmentary witnesses to the *Gospel of Thomas*.

6. See, for example, Robert Funk, *Honest to Jesus: Jesus for a New Millennium* (San Francisco: HarperSanFrancisco, 1996).

7. John Dominic Crossan, *The Historical Jesus: The Life of a Mediterranean Jewish Peasant* (San Francisco: HarperSanFrancisco, 1991); idem, *The Birth of Christianity: Discovering What Happened in the Years Immediately After the Execution of Jesus* (San Francisco: HarperSanFrancisco, 1998).

8. Robert W. Funk, Roy Hoover, and the Jesus Seminar, *The Five Gospels: The Search for the Authentic Words of Jesus* (New York: Macmillan, 1993).

9. Stephen J. Patterson, *The Gospel of Thomas and Jesus* (Foundations and Facets; Sonoma, CA: Polebridge, 1993).

The idea that *Thomas* is familiar with the Gospels can seem unwelcome. If *Thomas* derives much of the material it shares with the Synoptics from the Synoptics themselves, then one of the key elements in the *Trajectories* model disappears. No longer would *Thomas* be an early, independent witness to primitive Jesus tradition or to early, variant Christian ideologies. It is easy, in such circumstances, for a case in favor of *Thomas's* knowledge of the Synoptics to be seen as something of a recalcitrant, spoilsport attempt to hark back to a position that is now passé.[10] Unless there are new arguments, and new perspectives, the case for an autonomous *Thomas* remains a highly attractive one to anyone interested in exploring the diversity of early Christianity. Given the difficulty in making progress in scholarship, some might feel that the last thing we want is to undo the fine work of the last generation and to set back the clock to a bland, monochrome view of Christian origins.

If the case for *Thomas's* familiarity with the Synoptics is now sometimes regarded as old-fashioned or reactionary,[11] it is further damaged, in the minds of some, by its association with a particular ideological stance. *Thomas's* familiarity with the Synoptics is often regarded as an essentially conservative case, argued by those who are keen to police canonical boundaries and align the earliest forms of Christianity with emerging orthodoxy. The crucified and risen Savior then remains the heart of a unified early Christian kerygma, witnessed alike by the evangelists, Paul, the General Epistles, and Revelation. The perception is understandable.[12] Several scholars who identify themselves as evangelicals are among those who argue for a later, dependent *Thomas*,[13] and the relegation of *Thomas* to the second century is becoming a major theme in scholarly works of Christian apolo-

10. Cf. Ron Cameron, "Ancient Myths and Modern Theories of the *Gospel of Thomas* and Christian Origins," in Ron Cameron and Merrill P. Miller, eds., *Redescribing Christian Origins* (SBLSymS 28; Atlanta: Society of Biblical Literature, 2004), 89-108 (91): "The effects of subordinating the *Gospel of Thomas* to the canonical Gospels are especially pernicious, in that *Thomas* is not taken seriously as a Gospel worthy of study in its own right, but is reduced to the status of a textual variant in the history of the Synoptic tradition."

11. April DeConick, "Human Memory in the Sayings of Jesus," in Tom Thatcher, ed., *Jesus, the Voice, and the Text: Beyond the Oral and Written Gospel* (Waco: Baylor University Press, 2008), 135-80, "It is my firm opinion that the time has come for the theory of Thomas's literary dependence to be put to bed" (179).

12. See, for example, Klyne R. Snodgrass, "The Gospel of Thomas: A Secondary Gospel," *Second Century* 7/1 (1989-90): 19-38 (23); repr. in Craig A. Evans, ed., *The Historical Jesus*, vol. 4: *Lives of Jesus and Jesus Outside the Bible* (London: Routledge, 2004), 291-310 (page references throughout this book are to the original publication).

13. Most recently Nicholas Perrin, *Thomas: The Other Gospel* (Louisville: Westminster

getics.[14] We should be wary of the notion, however, that a late or dependent *Thomas* always and inevitably proceeds from a conservative or apologetic scholarly stance. Assessing scholarly trends is rarely straightforward and it is frequently unhelpful. The easy categorizing of viewpoints into one camp or another can lead to summary dismissals and failure to study the evidence.

Although *Thomas* has a clearly defined role in evangelical Christian apologetics, it does not follow that all those arguing for *Thomas*'s familiarity with the Synoptics are motivated by the desire to defend the faith. Some scholars known as broadly conservative in some areas are advocates of an early, independent *Thomas*,[15] and there are well-known skeptics who see it as a later, Gnostic text.[16] In other words, the expectation of a necessary alignment between a particular ideological stance and a given view on *Thomas*'s relationship to the Synoptics is oversimplifying and unhelpful. At the risk of sounding hackneyed or even naïve, it remains important to underline that whatever the presuppositions of the scholars involved, it has always been argument and evidence that matter. Scholarship on the *Gospel of Thomas* is at its worst when those perceived to be on different sides simply retreat into entrenched positions without engaging carefully what is actually being said by one another. This is not to argue for a return to modernist delusions about the possibility of a neutral and objective perspective on history, but rather to remind ourselves that the presence of presupposi-

---

John Knox, 2007); idem, *Thomas and Tatian: The Relationship between the Gospel of Thomas and the Diatessaron* (Academia Biblica 5; Atlanta: Society of Biblical Literature, 2002).

14. For example, Craig A. Evans, *Fabricating Jesus: How Modern Scholars Distort the Gospels* (Downers Grove, IL: InterVarsity Press, 2006), lists the following in the front matter (7) as "fact": "The *Gospel of Thomas* . . . is late, not early; secondary, not authentic. Contrary to what a few scholars maintain, the *Gospel of Thomas* originated in Syria and probably no earlier than the end of the second century." The discussion of *Thomas* is in chapter 3 (52-77). See similarly Darrell L. Bock and Daniel B. Wallace, *Dethroning Jesus: Exposing Popular Culture's Quest to Unseat the Biblical Christ* (Nashville: Nelson, 2007), 105-30, devoted to refuting the claim that "The *Gospel of Thomas* radically alters our understanding of the real Jesus."

15. For example, Gerd Theissen; see further below, 8-9.

16. For example, Michael Goulder, *Luke: A New Paradigm* (JSNTSup 20; Sheffield: Sheffield Academic Press, 1989), 23, 25, 181-82 n. 40; and Bart Ehrman, *Jesus, Apocalyptic Prophet*, 71-78. Ehrman holds open the possibility that *Thomas* preserves independently attested sayings of Jesus but does not think that it provides any significant help in the historical Jesus quest. See also Ehrman's *Lost Christianities: The Battle for Scripture and the Faiths We Never Knew* (Oxford: Oxford University Press, 2003), "The Discovery of an Ancient Forgery," 47-66.

tions should not be used as an excuse to ignore uncongenial evidence or to engage in easy dismissal of opposing views.

Dependence or Familiarity?

In the early days of *Thomas* scholarship, following the publication of the Coptic text in 1959,[17] the majority view was that *Thomas* knew the Synoptic Gospels.[18] These days, essays on the state of the question tend to represent the debate as a scholarly split, half on the side of *Thomas*'s independence, half on the side of its dependence on the Synoptics,[19] though some claim that the scales are tipping in favor of Thomasine independence,[20] or that there is a kind of geographical split, with those in North America more inclined to see *Thomas* as independent, and those in Europe more inclined to

---

17. A. Guillaumont, H.-Ch. Puech, G. Quispel, W. Till, and Yassah 'Abd al Masih, eds., *The Gospel According to Thomas: Coptic Text Established and Translated* (Leiden: Brill, 1959).

18. See in particular Robert M. Grant, David Noel Freedman, and William R. Schoedel, *The Secret Sayings of Jesus: The Gnostic Gospel of Thomas* (London: Collins, 1960); and Wolfgang Schrage, *Das Verhältnis des Thomas-Evangeliums zur synoptischen Tradition und zu den koptischen Evangelien-übersetzungen: Zugleich ein Beitrag zur gnostischen Synoptikerdeutung* (BZNW 29; Berlin: Töpelmann, 1964); but note also Harvey K. McArthur, "The Gospel According to Thomas," in Harvey K. McArthur, ed., *New Testament Sidelights: Essays in Honor of Alexander Converse Purdy* (Hartford: Hartford Seminary Foundation Press, 1960), 43-77. The key early works to argue against a simple dependence on the Synoptics were by G. Quispel; see especially "The Gospel of Thomas and the New Testament," *VC* 11 (1957): 189-207; "L'Evangile selon Thomas et le Diatessaron," *VC* 13 (1959): 87-117; "L'Evangile selon Thomas et le 'Texte Occidental' du Nouveau Testament," *VC* 14 (1960): 204-15; and "Some Remarks on the Gospel of Thomas," *NTS* 5 (1958-59): 276-90.

19. James D. G. Dunn, *Jesus Remembered* (Christianity in the Making 1; Grand Rapids: Eerdmans, 2003), for example, says, "From early days following its initial publication (1959), opinion has been almost equally divided as to whether the *Gospel of Thomas* knew and drew from the Synoptics (and John) or is a witness to an early form of the Jesus tradition prior to the Synoptics and independent of the Synoptics as such" (161-62).

20. Stephen J. Patterson, "Understanding the Gospel of Thomas Today," in Stephen J. Patterson, James M. Robinson, and Hans-Gebhard Bethge, *The Fifth Gospel: The Gospel of Thomas Comes of Age* (Harrisburg: Trinity Press International, 1998), 33-75, "Most scholars working on *Thomas* today share this view," viz. that the evidence does not support the idea that "*Thomas* was generated out of the synoptic texts through wholesale borrowing of material" (67-68). Already in 1988, Christopher Tuckett warned about the differing claims made about what constitutes the majority view, "Thomas and the Synoptics," *NovT* 30/2 (1988): 132-57 (132).

see *Thomas* as familiar with the Synoptics.[21] Others claim that the question itself is fundamentally wrongheaded, and that we should instead be asking about the evolution of the document, and its complex interactions with synoptic-like traditions across many years.[22] The one view that is rarely canvassed is that *Thomas* was used by one or more of the Synoptic Gospels, perhaps surprising given the number of scholars who wish to date *Thomas* early.[23]

One of the difficulties with these discussions is that they are often framed in terms of "literary dependence" and "independence,"[24] but these terms can be unhelpful. The term "literary" inevitably makes us think about scribes, books, and copying, imagery that may be inappropriate for a book like *Thomas* that gives so clear an impression of orality and aurality. The book is filled with what is said and heard, with mouths and speaking, with ears and listening. Writing and reading are seldom mentioned.[25] Could a

---

21. Patterson, *Gospel of Thomas and Jesus*, 10, spoke in 1993 of "a certain 'continental drift,'" but Plisch, who characterizes the original divide as between an "Anglo-Saxon and especially American front" represented by Koester and Robinson, and "the German front" represented by Schrage, sees the older controversies as "rather fruitless" and "increasingly irrelevant" (Uwe-Karsten Plisch, *The Gospel of Thomas: Original Text with Commentary* [Stuttgart: Deutsche Bibelgesellschaft, 2008], 15). He rightly notes, "The geographical distribution of research provides only a tendency; there have always been exponents of each view on both sides of the Atlantic," 15 n. 17. Recent German publications on *Thomas* include those on both sides of the issue: Enno Edzard Popkes, *Das Menschenbild des Thomasevangeliums* (WUNT 206; Tübingen: Mohr Siebeck, 2007), on the side of *Thomas*'s familiarity with the Synoptics; and Thomas Zöckler, *Jesu Lehren im Thomasevangelium* (Nag Hammadi and Manichaean Studies 47; Leiden: Brill, 1999), on the side of independence.

22. This approach is especially characteristic of April DeConick, who sees the Gospel as a "rolling corpus," beginning as a "Kernel Gospel" and accreting materials over years to produce our *Thomas*. There were some contacts with Synoptic materials in this process, but that contact is rarely determinative for *Thomas*'s content. See most fully April DeConick, *Recovering the Original Gospel of Thomas: A History of the Gospel and Its Growth* (LNTS 286; London: T & T Clark, 2005); idem, *The Original Gospel of Thomas in Translation: With a Commentary and New English Translation of the Complete Gospel* (LNTS 287; London: T & T Clark, 2006).

23. See Stevan L. Davies, "Mark's Use of the Gospel of Thomas," *Neotestamentica* 30 (1996): 307-34, for a useful exception to this general rule. See too Gregory J. Riley, "Influence of Thomas Christianity on Luke 12:14 and 5:39," *HTR* 88/2 (1995): 229-35.

24. Patterson, for example, characterizes it as "the dependency thesis," *Gospel of Thomas and Jesus*, 10; and in the pages that follow he speaks about "literary dependence," "patterns of dependence," and so on.

25. The only exception, however, is important — the Incipit. See below, 144-45 and 173-79.

text that is apparently so oral in nature be literarily dependent on other texts?

Moreover, the term "dependent" can be taken to suggest that *Thomas* is a fundamentally derivative gospel, and that the most important thing about it is its relation to the Synoptic Gospels. Given that only about half of *Thomas* has parallels with the Synoptics, it may be that the most important thing about *Thomas* is not the Synoptic parallel material but rather the non-Synoptic material.[26] Perhaps it is in the non-Synoptic half that we will learn most about the origins and nature of the *Gospel of Thomas*. It may be preferable, therefore, to move the terminology away from "dependence" or "independence" and instead to talk about "familiarity," "knowledge" or "use." These terms allow us to ask whether *Thomas* knows the Synoptic Gospels, without prejudging the extent of their influence on its author's thinking. It could be that *Thomas* uses the Synoptic Gospels as source material, but that the author does so critically and creatively, and not in a "dependent" or derivative way.

The same kind of issue rears its head in discussions of John and the Synoptics, in which one can argue that the links between the texts amount to John's "knowledge of" rather than "dependence on" the Synoptics. Similar issues are relevant also in discussion of second-century texts that are familiar with but not necessarily dependent on the canonical Gospels.[27] Even in discussions of the Synoptic Gospels, with their very high level of verbatim agreement, many prefer to talk about "knowledge" rather than "dependence" given the rather loaded nature of the latter term.[28] The term "dependence" is therefore best avoided in discussions of *Thomas*'s relationship to the Synoptics given its potential to mislead rather than to clarify.

---

26. Cf. Snodgrass, "Gospel of Thomas," 19: "Dependence on the canonical Gospels by itself will not explain the character of the *Gospel of Thomas*. In fact, it may explain only a relatively small portion of the collection. That *Thomas* is dependent in some sayings does not mean that it is dependent in all its sayings." Note the similarly cautious comments of Tuckett, "Thomas and the Synoptics," 156-57; but contrast Charles W. Hedrick, "Thomas and the Synoptics: Aiming at a Consensus," *Second Century* 7/1 (1989-90): 39-56, who speaks about "those who argue that *Thomas* depends only on the Synoptic Gospels" (52).

27. For the latter, see particularly Andrew Gregory, "Reflections on Method: What Constitutes the Use of the Writings That Later Formed the New Testament in the Apostolic Fathers?" in Andrew Gregory and Christopher Tuckett, eds., *The Reception of the New Testament in the Apostolic Fathers* (Oxford: Oxford University Press, 2005), 61-82.

28. As one among many examples, Michael Goulder regularly speaks about Luke's "knowledge of" Matthew rather than his dependence on him, e.g., "Luke's Knowledge of Matthew," in Georg Strecker, ed., *Minor Agreements: Symposium Göttingen 1991* (Göttinger theologische Arbeiten 50; Göttingen: Vandenhoeck & Ruprecht, 1993), 143-60.

The Case for Thomasine Independence

Discussions of the state of play in scholarship are, of course, only ever a prelude to the examination of the key questions, and it is necessary to turn to the arguments themselves. Many find the case for *Thomas*'s independence of the Synoptic Gospels appealing. Those dipping into the discussion through textbooks, popular introductions, summaries, and websites will encounter some general-level arguments that sound impressive. While detailed exegetical work is of course important, it is also necessary to address the introductory level and summary arguments that are so often found persuasive. For many, the case is settled before the detailed work has begun, not least because of the forthright statement of the case. Indeed, the standard scholarly edition of the *Gospel of Thomas* provides an introduction to the issue that simply asserts the independence view as if it is self-evidently plausible. It does not even mention the alternative, that *Thomas* knew and used the Synoptics.[29]

Similarly, Gerd Theissen and Annette Merz, in their popular textbook on the historical Jesus, state the case for independence with no consideration of the alternative. They offer three primary reasons for seeing *Thomas* as independent of the Synoptics under the headings of genre, order, and tradition history.[30] On genre, they write: "As a collection of sayings, the Gospel of Thomas embodies one of the earliest genres of framework in which the Jesus tradition was handed down."[31] On order, they say: "The order of the

29. "The Gospel According to Thomas," in Bentley Layton, ed., *Nag Hammadi Codex II, 2-7* (2 vols.; NHS 20-21; Coptic Gnostic Library; Leiden: Brill, 1989), 1:38-130; introduction by Helmut Koester, 38-49 (42). Koester's introductory textbook is similarly single-minded about *Thomas*'s independence, *Introduction to the New Testament*, vol. 2: *History and Literature of Early Christianity* (2nd ed.; Berlin: de Gruyter, 2000), 154-58.

30. Gerd Theissen and Annette Merz, *The Historical Jesus: A Comprehensive Guide* (ET; Minneapolis: Fortress, 1998), 38-40.

31. Theissen and Merz, *Historical Jesus*, 38. See Richard Valantasis, *The Gospel of Thomas* (New Testament Readings; London: Routledge, 1997), 2, for a good example of this argument in practice: "The Synoptic Sayings Source Q that Matthew and Luke used was considered a collection of sayings of Jesus *without any narrative frame*. The content of this Synoptic Sayings Source Q could only be established by comparing *the sayings* common to Matthew and Luke and by then reconstructing the common text; the genre of collections of 'sayings of Jesus' remained theoretical. With the discovery of the Gospel of Thomas in Coptic, scholars finally had an actual document *in the same genre as had been theorized, an existent gospel composed only of sayings of Jesus in a collection of sayings*" (emphasis added). See similarly Plisch, *Gospel of Thomas*, 9.

logia in the Gospel of Thomas is completely independent of the Synoptic Gospels; this is a strong indication that the logia which they have in common have not been taken over from the Synoptic Gospels."[32] And on tradition history, they write: "Often the Gospel of Thomas offers logia in a form which in terms of the history of the tradition is earlier than the Synoptics."[33]

These general, popular-level assertions summarize arguments in favor of *Thomas*'s independence that are often found in the literature. There are problems with each of them, and it will be helpful to take each in turn.

Genre

The argument from the genre of *Thomas* requires appeal to the existence of the hypothetical Synoptic source Q, which by definition predates both Matthew and Luke since, according to the Two-Source Theory, it is a major source for both. The argument will be unimpressive to those who are not persuaded by arguments for the existence of Q, for whom a direct link between Matthew and Luke is more plausible than their independence of one another.[34]

But Q skeptics should not be the only ones to have problems with this argument. The argument is circular. The problem with using the Q hypothesis to support an early *Thomas* is that it reverses the usual way that this argument is configured. As it is normally expressed, the existence of a sayings gospel like *Thomas* makes the existence of Q more likely. In other words, doubts about the existence of sayings gospels like Q are put to rest with the discovery of *Thomas*.[35] But if *Thomas* is to be used as evidence in favor of the existence of sayings gospels, and so to support the existence of Q, it is circular to argue that the existence of Q bolsters the idea of an early *Thomas*. The matter might be different if there were other extant examples

32. Theissen and Merz, *Historical Jesus*, 39.

33. Ibid.

34. See further my *Case Against Q: Studies in Markan Priority and the Synoptic Problem* (Harrisburg: Trinity Press International, 2002).

35. See, for example, Robert E. Van Voorst, *Jesus Outside the New Testament* (Grand Rapids: Eerdmans, 2000), 157, "The discovery of *The Gospel of Thomas* in 1945 silenced those who claimed that there was no analogy in early Christianity for a collection of Jesus sayings without a narrative framework." Van Voorst does not, however, name these scholars who were "silenced."

of first-century sayings gospels like *Thomas*, but there are not.[36] Appeals to "the collection of logia behind Mark 4"[37] simply beg the question. What we have are first-century narrative gospels in which sayings clusters like Mark 4 are embedded. We do not have extant examples of the kind of gospel sayings collections that the genre argument requires. Of course they may have existed, but arguments like this, based only on what may have been the case, are inevitably weaker than arguments that draw on extant materials.

Even if Q theorists are right about the existence of the hypothetical document, though, the argument that aligns *Thomas* and Q cannot be particularly strong. It is true that there are certain basic generic similarities between *Thomas* and what is known of Q. As Q is reconstructed, it is rich in sayings material, and *Thomas* is almost entirely made up of sayings. Neither has a Passion Narrative. Beyond the introductory-level sketch, however, it may be the generic differences, rather than the similarities, that prove revealing. It is not just that the reconstructed Q features discourses that contrast with the enigmatic and pithy sayings in *Thomas*, but it is also a question of order. *Thomas* is made up of a series of loosely arranged sayings with no overarching narrative structure of any kind. By contrast, a careful reading of the text of Q as reconstructed by the International Q Project[38] reveals a narrative sequence, with one incident building on top of another, with later incidents presupposing earlier incidents. Thus John the Baptist is introduced (Q 3:2)[39] and located in the region around the Jordan (Q 3:3);

36. There are, on the other hand, many examples of tractates that focus on sayings among the Nag Hammadi documents. Werner Kelber, "Sayings Collection and Sayings Gospel: A Study in the Clustering Management of Knowledge," *Language & Communication* 9 (1989): 213-24 (215), counts nine that "are either in part or *in toto* structured around the model of sayings, or dialogue genre," listing the *Apocryphon of James*, the *Apocryphon of John*, the *Gospel of Thomas*, the *Book of Thomas the Contender*, the *Sophia of Jesus Christ*, the *Dialogue of the Savior*, the *First Apocalypse of James*, the *Second Apocalypse of James*, and the *Letter of Peter to Philip*. However, Kelber aligns *Thomas* not with those tractates in the Nag Hammadi library but with "those early Christian sayings collections which were in part used and revised by the narrative gospels, as was the case with Q" (221).

37. Theissen and Merz, *Historical Jesus*, 38; and many others, e.g., Koester, "Introduction," 42; Patterson, *Gospel of Thomas*, 117; and see further below, 160.

38. James M. Robinson, Paul Hoffmann, and John S. Kloppenborg, *The Critical Edition of Q: Synopsis Including the Gospels of Matthew and Luke, Mark and Thomas with English, German, and French Translations of Q and Thomas* (Hermeneia; Minneapolis: Fortress, 2000).

39. In this context, in which I am taking for granted the existence of Q and the reconstruction of the IQP, it makes sense to use the convention of representing Q verses by their Lukan enumeration, though it is a convention with which, as a Q skeptic, I have some difficulties. See further my "When Is a Text not a Text? The Quasi-Text-Critical Approach of the

crowds come to him for baptism (Q 3:7); he speaks to them about repentance (Q 3:7b-8); and he prophesies a "coming one" to whom he is subordinated (Q 3:16-17). Jesus is introduced and the Spirit descends on him, and he is called God's Son (Q 3:21-22); the Spirit then sends him to the wilderness, where he is tested as God's Son (Q 4:1-13); he is in Nazara (Nazareth; Q 4:16); he preaches a major Sermon (Q 6:20-49); and after he has finished speaking, he enters Capernaum (Q 7:1), where he heals a centurion's boy (Q 7:1b-10). Messengers from John the Baptist, who is now imprisoned, ask about whether Jesus is indeed the "coming one" (Q 7:18-35), and the ensuing discourse takes for granted that Jesus heals people and preaches good news to the poor, all in fulfillment of the Scriptures, and likewise the teaching presupposes that Jesus associates with tax collectors and sinners, and that he is criticized for doing so.

This narrative sequence is quite unlike anything in *Thomas*. The best explanation for the differences is source-critical rather than genre-critical.[40] Among the transitional editorial connections (Q 3:2, 21-22; 4:1, ?16; 7:1, 18-24) is one that has the clear residue of Matthean redaction, Q 7:1, "And it came to pass when he . . . ended these sayings. . . ." This narrative segue echoes the first of the five typically Matthean end-of-discourse editorial markers (Matt. 7:28; 11:1; 13:53; 19:1; 26:1). A source-critical solution accounts for the narrative sequence, with Luke paralleling elements in Matthew's non-Markan sequence (Matt. 3–11; Luke 3–7), a sequence that dissipates as Matthew follows closely the Markan sequence from Matt. 12 to the end of his Gospel.

But a commitment to a Q-skeptical solution to this problem is not necessary to see the clear contrast between Q and *Thomas*. The genre argument for the early, independent nature of *Thomas* breaks down when it emerges that Q and *Thomas* are so dissimilar.

The contrast between Q and *Thomas* should not be underestimated given that narrative elements are generally much less likely to make it into a reconstruction of a hypothetical document like Q than are sayings. Overall, the evangelists are inclined to be more conservative with sayings material than they are with narrative material.[41] Moreover, a lot of the Q sayings presuppose the narrative development of the Synoptics: John the

---

International Q Project," in Mark Goodacre and Nicholas Perrin, eds., *Questioning Q* (Downers Grove, IL: InterVarsity Press, 2005), 115-26.

40. For the full argument, see my *Case Against Q*, chapter 9.

41. See, for example, the figures in Charles E. Carlston and Dennis Norlin, "Once More — Statistics and Q," *HTR* 64 (1971): 59-78 (71).

Baptist's introduction, preaching, baptism of repentance, prophecy about
Jesus, criticism of Herod, arrest, and imprisonment; Jesus' progress from
Nazara to Capernaum to Jerusalem; his call of the Twelve, his healing
activity, his preaching to the poor, his quoting of Scripture, his associ-
ating with tax collectors and sinners, his death, exaltation, and return.
While *Thomas* has at best narrative fragments,[42] loose shards of minimal
context of the kind that give certain sayings some coherence, Q has a sustained narrative sequence, a flow of cause-and-effect action presupposed
and illustrated in saying after saying, especially in the first third of the
document.[43]

Perhaps the danger with these observations is that they work at the detailed, nuanced level, where the point about the generic similarity of *Thomas*
and Q is often made at a fairly basic level of appeal, one of those "first impressions" that make an impact on new students. Such appeals have two simple
points: both *Thomas* and Q are predominantly made up of sayings,[44] and
both *Thomas* and Q lack a Passion Narrative. Helmut Koester, for example,
frames it as follows:

> One of the most striking features of the *Gospel of Thomas* is its silence
> on the matter of Jesus' death and resurrection — the keystone of Paul's
> missionary proclamation. But Thomas is not alone in this silence. The
> Synoptic Sayings Source (Q), used by Matthew and Luke, also does not
> consider Jesus' death a part of the Christian message. And it is like-
> wise not interested in stories and reports about the resurrection and
> subsequent appearances of the risen Lord. The *Gospel of Thomas* and
> Q challenge the assumption that the early church was unanimous in
> making Jesus' death and resurrection the fulcrum of Christian faith.

42. For an interesting take on these narrative fragments, arguing that *Thomas*'s sayings
are extracted from a commentary, see Hans-Martin Schenke, "On the Compositional History
of the Gospel of Thomas," *Foundations and Facets Forum* 10/1-2 (1994): 9-30.

43. It is worth underlining that there are narrative elements found within certain sayings
in *Thomas*, most clearly in the key conversation in *Thom.* 13, on which see especially Valantasis, *Gospel of Thomas*, 74-78. The key difference between Q and *Thomas* is over the developing
narrative sequence.

44. Note, for example, Stevan L. Davies's summary statement, "Because of its primitive
literary form (the list) and its lack of elaborate theories of Christ, and because it does not
quote the New Testament verbatim, the Gospel of Thomas appears to be a very early text,
perhaps one of the earliest pieces of Christian writing," in *The Gospel of Thomas and Christian
Wisdom* (2nd ed.; Oregon House, CA: Bardic Press, 2005), xi. For the claim about verbatim
quotation, see chapter 2 below.

Both documents presuppose that Jesus' significance lay in his words, and in his words alone.[45]

This is a helpful description of *Thomas*, which is well characterized as a "sayings gospel" in which salvation is found in the hearing and interpreting of Jesus' words. It is emphasized right at the beginning of the document, in *Thom.* 1, "Whoever finds the interpretation of these sayings will not experience death"; and the theme continues throughout the book, with repeated references to Jesus' words,

> "If you become my disciples and listen to my words, these stones will minister to you." (*Thom.* 19)

> "Many times have you desired to hear these words which I am saying to you, and you have no one else to hear them from." (*Thom.* 38)

It is brought home with the repetition of "Whoever has ears to hear, let them hear!" on frequent occasions (*Thom.* 8, 21, 24, 63, 65, 96). For *Thomas*, what Jesus says and how the interpreter hears are paramount. In Koester's words, it is indeed the case that its interest is in "his words, and his words alone."

There are major problems, however, with seeing Q in the same way. It illustrates the danger of trying to force the one, hypothetical document into the generic straitjacket of the other, extant document. While Jesus' words are clearly important in Q, Jesus' deeds appear to be equally important, with illustrations of Jesus' wonder-working activity (Q 7:1-10, Centurion's Boy; Q 7:22, Healing of Many; Q 11:14, Exorcism) alongside reflections on what they tell the readers about Jesus. When John the Baptist's messengers want to find out if Jesus is indeed the "coming one" their master prophesied, Jesus confirms his identity not primarily by means of his teaching but instead by means of his wonder-working activity (Q 7:22). When Chorazin and Bethsaida are condemned, it is for rejecting Jesus' mighty works, not his words (Q 10:13-15).[46]

There is a further difficulty with the generic comparison between *Thomas* and Q — it functions to deflect attention away from generic comparisons

---

45. Helmut Koester, *Ancient Christian Gospels: Their History and Development* (Harrisburg: Trinity Press International, 1990), 86.

46. The only hint of this in *Thomas* is *Thom.* 14, in which Jesus commands the disciples to "heal the sick."

between *Thomas* and similar materials from the second century. There is no shortage of analogous works, as has long been recognized. Koester and Robinson themselves noted the generic parallels to *Thomas* among second-century texts and suggested that the *Gattung* of *logoi sophōn* (sayings of the wise) had a "gnosticizing proclivity."[47] Q functions in this model to help anchor *Thomas* to the earlier period. Without it, *Thomas* loses that anchor, and finds itself on a current heading for the early to middle second century.

Caution is necessary, in any case, over inventories that compare narratives with sayings collections and then assign greater antiquity to the latter.[48] It is an appeal of such generality and vagueness as to be unhelpful. After all, narratives had been around for centuries, as had books of sayings. Neither has an obviously greater antiquity, and there is no reason to imagine that the earliest Christians began with sayings collections and only later moved on to narrative books. Nor is the situation any different when we look for hints about the types of traditional material in early circulation. One of our earliest extant Christian texts, 1 Corinthians, shows knowledge of both narrative material about Jesus (1 Cor. 11:23-26; 15:3-7) and individual sayings (7:10-11; 9:14), just as we might have expected. All in all, the argument for *Thomas*'s antiquity based on its supposed generic similarity to Q is not strong. This comparison between a hypothetical source and an extant text only works on a sketchy level, assuming an unproven greater antiquity for sayings books over narrative books that detracts attention from more fruitful parallels in the second century.

Order

The argument from the difference in order between the Synoptics and *Thomas* is at first sight impressive. Given the large number of parallel say-

47. James M. Robinson, "LOGOI SOPHON: On the Gattung of Q," in Robinson and Koester, *Trajectories*, 71-113.

48. Already made in Oscar Cullmann, "The Gospel of Thomas and the Problem of the Age of the Tradition Contained Therein: A Survey," *Interpretation* 16 (1962): 418-38, "In general, such collections of Logia were probably, along with Testimonia from the Old Testament, the oldest Christian literary types. The rabbinical Pirke Aboth could be cited as an analogy. . . . It is, finally, very natural that before the narrative of his life was drawn up the words of Jesus would have been handed on" (433). Contrast Tjitze Baarda, "The Gospel of Thomas," *PIBA* 26 (2003): 46-65, "The idea — that sayings traditions precede narratives — is merely an unproven hypothesis" (54).

ings in *Thomas* and the Synoptics, it is surprising that there are so few parallels in order. Yet the argument proceeds in large part from the unrealistic expectations that are thrown up by our familiarity with the Synoptics, where parallels in order are so frequent and sustained. It is easy to default to thinking that the remarkable extent of the parallel order among Matthew, Mark, and Luke is somehow the norm. Stephen Patterson thus begins his discussion of the question by looking at the agreements in wording and order among the Synoptics, looking for the same kind of thing in relation to *Thomas* and the Synoptics. He regards it as a requirement in a theory of literary dependence for the scholar to demonstrate that "the sequence of individual pericopae in each text is substantially the same."[49]

The extraordinary degree of agreement among the Synoptics has spoiled us. It has created unrealistic expectations when we look at other similar documents.[50] Moreover, the argument essentially reverses a valid positive argument about literary relationships such that it becomes a flawed negative argument about literary relationships. It is true, in discussions of the common order among the Synoptics, that the substantial agreement in order among Matthew, Mark, and Luke necessitates theories of a literary relationship. But one cannot legitimately reverse that positive argument and make the absence of substantial agreement in order a sign of the lack of literary relationship. The relative lack of agreement in order between *Thomas* and the Synoptics of course leaves a literary link still to be demonstrated, but it does not show the absence of a literary link.

It is important to remind ourselves also that one of the reasons for the sustained agreements in order among the Synoptics is the key presence of common narrative sequence. The Synoptic evangelists are much more conservative in the order of narrative material than they are in the order of sayings material. This is particularly the case in the double tradition material, which often appears in different contexts in Matthew and Luke. Either Matthew or Luke (or both) has removed a lot of double tradition sayings material from the contexts in which he found it. Given that *Thomas* has no narrative contexts into which to slot its sayings material, it is not surprising that its sayings appear in a very different order from that found in the Synoptics.

---

49. Patterson, *Gospel of Thomas*, 16.

50. Some might argue that the same is true with respect to the relationship between John and the Synoptics. Patterson's analogy between *Thomas*-Synoptic comparison and John-Synoptic comparison (*Gospel of Thomas*, 12-16) may be an unhelpful analogy for this reason.

Furthermore, the abbreviated, disconnected nature of the Thomasine sayings lends itself to a looser structure. The form of the sayings relates directly to *Thomas*'s redactional profile, the mysterious Gospel in which enigmatic, self-contained sayings, at best only loosely related to one another, are stacked up in baffling succession. The very success of the Gospel lies in its attempt to unnerve the reader, especially the outsider. This disconcerting aim reinforces the necessity for mysterious, pithy sayings, largely devoid of contextual clues to their interpretation. If *Thomas*'s redactional aims require particular forms, those forms themselves cohere with *Thomas*'s order, or lack of it.

This is a point to which we will return, and one that requires a little more exploration. For the purposes of this discussion about order, the important thing is to notice the way in which the author of *Thomas* is able to compound the nature of his enigma by surprising the hearer with constant changes of gear. It is not just the sayings themselves that shock and surprise, but also the bizarre juxtaposition of apparently contrasting ideas, side by side. This is a key point: if the author of *Thomas* is aiming at coherence, he has failed. It is unlikely, however, that he is attempting to be coherent. Rather, his Gospel is aiming at enigma, and this is why it announces itself as an enigma from the beginning (Incipit, 1), and why it orders sayings in this apparently incomprehensible way. If one thing is clear about *Thomas*, it is that it is not clear. Modern interpreters with their bright ideas about *Thomas*'s arrangement run the risk of attempting to explain what the author wishes to leave unexplained, blunting the author's purpose by artificially conjoining and deciphering sayings that resist that kind of work.

In other words, we are rightly surprised by the difference between the order of sayings in *Thomas* and the Synoptics, but this difference does not need to be explained as due to *Thomas*'s ignorance of the Synoptics. It may be that the author wishes to retain elements from the Synoptics in order to give his Jesus the sound of authenticity, while depriving the reader of the kind of interpretive contextual clues that lead the reader of the Synoptics in particular directions. It could be that the difference in order between *Thomas* and the Synoptics says much more about the author's redactional agenda than it does about the author's source material.[51]

51. See also the useful comments in Tuckett, "Thomas and the Synoptics," 139-40, especially 140, "Further, the claim that Th has no logical order of its own, and hence the order of Th must reflect the order of a source (which therefore cannot be the synoptic gospels), really only pushes the problem one stage further back. What are we to make of the equally formless source(s) which lie(s) behind Th? If the formlessness of Th is problematic, ascribing the order to a prior source merely transfers the problem. It does not solve it."

Two further points are relevant in this context. First, as everyone acknowledges, there are certain key agreements in order between *Thomas* and
the Synoptics (most notably 16.1-2 and 3; 55.1 and 2; 65 and 66), and these
require explanation.[52] These agreements may be the result of the kind of
familiarity with the texts that is so great that they went almost unnoticed
by the author of *Thomas*, whose policy was elsewhere to decontextualize
Synoptic sayings.

Second, the lack of common order in *Thomas*'s sayings may simply be
a corollary of the first argument for Thomasine independence discussed
above, concerning *Thomas*'s genre. The assumption that sayings gospels
would tend to have major agreements in order with the Synoptics proceeds
in part from the Q hypothesis, according to which Matthew and especially
Luke retain the order of many of the sayings from their source document.
In the absence of Q, though, we do not have another extant example of a
first-century sayings gospel that shares sayings with the Synoptics, and so it
is difficult to know what exactly we ought to expect.

The argument from lack of common order, then, does not necessarily
point to *Thomas*'s independence. It imposes an expectation derived from the
sustained agreements in order among Matthew, Mark, and Luke, agreements
that are unusually strong and result in part at least from their shared narrative
structure. The self-consciously enigmatic nature of *Thomas*'s sayings collection precludes the likelihood of that kind of sustained logical sequence.

Tradition History

The third major argument for the primitivity and independence of *Thomas*
is almost certainly the most influential, and it requires a good deal more
exploration than the previous two, and it will be a topic that will continue
to rear its head in a variety of ways throughout our study. It is worth paying some preliminary attention to the issues here, though, in an attempt to
make clear how the argument works, and what to look for as the discussion
develops.

The argument from tradition history is effectively stated by Patterson:

> If Thomas were dependent upon the synoptic gospels, it would be pos-
> sible to detect in the case of every Thomas-synoptic parallel the same

---

52. Noted by, among others, DeConick, *Original Gospel*, 17.

tradition-historical development behind both the Thomas version of the saying and one or more of the synoptic versions. That is, Thomas' author/editor, in taking up the synoptic version, would have inherited all of the accumulated tradition-historical baggage owned by the synoptic text, and then added to it his or her own redactional twist. In the following texts this is not the case. Rather than reflecting the same tradition-historical development that stands behind their synoptic counterparts, these Thomas sayings seem to be the product of a tradition-history which, though exhibiting the same tendencies operative within the synoptic tradition, is in its own specific details quite unique. This means, of course, that these sayings are not dependent upon their synoptic counterparts, but rather derive from a parallel and separate tradition.[53]

Like the previous two arguments for *Thomas*'s independence, this one has a certain basic appeal. It sounds persuasive, but closer examination reveals problems. The model Patterson assumes to be necessary for Thomasine dependence on the Synoptics is not in fact used by anyone, nor is it one that is required by the case. The issue under discussion is whether the author of *Thomas* is familiar with the Synoptic Gospels, and it is in principle likely that in taking over source material, he would not retain everything in the material he is using. Writers are not obliged to take over everything they find in their sources, and it is never surprising to see authors editing material to suit their needs. Indeed, one might expect the author of *Thomas* to edit source material in order to reflect his distinctive agenda, not least if the text is aiming to be enigmatic.

The model that Patterson argues against is one that imagines the snowball rolling down the hill, accreting fresh snow, but retaining what it already has. The image is an unhelpful one when one is dealing with authors and texts. Indeed, it is not particularly helpful even when one is dealing with oral tradition history.

The point is illustrated by the example of inter-Synoptic dependence. We have little trouble in seeing Matthew and Luke redacting Mark without inheriting all of the tradition-historical baggage owned by the Markan text. Even a relatively short amount of time with a Gospel synopsis will provide the reader with plenty of examples of Matthew and Luke radically

---

53. Patterson, *Gospel of Thomas and Jesus*, 18. For a succinct and forthright version of the same argument, see Koester, "Introduction," 42, "A comparison with the Synoptic parallels demonstrates . . . that the forms of the sayings in the *GTh* are either more original than they or developed from forms which are more original."

altering their source material. Where Matthew rewrites Mark's story of the Gerasene demoniac (Mark 5:1-20 // Matt. 8:28-34),[54] the bulk of that story is absent from his much shorter version, but few would take seriously the idea that Matthew is independent from Mark here. Or when Matthew retells the story of John the Baptist's death (Matt. 14:1-12), his far shorter version is demonstrably secondary to Mark's more primitive version (Mark 6:14-29),[55] and yet it lacks many of the latter's details. To use Patterson's terminology, Matthew has left lots of the "tradition-historical baggage" behind.

The situation is no different when it comes to sayings material. When one evangelist is working from a source, he may or may not carry over elements that illustrate that saying's tradition history. The double-barreled pronouncement in Mark 2:27-28, "The Sabbath is made for humanity, not humanity for the Sabbath; therefore the Son of Man is Lord even of the Sabbath," is revised by both Matthew (Matt. 12:8) and Luke (Luke 6:5) to include only the second half of the pronouncement. Neither apparently felt obliged to retain both halves of the saying that they inherited. Examples like this could be multiplied. It is simply not the case in Synoptic comparison that one pericope, when taken over by a later writer, necessarily drags with it all the traditional features from the earlier version. Indeed, it is a common fallacy in the discussion of the Synoptic Problem to assume that the evangelists' default position was to avoid omission of material from their sources. Sometimes they omitted material; sometimes they retained material; it is never straightforward to predict how they might behave on a given occasion.[56]

In other words, Patterson has raised the bar too high for the notion of Thomasine familiarity with the Synoptics, asking for a standard that would make Matthew independent of Mark, and Luke from both. It is unrealistic to expect *Thomas* to have taken over all "the accumulated tradition-historical baggage" from the Synoptics. The difficulty arises in part because the

---

54. I assume Markan priority here and throughout. My arguments in favor of Markan priority are found in *The Case Against Q*, chapter 2; *The Synoptic Problem: A Way Through the Maze* (Biblical Seminar 80; Sheffield: Sheffield Academic Press, 2001), chapter 3; and "Fatigue in the Synoptics," *NTS* 44 (1998): 45-58.

55. "Fatigue in the Synoptics," 46-47, 52.

56. The fallacy arises in part because of the nature of the Two-Source Theory, one of the advantages of which is that it involves the least amount of large-scale omission of any of the major theories. Matthew and Luke both include most of Mark and Q. However, even on the Two-Source Theory, Matthew and Luke are both involved in some large-scale omission and a great deal of smaller-scale, intra-pericope omission.

model being used is an evolutionary one, a model with too great a debt to classical form criticism and too little attention to *Thomas*'s redactional interests. Even granted the self-consciously enigmatic nature of the *Gospel of Thomas*, it is possible to isolate several important redactional traits that control its author's selection and editing of the material it has in parallel with the Synoptics.

These three general arguments, from genre, order, and tradition history, are less persuasive on closer inspection than they might appear at first. If there are question marks against the persuasiveness of these arguments for *Thomas*'s independence, it is worth turning more directly to the case for *Thomas*'s knowledge of the Synoptics. The best beginning point is a strong general observation about the parallels between *Thomas* and the Synoptics.

The Spread of Traditions

Not everyone who argues in favor of *Thomas*'s familiarity with the Synoptics devotes a whole book to the topic; a few pages are often considered sufficient. One such example is John P. Meier, who in the first volume of his major, multivolume project on the historical Jesus, explains why he does not make *Thomas* one of his major sources in the quest. He makes an observation that deserves serious attention: there are broad parallels to many different strands in the Synoptic Gospels (and John) in *Thomas*.[57] He writes:

> This broad "spread" of Jesus' sayings over so many different streams of canonical Gospel tradition (and redaction!) forces us to face a fundamental question: Is it likely that the very early source of Jesus' sayings that the *Gospel of Thomas* supposedly drew upon contained within itself material belonging to such diverse branches of 1st-century Christian tradition as Q, special M, special L, Matthean and Lucan redaction, the triple tradition, and possibly the Johannine tradition? What were the source, locus,

---

57. This argument is not often taken seriously in the literature. The exceptions are J.-D. Kaestli, "L'utilisation de l'Évangile de Thomas dans la recherche actuelle sur les paroles de Jésus," in D. Marguerat, E. Norelli, and J.-M. Poffet, eds., *Jésus de Nazareth: Nouvelles approches d'une énigme* (Monde de la Bible 38; Geneva: Labor et Fides, 1998), 373-95 (382-83); David E. Aune, "Assessing the Historical Value of the Apocryphal Jesus Traditions: A Critique of Conflicting Methodologies," in J. Schröter and R. Brucker, eds., *Historische Jesus* (BZNW 114; Berlin: de Gruyter, 2002), 243-72 (255-56); and Stevan Davies, *Gospel of Thomas*, xx-xxii. On all three, see below.

and composition of this incredibly broad yet very early tradition? Who were its bearers? Is it really conceivable that there was some early Christian source that embraced within itself all these different strands of what became the canonical Gospels?[58]

Meier's observation, that *Thomas* apparently has parallels with every type of Synoptic material,[59] repays some additional reflection. If anything, Meier's statement of the spread of parallels is somewhat conservative, since *Thomas* features more than just triple tradition, double tradition, M, L, Matthean redaction, and Lukan redaction. *Thomas* also has parallels to Special Mark (Mark 4:29 // *Thom.* 21.10, Sickle and Harvest) and to triple tradition material in which there are major agreements between Matthew and Luke (Matt. 13:31-32 // Mark 4:30-32 // Luke 13:18-19 // *Thom.* 20, Mustard Seed; Matt. 12:31-32 // Mark 3:28-30 // Luke 12:10 // *Thom.* 44, Blasphemy against the Spirit; Matt. 10:8-13 // Mark 6:7-12 // Luke 9:1-6 // Luke 10:5-9 // *Thom.* 14.4, Mission Instruction).[60] The parallel to Special Mark material is particularly noteworthy given that Special Mark is such a small set of material.

The strands of Synoptic material found in *Thomas*, therefore, are the following:

- Triple tradition (Matthew // Mark // Luke)
- Double tradition (Matthew // Luke, not Mark)
- Triple tradition in which Mark is not the middle term (Matthew // Mark // Luke with major agreements between Matthew and Luke)
- Special Matthew
- Special Luke
- Special Mark

58. John P. Meier, *A Marginal Jew: Rethinking the Historical Jesus* (4 vols.; New York: Doubleday, 1991-2009): 1:137.

59. Snodgrass makes the same kind of argument, but more briefly, "Gospel of Thomas," 24-25, though with more stress on John. See also Craig L. Blomberg, "Tradition and Redaction in the Parables of the Gospel of Thomas," in David Wenham, ed., *Gospel Perspectives*, vol. 5: *The Jesus Tradition Outside the Gospels* (Sheffield: JSOT Press, 1984), 177-205 (180-81); and Craig Evans, *Ancient Texts for New Testament Studies: A Guide to the Background Literature* (Peabody, MA: Hendrickson, 2005), 258.

60. This material is more commonly called "Mark-Q overlap" but the use of this descriptor actually prejudges the question of the origin of this material. The more neutral description of this material notes that this is triple-tradition material in which there are major agreements between Matthew and Luke. See my *Case Against Q*, 52-54 and 163-65.

- Matthean redaction of Mark (material found only in Matthew's apparent additions to Mark)
- Lukan redaction of Mark (material found only in Luke's apparent additions to Mark)

The most questionable pieces here are, of course, "Matthean and Lukan redaction" because these might seem to beg the question. If it were agreed that *Thomas* features Matthean and Lukan material that is clearly redactional, then the discussion could end at that point. Under these circumstances, *Thomas* would be taking over material that Matthew and Luke had themselves contributed to their Gospels and it would be clear that *Thomas* is familiar with their Gospels rather than their traditions. In this context, however, the terms can be used without prejudice, as referring simply to material in Matthew's or Luke's triple tradition that is not found in Mark, whatever the explanation for that material might be.[61] It is a fact that this material is present in *Thomas*. The dispute is over the origin of this material, whether in oral traditions shared by *Thomas* with Luke and Matthew[62] or in *Thomas*'s knowledge of Matthew's and Luke's Gospels.

The spread is remarkable since it touches on every strand of Synoptic data. No group of material is absent.[63] How can this be explained? For Meier, it is clear evidence of *Thomas*'s familiarity with the Synoptics and it is unsurprising because *Thomas* is simply deriving the material from a range of different contexts in the Synoptic texts. If *Thomas* were independent, Meier argues, it would be remarkable that the author had access to multiple source materials that went on to form the basis of all three Synoptics.

This certainly sounds like a strong argument. How plausible is it that *Thomas* could have known so full a range of traditions at an early date, independently of the Synoptics? David Aune offers several points in response to Meier, but most are in the nature of corrections and clarifications.[64] He notes that those defending an independent *Thomas* do not presuppose "a

61. For full discussion of MattR and LukeR material in *Thomas*, see further chapters 3–6 below.

62. This explanation is used frequently by Sieber, e.g., below, 71. Cf. Patterson, below, 83.

63. Cf. the related phenomenon pointed out by H. K. McArthur, "The Dependence of the Gospel of Thomas on the Synoptics," *ExpT* 71 (1959-60): 286-87, "Again, if the Gospel of Thomas was completely independent of Matthew is it not a curious coincidence that it includes all seven of the Parables of the Kingdom found in Mt 13? (see Logia 8, 9, 20, 57, 76, 96, 109)" (287).

64. Aune, "Assessing," 255-56.

single, very early source," in Meier's phrase,[65] and he doubts *Thomas's* dependence on John, both useful clarifications to Meier's framing of the argument. More substantively, he goes on to note that *Thomas* is the first document to feature parallels to this range of Synoptic material, and that "the next author to exhibit a similar pattern of dependence on the Synoptics is Justin Martyr," an analogy that may shed light on *Thomas's* own familiarity with the Synoptics.[66] Further, Aune places a question mark against Meier's assertion that the M material paralleled in *Thomas* might be Matthew's redactional creations, noting that this is only a possibility.[67]

There are few other critical responses to Meier's argument in the literature. *Thomas* scholars either do not know the argument or they do not appreciate it. How else might it be answered? Some might say that the very way that the argument is set up depends on its conclusion. Is it circular? Meier's argument defines the different strands of tradition intrasynoptically and then proceeds to extrasynoptic comparison with *Thomas*. Perhaps one could do the same with the other Gospels. If one were to take any one Gospel out of the mix, and compare it with the different strands in the remaining three, would each one extracted not show the same parallels with every one of the isolated strands? Under this kind of argument, could one make a case for any one of the Gospels to be dependent on all the others?[68]

A counterargument like this would fail to get to the heart of Meier's argument. He is contrasting two differing scenarios, and attempting to show why one is more plausible than the other. One scenario, the one he sup-

65. Similarly Kaestli, "L'Utilisation," 383.

66. See below, 123-27.

67. Aune goes on (256), "Further, Meier's view that a single attested instance of the dependence of *Thomas* on a passage which is a Matthean creation or exhibits Matthean redactional features proves that *Thomas* knew and used the Gospel of Matthew is simply not correct. The complex origins and redactions of *Thomas* are such that the dependence of a single logion on the Gospel of Matthew proves only the dependence of that logion." But if *Thomas* shows knowledge of a pericope that is Matthew's own creation, this greatly increases the likelihood that *Thomas* knows Matthew's Gospel. There are in fact good examples of *Thomas's* familiarity with M material; see below, 73-80.

68. In practice, it does not work because there are no parallels that occur exclusively in Mark, Luke, and *Thomas*. If one were to take Matthew, Mark, and *Thomas* together, for example, and look for patterns of agreement and disagreement, with a view to isolating the strands, one would find that Luke has parallels with Matthew alone, Mark alone, *Thomas* alone, Matthew // Mark, and Matthew // *Thomas* (but not Mark // *Thomas*). So too if we were to take Mark out of the equation, work out the different agreements and disagreements among Matthew, Luke, and *Thomas*, we would then find agreements with Matthew alone, Luke alone, *Thomas* alone, Matthew // Luke, Matthew // *Thomas* (but not Luke // *Thomas*).

ports, explains the parallels with the multiple strands by suggesting that *Thomas* has taken varieties of materials from across all three Synoptics, thereby picking up material from each of the different strands. The other scenario is that *Thomas* is independent and early, and on this scenario the only way that its author can have gained access to this range of differing strands is through having access to a comprehensive range of oral traditions, working on the assumption that at least some of the differing strands come from a disparate range of materials. [69]

Of course it may be the case that *Thomas* accesses these traditions before they have divided into the differing strands,[70] but if this is the case, then early Christian oral tradition was considerably more unified and homogeneous than is usually thought, especially by those advocating Thomasine independence.[71] It seems that advocates of Thomasine independence have two available paths for the origins of *Thomas*'s Synoptic material. Either it emerges from a large body of oral tradition at a point before it separated into different strands, in which case early Christian tradition is considerably more homogeneous and all-encompassing than was previously thought, or *Thomas* is indeed familiar with a remarkably diverse set of traditions, able to dip into every pot of tradition that fed the later Synoptic Gospels. Neither path is likely to be attractive to advocates of Thomasine independence, for whom *Thomas* is often seen as "the offspring of an autonomous stream of early Christian tradition."[72] *Thomas*'s familiarity with the Synoptic Gospels provides the more economical and persuasive model here.[73]

69. Stevan Davies's response, *Gospel of Thomas*, xxi, misses this point when he says, "If we look for another ancient Christian text that contains 'such an incredibly broad range of traditions' . . . we do find one, and it is the Gospel of Matthew!" Davies repeats the claim for Luke. But for Meier, Matthew is dependent on Mark, Q, and M, and this range of traditions results from Matthew's knowledge of those texts. His argument is that if *Thomas* is independent, its author knows a broader range of traditions at an earlier date.

70. This is effectively Kaistli's response, "L'utilisation," 383, "Les parallèles avec Q, M, and L et la triple tradition peuvent très bien avoir coexisté dans une tradition antérieure à la rédaction des évangiles synoptiques."

71. Risto Uro, "*Thomas* and the Oral Gospel Tradition," in Risto Uro, ed., *Thomas at the Crossroads: Essays on the Gospel of Thomas* (Studies of the New Testament and Its World; Edinburgh: T & T Clark, 1998), 8-32 (20), makes this point in criticism of Patterson and others, "To argue that such an amount of common material entered into the *Gospel of Thomas* basically through an 'unmixed' oral transmission presupposes a view of a very solid tradition."

72. Patterson, *Gospel of Thomas*, 110.

73. DeConick's model of a "rolling corpus" (*Recovering*, passim; *Original Gospel*, passim) might at first seem to be exempt from the problems here because, on an evolutionary model, one could argue that different pieces accrete and accrue at different times and in different

*   *   *

The apparent spread of different strands of Synoptic material in *Thomas* is highly suggestive. It makes better sense on the assumption that *Thomas* is familiar with the Synoptic Gospels than on the assumption that its author had independent access to every traditional stream that ultimately fed into the Synoptics. However, the discussion about *Thomas*'s familiarity with the Synoptics will not be settled by general observation and argument. Much of the scholarly debate has involved detailed, exegetical analysis, and the plausibility of any case for *Thomas*'s knowledge of the Synoptics stands or falls on the basis of the analysis of the parallels. The first key step, often missed in these discussions, is to take a close look at *Thomas* for verbatim agreement with the Synoptic Gospels. Are the texts close enough to establish familiarity? If the only commonalities are a word here and a phrase there, perhaps some kind of mutual knowledge of oral tradition will be the best option. If, on the other hand, there are cases where *Thomas* and the Synoptic Gospels show verbatim agreement over more extended passages, then the case for a direct link between the texts will be stronger.

---

places, leading to a diversity of traditions. However, almost all of the Synoptic parallels to *Thomas* occur in DeConick's "Kernel Gospel," i.e., at the earliest point in the Gospel's development, and before any exposure to the Synoptic Gospels. (Exceptions include *Thom.* 3 // Luke 17:20-21, L; and *Thom.* 14.5 // Matt. 15:11, MattR.) Thus the Kernel Gospel appears to have links to the full range of different groups of material, Mark, Q, M, L, and so on, at a very early stage, a scenario that becomes even more unlikely when one bears in mind that DeConick does not see the "Kernel Gospel" as a source for the Synoptics. The "Kernel Gospel" therefore highlights the range of traditions problem in a striking way.

CHAPTER 2

Verbatim Agreement between *Thomas* and the Synoptics

Nag Hammadi and Oxyrhynchus

The usual starting point for modern discussion of the *Gospel of Thomas* is 1945,[1] when Muhammad 'Ali, his brothers, and others[2] stumbled upon an ancient jar containing twelve leather-bound codices[3] while they were out searching for fertilizer near Nag Hammadi in Egypt.[4] It is, in a sense, an obvious starting point because it represents the moment at which a complete textual witness to the *Gospel of Thomas* is finally unearthed after cen-

---

1. See, for example, Patterson et al., *Fifth Gospel*, 1.

2. It is practically impossible to work out who was present with 'Ali at the discovery; see further n. 6 below. For what follows, see James M. Robinson, "The Discovery of the Nag Hammadi Codices," *BA* 42/4 (1979): 206-24; idem, "From Cliff to Cairo: The Story of the Discoverers and the Middlemen of the Nag Hammadi Codices," in Bernard Barc, *Colloque international sur les textes de Nag Hammadi: Québec, 22-25 août 1978* (Bibliothèque copte de Nag Hammadi 1; Québec: Presses de l'Université Laval, 1981), 21-58; idem, ed., *The Nag Hammadi Library in English*, 3rd ed. (Leiden: Brill, 1988); idem, ed., *The Facsimile Edition of the Nag Hammadi Codices: Introduction* (Leiden: Brill, 1984).

3. It is often said that the jar contained thirteen codices, which may not be strictly correct. There are twelve extant codices, and one tractate from a thirteenth was found inside Codex VI. See Robinson, *Nag Hammadi Library*, 10; idem, "Discovery," 214. However, the question of the number of codices found in the different versions of the story is not straightforward. See further my forthcoming article, "How Reliable Is the Story of the Nag Hammadi Discovery?"

4. Although widely used in the earlier literature, the town name Chenoboskion eventually gave way to Nag Hammadi as the more memorable place association for the discoveries.

turies of having been lost. Moreover, in a field like this, so often a matter of books, libraries, studies, and texts, the story of the Nag Hammadi discovery injects a little bit of sensation. It has a memorable date, the year the Second World War ended;[5] its discoverer has a memorable name, one shared with the most famous boxer of the twentieth century;[6] and it has an exotic and dramatic story. James Robinson's brilliantly told narrative is one of the most memorable tales in the history of the search for ancient texts, the rival of the best kind of historical fiction. Robinson himself has retold the story on countless occasions,[7] and others have followed his lead.[8]

The most memorable passage relates to events that took place not long after the discovery of the Nag Hammadi codices, events that prevented 'Ali from revisiting the site of their discovery for decades until accompanied by Robinson. 'Ali's father was murdered in May 1945, and he got the chance to avenge the killing in early 1946:

> Sometime between a few days and a month after the discovery of the codices, Ahmad [the alleged murderer] was sitting beside the road near Muhammad 'Ali's home in al-Qasr. He was asleep with his head between his knees and a jug of sugarcane molasses for sale beside him. On learn- ing that their victim slept defenceless nearby, 'Ali Muhammad Khalifah's widow, 'Umm Ahmad — who had told her seven sons to keep their mat-

---

5. The end of the war is mentioned in the account given in John Dart, Ray Riegert, and John Dominic Crossan, *Unearthing the Lost Words of Jesus: The Discovery and Text of the Gospel of Thomas* (Berkeley: Seastone, 1998), 85. Robinson settled on the date December 1945 after considerable uncertainty in earlier literature. It is now universally given as the date of discovery. The date is worked out on the basis that Muhammad 'Ali reports having discovered the documents about six months after the murder of his father, which Robinson is able to date through official documentation to 7 May 1945. 'Ali claimed to have been digging for fertilizer before Coptic Christmas (6 January), which brings the discovery to "about December 1945" ("Discovery," 209). The date is plausible but not watertight — Robinson does not report of- ficial documentation for the subsequent revenge murder, and 'Ali's memory of thirty years previously was demonstrably deficient in other respects (see n. 6 below).

6. In several of Robinson's accounts, the person who actually unearthed the pot contain- ing the texts, 'Ali's younger brother, had the much less memorable name, Abū al-Majd (Rob- inson, "Discovery," 208, 213). In others of Robinson's accounts, Abū al-Majd is not present; only 'Ali and Khalifah are there (*Nag Hammadi Library*, 21). In the alternative, more recent version provided in Tobias Churton, *The Gnostics* (London: Weidenfeld & Nicolson, 1987), 9, only 'Ali is present.

7. See n. 2 above for details.

8. Compelling versions include Elaine Pagels, *The Gnostic Gospels* (New York: Random House, 1979): xiii-xv; and Dart et al., *Unearthing*, 3-9.

tocks sharp — handed these instruments to her sons to avenge her. They fell upon Ahmad Isma'il pitilessly. Abu al-Majd, then a teenager, brags that he struck the first blow straight to the head. After having hacked Ahmad Isma'il to pieces limb by limb, they cut out his heart and consumed it among them — the ultimate act of blood revenge.[9]

The outrageous and appalling story provides a sensational introduction to the study of the *Gospel of Thomas,* and it is difficult to resist bringing it forward as a supporting feature before presenting *Thomas,* the main event, whether in the classroom or in the introductory essay.

Yet the discovery of the Nag Hammadi codices is not really where the story of the modern study of the *Gospel of Thomas* begins. Bernard Grenfell and Arthur Hunt's discovery of the Oxyrhynchus papyri half a century earlier[10] does not have the drama of Robinson's account of the Nag Hammadi discovery with its illiterate peasants stumbling upon texts of great value without realizing what they have found, let alone the associated drama of blood feuds. Rather, their story is one of two Oxford fellows meticulously excavating an old Egyptian rubbish dump, looking for scraps of manuscripts. Its main moment of drama comes not from any cannibalism but from spotting a piece of papyrus with a rare word, κάρφος ("speck"), and immediately thinking of Jesus' saying about specks and beams.[11] Altogether they found three fragments of *Thomas,* P.Oxy. 1, P.Oxy. 654, and P.Oxy. 655, though it was only after the Nag Hammadi find that scholars really knew what they were.

At the center of the Oxyrhynchus finds are people a little more like most of us, literate, middle-class, Western academics with an interest in ancient texts, but the import of their discovery should not be downplayed. The Oxyrhynchus fragments of *Thomas* are in Greek rather than Coptic; they are far earlier than the Nag Hammadi codices;[12] they come from three

---

9. Robinson, "Discovery," 209.

10. B. P. Grenfell and Arthur S. Hunt, *ΛΟΓΙΑ ΙΗΣΟΥ: Sayings of Our Lord from an Early Greek Papyrus Discovered and Edited, with Translation and Commentary* (Egypt Exploration Fund; London: H. Frowde, 1897); idem, *New Sayings of Jesus and Fragment of a Lost Gospel from Oxyrhynchus* (Egypt Exploration Fund; London: H. Frowde, 1904); idem, *The Oxyrhynchus Papyri,* vols. 1 and 4 (London: Egypt Exploration Fund, 1893, 1904).

11. Bernard P. Grenfell, "The Oldest Record of Christ's Life," *McClure's Magazine,* Oct. 1897, 1022-30 (1027).

12. Harold W. Attridge, "The Gospel According to Thomas: Appendix: The Greek Fragments," in Layton, ed., *Nag Hammadi Codex II, 2-7,* 1:95-128 (96-98), suggests the following

separate witnesses to the *Gospel of Thomas*; and they are likely to represent earlier witnesses to the *Gospel of Thomas*.[13]

The difficulty is, of course, that the Oxyrhynchus papyri are so much more fragmentary than Nag Hammadi Codex II. Taking the three Greek witnesses together, they comprise less than half of what we know of *Thomas* from the Coptic witness, and they are all in the first half of the book.[14] But textual scholarship involves the scrutiny of all the earliest and best evidence, and since the extant witnesses of *Thomas* are so few, we cannot afford to be fussy. The Greek evidence should be given its proper place, and the tendency to play it down should be resisted.[15] The tendency among some scholars to describe the book as "Coptic *Thomas*," for example, is unfortunate since it confuses the literary work with one of its textual witnesses.[16] The term *Gospel of Thomas* should be used for the literary work, and its textual witnesses can then be accurately identified.

The marginalization of the Greek textual witnesses has several damaging effects on *Thomas* scholarship, the most important of which is the tendency to neglect the verbatim agreement, in Greek, between *Thomas* and the Synoptic Gospels. The more that scholars give special attention to the Coptic, the less they are inclined to realize the striking nature of *Thomas*'s parallels with the Synoptics. In order to underline the point, it will be worth beginning with the first and most extensive of the agreements, an agreement that deserves more notice than it has been given. Indeed, we can begin at the very beginning, with the first piece of the first fragment found by Grenfell and Hunt in 1897.[17]

---

dates: P.Oxy. 1: shortly after 200; P.Oxy. 654: mid-third century; P.Oxy. 655: 200-250. Broadly, these follow Grenfell and Hunt's original suggestions.

13. There is also a tendency in the scholarship to homogenize the three Greek witnesses as if they come from the same textual witness rather than from three separate textual ones.

14. The exception is *Thom.* 77.2-3, which occurs alongside *Thom.* 30 in P.Oxy. 1.

15. One of the major exceptions to the tendency is Valantasis, *Gospel of Thomas*, who begins by studying the Greek evidence as "A Window on the Gospel of Thomas" (chapter 2), only subsequently to move on to the Coptic witness (chapter 3). Valantasis complains, "These have recently received little attention in the scholarly literature and they have been virtually ignored by the popular press" (27).

16. For example, Armin D. Baum, "The Anonymity of the New Testament History Books: A Stylistic Device in the Context of Greco-Roman and Ancient Near Eastern Literature," *NovT* 50 (2008): 120-42 (122).

17. Grenfell and Hunt, ΛΟΓΙΑ ΙΗΣΟΥ.

Verbatim Agreement in *Thomas*: The Case of P.Oxy. 1.1-4

Saying 26 of the *Gospel of Thomas* is witnessed in P.Oxy. 1.1-4, and it features a thirteen-word verbatim agreement with Luke 6:42, differing only in the placement of a single word:

Matt. 7:5	Luke 6:42	P.Oxy. 1.1-4 (*Thom.* 26)
ὑποκριτά, ἔκβαλε πρῶτον ἐκ τοῦ ὀφθαλμοῦ σοῦ τὴν δοκόν <u>καὶ τότε διαβλέψεις</u> <u>ἐκβαλεῖν τὸ κάρφος</u> <u>ἐκ τοῦ ὀφθαλμοῦ τοῦ</u> <u>ἀδελφοῦ σου</u>	ὑποκριτά, ἔκβαλε πρῶτον τὴν δοκὸν ἐκ τοῦ ὀφθαλμοῦ σοῦ <u>καὶ τότε διαβλέψεις</u> <u>τὸ κάρφος τὸ</u> <u>ἐν τῷ ὀφθαλμῷ τοῦ</u> <u>ἀδελφοῦ σου ἐκβαλεῖν</u>	<u>καὶ τότε διαβλέψεις</u> <u>ἐκβαλεῖν τὸ κάρφος τὸ</u> <u>ἐν τῷ ὀφθαλμῷ τοῦ</u> <u>ἀδελφοῦ σου</u>
Hypocrites! First cast out the beam from your own eye, <u>and then you will see clearly</u> to cast out the speck from <u>your brother's eye.</u>	Hypocrites! First cast out the beam from your own eye, <u>and then you will see clearly</u> to cast out the speck that is in <u>your brother's eye.</u>	<u>and then you will see clearly</u> to cast out the speck that is in <u>your brother's eye.</u>

The only difference between *Thomas* and Luke 6:42 (NA[27]) is the position of ἐκβαλεῖν ("to cast out"), at the end of the sentence in Luke 6:42, but after διαβλέψεις ("you will see") in P.Oxy. 1, apparently agreeing with Matt. 7:5. Of course, one has to be wary in comparing a manuscript fragment with a critical edition, and it is worth bearing in mind that when Grenfell and Hunt looked at P.Oxy. 1, they saw a text that "agrees exactly" with Luke.[18]

---

18. *ΛΟΓΙΑ ΙΗΣΟΥ*, 10. Henry Barclay Swete offered a swift corrective here, "The editors say that the *logion* agrees exactly with Luke. It does agree exactly with the R.T. of Luke, but not with WH, who following B and some important cursives, place ἐκβαλεῖν at the end of the sentence; nor with the 'Western' text, which has ἐν τῷ ὀφθαλμῷ for τὸ ἐν τῷ ὀφθαλμῷ, and thus assimilates Luke to Matthew. This is a point of no little interest, and ought to be weighed before we infer a Lucan tendency in the new *logia*" ("The Oxyrhynchus Fragment," *ExpT* 8 [1897]: 540-50, 568 [546]). Cf. Charles Taylor, *The Oxyrhynchus Logia and the Apocryphal Gospels* (Oxford: Clarendon, 1899), 6-7. Simon Gathercole, "Luke in the *Gospel of Thomas*," *NTS* 57 (2010): 114-44 (135-36), speculates that there may have been three stages in the development of the text, from the form witnessed in P[75] B W (= NA[27]) to the version witnessed in ℵ A C, perhaps influenced by Matthew, to *Thomas*'s reproduction of the latter; but he rightly

What is clear, though, is that the degree of agreement between *Thomas* and Luke here is impressive.

The agreement between *Thomas* and Luke (// Matthew) is all the more striking in that the witness to *Thomas* is fragmentary. Although caution is required about considering what is not present in the papyrus, it is worth noting that the P.Oxy. 1 fragment here begins halfway through a sentence. The structure, beginning with καὶ τότε διαβλέψεις ("and then you will see"), implies the presence of something very similar to what Matthew and Luke provide as the first clause in the sentence.[19]

This example is all the more remarkable in that it is not the kind of agreement that comes from liturgical recitation, creedal formula, or familiar phrase. The agreement includes several rare words of the kind that are traditionally used to make the case for a literary link between the Synoptic Gospels.[20] κάρφος ("speck") occurs only here in the New Testament, and διαβλέπω ("see") occurs only here and in Mark 8:25.[21] It is the kind of agreement that points to direct contact between the texts in question.

The importance of the verbatim agreement here is generally overlooked in the literature, in line with the tendency in *Thomas* scholarship to focus on Coptic *Thomas* and to relegate discussion of the Oxyrhynchus fragments to the footnotes. Stephen Patterson, for example, mentions P.Oxy. 1.1-4 only in order to explain its deficiency in helping to ascertain the Greek *Vorlage*

---

underlines the key point, "What this saying does confirm is the extreme likelihood of a literary relationship between Thomas and the Synoptics at the Greek stage: the striking string of very similar Greek words is surely instructive on this point" (136).

19. Already seen in Joseph A. Fitzmyer, "The Oxyrhynchus Logoi of Jesus and the Coptic Gospel According to Thomas," *Theological Studies* 20 (1959): 505-60; repr. in *Essays on the Semitic Background of the New Testament* (London: Geoffrey Chapman, 1971), 355-433 (388-89). See too R. McL.Wilson, *Studies in the Gospel of Thomas* (London: Mowbray, 1960), 58. Cf. Plisch, *Gospel of Thomas*, 92, who notes that the Greek text here is closer to Matthew and Luke than is the Coptic and concludes that "the similarity between the two versions must originally have been greater."

20. John Hawkins, *Horae Synopticae: Contributions to the Study of the Synoptic Problem* (2nd ed.; Oxford: Clarendon, 1909), part II, section I, is devoted to "Identities in Language" that contain "constructions or words which are so very unusual or even peculiar, that the use of written Greek documents is prima facie suggested by them" (54). Hawkins also notes the oddity of the insertion of words between the article and its noun, τὴν δὲ ἐν τῷ σῷ ὀφθαλμῷ δοκόν (Matt. 7:3) // τὴν ἐν τῷ ὀφθαλμῷ σου δοκόν (Luke 6:42), as evidence for a literary link (*Horae Synopticae*, 57). Sadly, the P.Oxy. 1 parallel is lacking here, and it is impossible to tell from the Coptic how the phrase might have been constructed in its source.

21. Cf. Hawkins, *Horae Synopticae*, 64. Hawkins also notes that κάρφος occurs once in the LXX (Gen. 8:11) and that διαβλέπω is absent from the LXX.

of Coptic *Thom.* 26, without noting how far the extant text agrees with Luke (and Matthew).[22] April DeConick speaks of "the fact that the saying also reflects the characteristics of orally transmitted materials, common words and phrases with varying sequences and inflections," but this is weak.[23] The texts, in Greek, are practically identical. Verbatim agreement like this is actually characteristic of direct contact between texts and not of "orally transmitted materials." Indeed, it is diagnostic of that contact. And even if the Greek were to show variation in sequence and inflection, this would hardly point to oral contact since it is the very stuff of synoptic dependence, where verbatim agreement is interspersed with minor editorial variations. The reason we know that there is a literary relationship among the Synoptic Gospels is exactly this kind of evidence, verbatim agreement between texts.

After all, no one seriously thinks that the verbatim agreement between Matt. 7:3-5 and Luke 6:41-42 is due to oral tradition. A literary explanation, whether in terms of Luke's knowledge of Matthew or in terms of their mutual knowledge of Q, is rightly the consensus in the literature.[24] Those arguing the contrary would have a difficult job. And yet this Greek fragment of *Thomas* shows the same degree of verbatim agreement. We would be well advised to treat the text of *Thomas* here as we treat the texts of Matthew and Luke, and to conclude that strong verbatim agreement does indeed illustrate a direct link between texts.

The oversight on this agreement is particularly surprising given that *Thom.* 26 was the first piece of *Thomas* to see the light of day back in January 1897, forming the first four lines of the first fragment of *Thomas* to have been seen by anyone, as far as we know, for over a millennium. It is a reminder of the importance of beginning the story of the discovery of *Thomas*

---

22. Patterson, *Gospel of Thomas*, 29-31.

23. DeConick, *Original Gospel*, 128. DeConick's discussion (*Original Gospel*, 127-29) focuses unnecessarily strongly on the Coptic. DeConick is here discussing John Sieber, "A Redactional Analysis of the Synoptic Gospels with regard to the Question of the Sources of the Gospel according to Thomas" (PhD diss., Claremont Graduate School, 1966; Ann Arbor: University Microfilms International, 1976), 72-74, who argues for oral transmission. If verbatim agreement of this nature does not point to direct contact between texts, then there is no literary relationship among the Synoptic Gospels. Her English translations of the texts in synopsis (303) do not show how close *Thomas* is in P.Oxy. 1 to Luke; for example, "and" and "that is" are not underlined in Luke 6:42.

24. Those arguing for an oral component to Q admit that passages like this, with high verbatim agreement, must have been the result of direct contact between texts, e.g., Dunn, *Jesus Remembered*, 231, "the degree of closeness is such that the passages qualify as good evidence for the existence of a Q document."

in the right place. Grenfell describes the dramatic moment when his colleague Hunt noticed the word κάρφος ("speck") in P.Oxy. 1, as he was sifting through the fragments discovered on the second day of their excavations.[25] Knowing it to be a rare word, he immediately thought of Matt. 7:3-5 // Luke 6:41-42.[26] In the early scholarship on the fragments, the verbatim agreement here between Matthew, Luke, and P.Oxy. 1 was often mentioned, and it was taken for granted that the similarity was striking.

As time has passed, the remarkable similarity of these parallel texts has been forgotten and its significance ignored. The reason for this may lie not only in the marginalization of the Greek witness but also in a failure to appreciate the importance of verbatim agreement, and what it can tell us about the relationship between literary works. It will be worth pausing to consider the role that verbatim agreement should play in these discussions.

Appreciating the Importance of Verbatim Agreement

In any study of the relationship between texts, it is essential to ask the question about the degree of similarity between the texts. It is a key element in beginning discussion of the Synoptic Problem, for example, to establish just how similar the Synoptics are to one another. Likewise in discussions of the relationship between John and the Synoptics, much time is spent analyzing the minor verbal agreements between the texts, and the divided opinions on that issue often come down to how significant one finds those agreements.[27] Surprisingly, this vital first step is almost always missed out in discussions of the relationship between *Thomas* and the Synoptics. Most proceed straight to the second step, which asks whether possible Synoptic redactional elements are present in *Thomas*.[28]

25. Grenfell, "Oldest Record," 1027.

26. See n. 18 above.

27. See, for example, D. Moody Smith, *John Among the Gospels* (2nd ed.; Columbia, SC: University of South Carolina Press, 2001), 2-3. It is worth noting that John does not contain anything like the string of words in agreement that one finds, on occasion, between *Thomas* and the Synoptics. The longest strings of agreement between John and the Synoptics are five to seven words (e.g., Mark 2:9,Έγειρε καὶ ἆρον τὸν κράβαττόν σου καὶ περιπάτει; John 5:8, Έγειρε ἆρον τὸν κράβαττόν σου καὶ περιπάτει). There is also a nine-word agreement, ἀμὴν λέγω ὑμῖν ὅτι εἷς ἐξ ὑμῶν παραδώσει με, at John 13:21 and Mark 14:18 = Matt. 26:21.

28. For example, John Dominic Crossan, *Four Other Gospels: Shadows on the Contours of Canon* (Minneapolis: Seabury, 1985), 36. In spite of speaking of the need for "proper methodology," Crossan begins by asking whether redactional traits from one text are present in

To an extent, the omission is understandable. Our only complete textual witness of *Thomas* is in Coptic, and comparisons between Greek texts of the Synoptics and the Coptic text of *Thomas* are far from straightforward. There is the danger that the interpreter keen to stress similarities might inadvertently introduce parallel wording into retroversions from the Coptic to the Greek, just as the interpreter who is keen to stress differences might create greater distance between the texts.[29] But the difficulties in the task should not be our invitation to sidestep something so important. It is easy to overstate the complexity of the process of comparing Coptic texts with Greek ones; and, more importantly, the Oxyrhynchus fragments of *Thomas*, P.Oxy. 1, 654, and 655, need to be taken seriously.[30]

If there is some direct contact between the texts in the Log and Speck saying, it is worth searching for direct contact in other sayings too. Indeed, direct contact becomes more persuasive if there are further examples of verbatim agreement. Finding other examples of verbatim agreement with the Synoptics among the relatively small sample of *Thomas* that is contained in P.Oxy. 1, 654, and 655 might sound like a tall order, but in fact there are several more noteworthy agreements of six to eight words. Moreover, several of these feature words or expressions that are rare enough to raise attention.[31] The first of these is in the Oxyrhynchus text of *Thomas* 3, in comparison with Luke 17:21:

---

another. The prior question is surely: is there any verbatim or near-verbatim agreement between the texts in question such as to suggest the possibility of direct knowledge one way or the other? Similarly, Koester, *Ancient Christian Gospels*, 84-85, begins his discussion of *Thomas*'s relationship to the Synoptics without any analysis of the degree of agreement between the texts.

29. DeConick, *Original Gospel*, 299-316, attempts to overcome the difficulty by producing a synopsis of "Verbal Similarities between *Thomas* and the Synoptics." This synopsis is useful in enabling one to see quickly the range and extent of the parallels, though a closer look at the parallels in Greek is of course necessary for serious work on the issue.

30. I am persuaded that the original language of the *Gospel of Thomas* was Greek, but see Perrin, *Thomas and Tatian*, for the view that the work was originally in Syriac. Perrin's thesis is summarized in his *Thomas, the Other Gospel* (London: SPCK, 2007), 73-106. In response to Perrin's project, see especially P. J. Williams, "Alleged Syriac Catchwords in the Gospel of Thomas," *VC* 63/1 (2009): 71-82.

31. Again, this element is often ignored in discussions of *Thomas*-Synoptic relations, but see Snodgrass, "Gospel of Thomas," 26, "I would suggest that the appearance of *hapax legomena* or other rare words from one of the canonical Gospels in a parallel saying in *Thomas* should be considered as proof of dependence on the canonical Gospels."

P. Oxy. 654.15-16, *Thom. 3* // Luke 17:21

Luke 17:20-21	P.Oxy. 654.15-16, *Thom.* 3.1-3
ἐπερωτηθεὶς δὲ ὑπὸ τῶν Φαρισαίων πότε ἔρχεται ἡ βασιλεία τοῦ θεοῦ ἀπεκρίθη αὐτοῖς καὶ εἶπεν, οὐκ ἔρχεται ἡ βασιλεία τοῦ θεοῦ μετὰ παρατηρήσεως. 21 οὐδὲ ἐροῦσιν ἰδοὺ ὧδε ἤ ἐκεῖ ἰδοὺ γὰρ ἡ βασιλεία τοῦ θεοῦ ἐντὸς ὑμῶν ἐστιν	λέγει ᾽Ι[η(σοῦ)ς· ἐὰν] οἱ ἕλκοντες ἡμᾶς [εἴπωσιν ὑμῖν· ἰδοὺ] ἡ βασιλεία ἐν οὐρα[νῷ, ὑμᾶς φθήσεται] τὰ πετεινὰ τοῦ οὐρ[ανοῦ· ἐὰν δ᾽ εἴπωσιν ὅ]τι ὑπὸ τὴν γήν ἐστ[ιν, εἰσελεύσονται] οἱ ἰχθύες τῆς θαλά[σσης προφθάσαν]τες ὑμᾶς· καὶ ἡ βασ[ιλεία τοῦ θεοῦ]* ἐντὸς ὑμῶν [ἐ]στι [κἀκτός . . .
Once Jesus was asked by the Pharisees when the kingdom of God was coming, and he answered them, "The kingdom of God is not coming with things that can be observed; 21 nor will they say, "Behold here!" or "Behold there!" For the kingdom of God is within you."	Jesus says, "[If] those who lead us" [say to you, 'See], the kingdom is in heaven,' then the birds of heaven [will precede you. If they say,] 'It is under the earth,' then the fish of the sea [will enter it, preceding] you. And the [kingdom of God] is within you [and it is outside you]."

*I reconstruct the lacuna here with τοῦ θεοῦ, following Fitzmyer, "Oxyrhynchus Logoi," 376-77, and others. Grenfell and Hunt, *New Sayings*, 15-16, reconstructed the lacuna here with τῶν οὐρανῶν, and they are followed by DeConick, *Original Gospel*, 51-52, among others. DeConick rightly notes that "kingdom of God" appears in *Thomas* only in the Greek of *Thom.* 27, but this is unimpressive given that *Thom.* 27 and the saying under discussion are the only two references to "kingdom" anywhere in the Oxyrhynchus fragments of *Thomas*. In other words, there are no extant examples of "kingdom of heaven" in Greek *Thomas*. See also the discussion in W. Schrage, "Evangelienzitate in den Oxyrhynchus-Logien und im koptischen Thomas-Evangelium," in W. Eltester and F. H. Kettler, eds., *Apophoreta: Festschrift für Ernst Haenchen* (BZNW 30; Berlin: Töpelmann, 1964), 251-68 (258). Moreover, "kingdom of heaven" would not work well in context here, where Jesus has just denied that the kingdom is to be found in heaven (the sky). On "kingdom of heaven" as an example of Matthean redactional phrasing influencing *Thomas*, see further below, 66-69.

**ἡμᾶς is usually emended to ὑμᾶς in line with the Coptic ΝΗΤΝ (Fitzmyer, "Oxyrhynchus Logoi," 376), now often without comment in translations of the Greek (e.g., DeConick, *Original Gospel*, 51).

The text is incomplete here, but what we have suggests something like a seven-word verbatim agreement between Luke and *Thomas*, ἡ βασιλεία τοῦ θεοῦ ἐντὸς ὑμῶν ἐστιν . . . , "the kingdom of God is within you . . . ."[32] This is a striking and unusual expression, and one that has generated multiple different attempts at translation ("within you," "among you," "in your midst"),[33] an oddity that increases the likelihood of a direct link between

32. The uncertainty is over the fact that two and a half words are missing, ἡ βασ[ιλεία τοῦ θεοῦ], but "kingdom of God" is most likely here.

33. Plisch, *Gospel of Thomas*, 43, rightly notes: "The interpretation of the expression in

Luke and *Thomas*. The expression ἐντὸς ὑμῶν ἐστιν is not found anywhere in Greek literature prior to Luke 17:21 and *Thom.* 3. In other words, it is not a common, everyday expression of the kind that would be passed on naturally via oral tradition. It is exactly the kind of agreement that leads us, when looking at agreements among the Synoptics, to postulate a direct link.

Our own familiarity with the expression from Luke may explain why we do not find it striking, at first, when we see it in *Thomas*. Moreover, attempts to discount this striking agreement by appealing to differences between *Thomas* and Luke elsewhere miss the point. Patterson, for example, says that "apart from this final clause the two sayings have virtually no verbal correspondence, so that a direct literary relationship between them can be ruled out."[34] But absence of agreement for part of the saying says nothing about the presence of agreement for part of the saying.[35] The verbatim agreement here, featuring an unparalleled and unusual expression, is a sign of direct contact between texts.

P. Oxy. 654.25-26, *Thom.* 4.2-3 // Matt. 19:30 // Mark 10:31

Another example of verbatim agreement between the Synoptics and Greek *Thomas* is worth mentioning. It is at P.Oxy. 654.25-26:

Matt. 19:30	Mark 10:31	P.Oxy. 654, *Thom.* 4.2-3
πολλοὶ δὲ ἔσονται πρῶτοι ἔσχατοι καὶ ἔσχατοι πρῶτοι.	πολλοὶ δὲ ἔσονται πρῶτοι ἔσχατοι καὶ [οἱ] ἔσχατοι πρῶτοι.	ὅτι πολλοὶ ἔσονται π[ρῶτοι ἔσχατοι καὶ] οἱ ἔσχατοι πρῶτοι
And many who are first will be last and last first.	And many who are first will be last and the last first.	For many who are f[irst] will be [last and] the last first.

Luke . . . . has always been a major headache for scholars, especially the perception of the Greek adverb 'within' (*entos*)." For a helpful discussion, see Joseph Fitzmyer, *The Gospel According to Luke: Introduction, Translation, and Notes* (2 vols.; AB; Garden City, NY: Doubleday, 1981–85), 2:1161-62, who favors either "within your grasp" or "among(st) you" for Luke.

34. Patterson, *Gospel of Thomas*, 72. Patterson only quotes the *Coptic* in comparison with Luke's Greek, and the Oxyrhynchus fragment is relegated to only a footnote in English translation. The striking agreement in Greek is hidden from the reader.

35. This is what I call "the plagiarist's charter." See further on this point below, 54-56.

Matthew and Mark here differ only in the plural article (οἱ) that may appear in Mark, something that is shared with *Thomas*. If the article is read, eight out of *Thomas*'s nine words[36] agree with Mark. Without it, seven out of nine agree, likewise with Matthew. On its own, a memorable aphorism like this might not be enough to demonstrate a direct link between texts.[37] As part of a cumulative case, however, it adds weight to the other examples of verbatim agreement between Greek *Thomas* and the Synoptics.[38] That aphorisms like this are easier to hold in the memory does not of necessity mean that *Thomas* gained his knowledge of it from an oral tradition independent of the Synoptics. It begs the question to assume that the memory is of a version in oral tradition. The very memorability of aphorisms like this makes them good candidates for getting picked up, by *Thomas*, from a familiar text. Moreover, that there are variants of the same saying in the Synoptics (Matt. 20:16; Luke 13:30) illustrates that there is more than one way to say, "The first will be last and the last first."[39]

36. Grenfell and Hunt, *New Sayings*, 18, made this reconstruction, and it has been almost universally followed (Attridge, "Greek Fragments," 115). DeConick, *Original Gospel*, 57, reconstructs without the καί, "There is only room for 12 letters. So the 15 letters proposed by Attridge look to me to be implausible." But this kind of precision overreaches the evidence. P.Oxy. 654 is 7.8 cm. wide; Larry Hurtado, "The Greek Fragments of the *Gospel of Thomas* as Artefacts: Papyrological Observations on Papyrus Oxyrhynchus 1, Papyrus Oxyrhynchus 654 and Papyrus Oxyrhynchus 655," in Jörg Frey, Enno Edzard Popkes, and Jens Schröter, eds., *Das Thomasevangelium: Entstehung — Rezeption — Theologie* (Berlin: de Gruyter, 2008), 19-32 (25), follows Attridge ("Greek Fragments," 98) in estimating an original column about 9 cm. wide, which would give room for 26-36 letters per line. Grenfell and Hunt's reconstruction of line 25, followed by Attridge, adds 15 letters to the extant 18 (note that ὅτι is written above the line and should not be counted), producing a line of 33 letters. This is well within the stated range, and it avoids the odd sentence with no conjunction suggested by DeConick.

37. Note, however, John C. Poirier's important caution, "not only is the exact wording of an aphorism more easily remembered than the wording of nonaphorisms . . . but the precise wording of an aphorism is also more ingredient to the aphorism as a traditional/semantic unit and is therefore less dispensable" ("Memory, Written Sources, and the Synoptic Problem: A Response to Robert K. McIver and Marie Carroll," *JBL* 123 [2004]: 315-22). For a full and helpful discussion, see D. E. Aune, "Oral Tradition and the Aphorisms of Jesus," in H. Wanbrough, ed., *Jesus and the Oral Gospel Tradition* (JSNTSup 64; Sheffield: JSOT Press), 211-65, especially 237-38.

38. Cf. Michael Fieger, *Das Thomasevangelium: Einleitung, Kommentar und Systematik* (Neutestamentliche Abhandlungen n.f. 22; Münster: Aschendorff, 1991), 28-30, who argues for Thomasine dependence on Matt. 19:30 // Mark 10:31, in a passage partly derived from Schrage, *Verhältnis*, 32-34, but with the addition of a stronger consideration of the Greek evidence.

39. Patterson, *Gospel of Thomas*, 19-20, discusses only the Coptic evidence and so does

P.Oxy. 654.29-31, *Thom.* 5.2 // Luke 8:17

Luke 8:17	P.Oxy. 654.29-31, *Thom.* 5.2
οὐ γάρ ἐστιν κρυπτὸν ὃ οὐ φανερὸν γενήσεται, οὐδὲ ἀπόκρυφον ὃ οὐ μὴ γνωσθῇ καὶ εἰς φανερὸν ἔλθῃ.	[οὐ γάρ ἐσ]τιν κρυπτὸν ὃ οὐ φανε[ρὸν γενήσεται], καὶ τεθαμμένον ὃ ο[ὐκ ἐγερθήσεται]
For nothing is hidden that will not be made manifest, nor is anything secret that will not become known and come to light.	For nothing is hidden that will not be made manifest, nor buried that will not be raised.

The text of P.Oxy. 654 is fragmentary, but according to the standard and un-controversial reconstructions, there is an eight-word verbatim agreement between *Thomas* and Luke, once again the kind of agreement that points to a direct link between the texts.[40]

DeConick draws attention to the divergence between *Thom.* 5 and the other elements in Luke 8:17,[41] but this negates the impact made by areas of agreement by appealing to areas of disagreement.[42] The presence of non-agreement in a saying should not be allowed to detract from striking examples of verbatim agreement in the same saying. Patterson's suggestion that Coptic *Thomas* "represents the more original version" in sayings 5 and 6 leaves unexplained the verbatim agreement in the Greek.[43]

---

not deal with the close verbatim agreement in Greek. He provides an English translation of P.Oxy. 654.21-27 on 19 n. 6, but he does not discuss it.

40. Cf. Tuckett, "Thomas and the Synoptics," 145-46. McArthur, "Dependence," 287, drew attention to this example; see further below, 82-84.

41. *Original Gospel*, 61, "Is this phrase enough to *prove* Lukan dependence especially when the rest of Logion 5.2 is wildly divergent from Luke 8.17, particularly the final clause of the passage which is not known in the Thomasine parallel?"

42. On this "plagiarist's charter," see further below, 54-56.

43. Patterson, *Gospel of Thomas*, 22, "There is no reason to suppose that Thomas could not have composed the saying in this way without direct knowledge of Luke 8.17a." Patterson discusses the related texts and suggests influence from Q on Luke 8:17, but the range of parallels illustrates the range of different ways there are to construct a similar saying, so making the coincidental agreement here all the more striking.

P.Oxy. 655 (Col. 2.19-23), *Thom.* 39.3 // Matt. 10:16

Matt. 10:16	*Thom.* 39.3, P.Oxy. 655
<u>γίνεσθε</u> οὖν <u>φρόνιμοι ὡς οἱ</u> <u>ὄφεις καὶ ἀκέραιοι ὡς αἱ</u> <u>περιστεραί</u>	[ὑμεῖς] δὲ <u>γεί[νεσθε φρόνι]μοι ὡ[ς οἱ</u> <u>ὄφεις καὶ ἀ]κέραι[οι ὡς αἱ</u> <u>περιστε]ρα[ί]</u>

Matt. 10:16	*Thom.* 39.3, P.Oxy. 655
Therefore <u>be as wise as serpents and as innocent as doves.</u>	But <u>be as wise as serpents and as innocent as doves.</u>

Although the text of P.Oxy. 655 is highly fragmentary, the reconstruction here is not difficult, especially as there is no good reason to think that the Coptic fails to translate the Greek quite closely.[44] While caution is necessary where texts are fragmentary, it looks like the agreement here between Matthew and *Thomas* may have been close, possibly a nine-word consecutive string.[45]

There are, therefore, several examples of verbatim agreements between the *Gospel of Thomas* and the Synoptic Gospels in Greek.[46] Given that the Greek evidence for *Thomas* is so fragmentary, this is an important observation. It raises a further question. If there is major verbatim agreement in the Greek, is there any way of estimating the degree of verbatim agreement that might have existed in other sayings that do not have parallels in the Greek?

44. See Fitzmyer, "Oxyrhynchus Logoi," 414.

45. The spelling of γίνεσθε / γείνεσθε differs, but note that γείνεσθε is the spelling of Codex Vaticanus and several other uncials. It is possible also that Greek *Thomas* lacked the articles in οἱ ὄφεις and αἱ περιστεραί; the text is sometimes reconstructed this way, e.g., Plisch, *Gospel of Thomas*, 38; and DeConick, *Original Gospel*, 160.

46. P. Oxy. 1.36-41 (*Thom.* 31), οὐκ ἔστιν δεκτὸς προφήτης ἐν τῇ π(ατ)ρίδι αὐτοῦ, is also very close to Luke 4:24, οὐδεὶς προφήτης δεκτός ἐστιν ἐν τῇ πατρίδι αὐτοῦ. On this parallel, see further below, 84-86. Similarly, P.Oxy. 655.1-17 (*Thom.* 36) exhibits substantial signs of verbatim agreement with Matt. 6:25-30 // Luke 12:22-28. However, the text is too fragmentary for one to be confident about the degree of verbatim agreement. See further on this passage below, 60-63.

What about the Coptic?

Although the agreement between the extant Greek fragments of *Thomas* and the Synoptics is striking, especially given the fragmentary nature of those papyri, it is worth taking a look at Coptic *Thomas* to confirm that a similar pattern might be evidenced in its Greek *Vorlage*. This is not a straightforward task. Hypothetical retroversions can be a minefield, complicated by the fact that the Coptic text tends to be further removed from the language of the Synoptics than are the Greek fragments.[47] And there is always the thorny problem of experimental bias, the risk of retroverting to a Greek text that fits one's theory better.

Nevertheless, one can go for help to the Greek retroversions made by Heinrich Greeven[48] and, more recently, the team led by Hans-Gebhard Bethge.[49] By working with their retroversions rather than providing new ones, we can at least avoid the difficulty of deliberately choosing Greek wording that will enhance the verbatim agreement with the Synoptics.[50] It is important to acknowledge that this kind of comparison is an imprecise art and that care is necessary. But it can provide a cautious confirmation that the kind of verbatim agreement witnessed in the Oxyrhynchus fragments might also have obtained in the Greek *Vorlage* of Coptic *Thomas*. I will offer three illustrative parallels, the first of which is Matt. 15:11 // *Thom.* 14.5.[51]

47. See further below, 59-63.

48. Albert Huck, *Synopsis of the First Three Gospels*, 13th ed., fundamentally revised by Heinrich Greeven (Tübingen: Mohr [Siebeck], 1981).

49. "Appendix 1: Evangelium Thomae Copticum," in Kurt Aland, ed., *Synopsis Quattuor Evangeliorum* (15th ed.; Stuttgart: Deutsche Bibelgesellschaft, 2001), 517-46. Plisch (*Gospel of Thomas*, 35) notes that he and Judith Hartenstein prepared the Greek retroversion. It appears also in Plisch, *Gospel of Thomas*, *ad loc.*

50. It is, of course, necessary to be cautious with these Greek retroversions. Christopher Tuckett suggests care, "And, for example, in cases where the Greek and Coptic exist but differ from each other, it is by no means clear that the differences are due to a Greek version lying behind the present Coptic text; the differences could just as easily have arisen when the text was translated into Coptic" (review of Uwe-Karsten Plisch, *The Gospel of Thomas: Original Text with Commentary, RBL* [http://www.bookreviews.org] (2009).

51. For more on this example, see below, 70-72.

Matt. 15:11	*Thom.* 14.5 (Coptic)	*Thom.* 14.5 (retroversion)
<u>οὐ</u> <u>τὸ εἰσερχόμενον</u> <u>εἰς τὸ στόμα</u> <u>κοινοῖ τὸν ἄνθρωπον,</u> <u>ἀλλὰ τὸ ἐκπορευόμενον</u> <u>ἐκ τοῦ στόματος</u> <u>τοῦτο κοινοῖ τὸν</u> ἄνθρωπον.	ΠΕΤΝΑΒШΚ ΓΑΡ ΕϨΟΥΝ ϨΝ ΤΕΤΝ̄ΤΑΠΡΟ ϤΝΑΧШϨΜ̄ ΤΗΥΤΝ̄ ΑΝ ΑΛΛΑ ΠΕΤΝ̄ΝΗΥ ΕΒΟΛ ϨΝ ΤΕΤΝ̄ΤΑΠΡΟ Ν̄ΤΟϤ ΠΕΤΝΑΧΑϨΜ̄ ΤΗΥΤΝ̄.	<u>οὐ</u> γὰρ <u>τὸ εἰσερχόμενον</u> <u>εἰς τὸ στόμα</u> ὑμῶν <u>κοινώσει</u> ὑμᾶς, <u>ἀλλὰ τὸ ἐκπορευόμενον</u> <u>ἐκ τοῦ στόματος</u> ὑμῶν <u>τοῦτο κοινώσει</u> ὑμᾶς.

Matt. 15:11	*Thom.* 14.5
<u>Not what goes into</u> the <u>mouth</u> <u>defiles</u> a person, <u>but what comes out of</u> the <u>mouth</u>, <u>this</u> <u>defiles</u> a person.	For <u>not what goes into</u> your <u>mouth</u> will <u>defile</u> you, <u>but what comes out of</u> your <u>mouth</u> — <u>this</u> will <u>defile</u> you.

Bethge's Greek retroversion provides a text that is very close to Matt. 15:11, in structure and much of the detail. The adjustment to the second person plural in *Thomas* is necessary given the contextual second person plural throughout *Thom.* 14. Otherwise, the language is very close.[52] DeConick's English translations provide seventeen consecutive words in common between the two.[53]

A second example is *Thom.* 73.

Matt. 9:37-38 // Luke 10:2	*Thom.* 73 (Coptic)	*Thom.* 73 (retroversion)
τότε <u>λέγει</u> τοῖς μαθηταῖς αὐτοῦ·* <u>ὁ μὲν θερισμὸς</u> <u>πολύς, οἱ δὲ ἐργάται</u> <u>ὀλίγοι· δεήθητε</u> οὖν <u>τοῦ κυρίου</u> τοῦ θερισμοῦ ὅπως <u>ἐκβάλῃ ἐργάτας</u>** <u>εἰς τὸν θερισμὸν</u> αὐτοῦ.	ΠΕΧΕ ῙΣ̄ ΧΕ ΠШϨΣ ΜΕΝ ΝΑϢШϤ· Ν̄ΕΡΓΑΤΗΣ ΔΕ ΣΟΒΚ· ΣΟΠΣ̄ ΔΕ Μ̄ΠΧΟΕΙΣ ϢΙΝΑ ΕϤΝΑΝΕΧ· ΕΡΓΑΤΗΣ ΕΒΟΛ· ΕΠШϨΣ.	<u>λέγει</u> ᾿Ιησοῦς· <u>ὁ μὲν θερισμὸς</u> <u>πολύς, οἱ δὲ ἐργάται</u> <u>ὀλίγοι· δεήθητε</u> δὲ <u>τοῦ κυρίου</u> <u>ἵνα ἐκβάλῃ ἐργάτας</u> <u>εἰς τὸν θερισμὸν.</u>

---

52. On the resumptive οὗτος, see below, 71 n. 22.

53. DeConick, *Original Gospel*, 91, 301.

Matt. 9:37-38 // Luke 10:2	*Thom.* 73
Then he <u>says</u> to his disciples, "<u>The harvest is great, but the</u> workers are few; <u>pray</u> therefore <u>the Lord</u> of the harvest <u>to send workers into</u> his harvest."	Jesus <u>says</u>, "<u>The harvest is great but the workers are few</u>; and <u>pray the Lord to send workers into</u> the <u>harvest</u>."
*Luke 10:2, ἔλεγεν δὲ πρὸς αὐτούς. **Luke 10:2 NA²⁷ reverses the order, i.e., ἐργάτας ἐκβάλῃ.	

The agreement between *Thomas* and Matthew // Luke is very close. Sixteen out of eighteen words in the Greek retroversion (corresponding to fourteen out of sixteen in Coptic) agree with Matthew and Luke, and variations are only minor.[54] The agreement includes language that, while common in the Synoptics, is unusual in *Thomas*, ϭⲟⲡⲥ̄ ("pray," only here), ⲉⲣⲅⲁⲧⲏⲥ ("worker," only here), ⲙⲉⲛ . . . ⲇⲉ ("On the one hand . . . on the other," only here),[55] ⲛⲁϣⲱ ("great," only here), ⲥⲟⲃⲕ̄ ("small," only here and in *Thom.* 20, where it parallels Matt. 13:32 // Mark 4:31). The near identity of the language in Matthew // Luke and *Thomas* is an indicator of a direct relationship between the texts, and the relatively unusual nature of a lot of the language in *Thomas* already provides a suggestion of the direction of the relationship, from the Synoptics to *Thomas*.[56]

54. See Schrage, *Verhältnis*, 153-54, for discussion of the degree of similarity between Coptic *Thomas* and Sahidic Coptic Matthew and Luke; and cf. Patterson, *Gospel of Thomas*, 56, for a critique. Patterson rightly notes that the differences between the texts are likely to "reflect differences in the Greek texts which underlie these Coptic translations," but he goes on to suggest that "Thomas and the synoptics have appropriated this saying from the oral tradition independently of one another," a conclusion less likely given the close verbatim agreement between *Thomas* and Matthew // Luke, and the markedly un-Thomasine language, especially the ⲙⲉⲛ . . . ⲇⲉ structure.

55. See also *Thomas* 9, where ⲙⲉⲛ occurs without ⲇⲉ. The parallels Mark 4:4-5 // Luke 8:5-6 have μὲν . . . καί; Matt. 13:4-5 has μὲν . . . δέ.

56. The verbatim agreement is often noticed but is seldom discussed. Because Matthew and Luke are practically identical here, there is no room, for those who accept the Q hypothesis, for the discovery of redactional features in Matthew and Luke. Patterson, *Gospel of Thomas*, 61, says, "Neither Matthew nor Luke has likely changed a thing in the tradition they received from Q; therefore, it is simply impossible to show on the basis of content that Thomas made use of Matthew and / or Luke in acquiring this saying" (cf. also J. Sieber, "Redactional Analysis," 208-9; and DeConick, *Original Gospel*, 231). This illustrates the danger with searching solely for redactional features in the case for or against Thomasine familiarity with the Synoptics. The first step has to be the isolation of verbatim agreement of the kind

The third example is similar.

Matt. 8:20 // Luke 9:58*	*Thom.* 86 (Coptic)	*Thom.* 86 (retroversion)
καὶ λέγει αὐτῷ ὁ Ἰησοῦς, αἱ ἀλώπεκες φωλεοὺς ἔχουσιν καὶ τὰ πετεινὰ τοῦ οὐρανοῦ κατασκηνώσεις, ὁ δὲ υἱὸς τοῦ ἀνθρώπου οὐκ ἔχει ποῦ τὴν κεφαλὴν κλίνῃ	ⲡⲉⲝⲉ ⲓ̅ⲥ̅ ⲝⲉ [ⲛⲃⲁϢⲟⲣ ⲟ̅ⲩⲛⲧ̅]ⲁⲩ ⲛⲟⲩ[ⲃ]ⲏⲃ ⲁⲩⲱ ⲛ2ⲁⲗⲁⲧⲉ ⲟⲩⲛⲧⲁⲩ ⲙ̅ⲙⲁⲩ ⲙ̅ⲡⲉⲩⲙⲁ2 ⲡϢⲏⲣⲉ ⲁⲉ ⲙ̅ⲡⲣⲱⲙⲉ ⲙⲛ̅ⲧⲁϥ ⲛ̅ⲛ[ⲟ]ⲩⲙⲁ ⲉⲣⲓⲕⲉ ⲛ̅ⲧⲉϥ ⲁⲡⲉ ⲛ̅ϥⲙ̅ⲧⲟⲛ ⲙ̅ⲙ(ⲟ)ϥ	λέγει Ἰησοῦς· [αἱ ἀλώπεκες ἔχου]σιν (τοὺς) [φωλεοὺς (αὐτῶν)] καὶ τὰ πετεινὰ (ἔχει [τὴν]) κατασκήνωσιν (αὐτῶν), ὁ δὲ υἱὸς τοῦ ἀνθρώπου οὐκ ἔχει ποῦ τὴν κεφαλὴν (αὐτοῦ) κλίνῃ καὶ ἀναπαύσηται.

*Matthew and Luke are identical here; only the introduction differs, where Luke has εἶπεν for Matthew's λέγει.

Matt. 8:20 // Luke 9:58	*Thom.* 86
Foxes have holes and the birds of the air have nests, but the Son of Man has nowhere to lay his head.	Foxes have their holes and the birds have their nest, but the Son of Man has nowhere to lay his head and rest.

The degree of verbatim agreement between Matthew, Luke, and Greek *Thomas* here is likely to have been strong, with at most minor variations[57] alongside the distinctively Thomasine final twist, ⲛ̅ϥⲙ̅ⲧⲟⲛ ⲙ̅ⲙ(ⲟ)ϥ, "and rest." Advocates of Thomasine independence rarely comment on the degree of closeness between the texts here. The issue is bypassed because of the verbatim agreement (100 percent identity) between Matthew and Luke, which means, on the standard paradigm, that there is no redactional intervention from Matthew or Luke. As soon as this exact form of the saying is attributed to Q, there is no redactional Synoptic fingerprint that requires explanation;[58] and, as usual, the verbatim agreement simply goes without

we see here, verbatim agreement that is all the more striking when it features so much un-Thomasine language.

57. As Plisch points out (*Gospel of Thomas*, 196), "The many possessive articles in the Coptic text do not give information about the Greek *vorlage* [*sic*], since they are idiomatic in Coptic. The Coptic translation of Matt 8:20 and Luke 9:58 displays the same possessive articles."

58. Patterson, *Gospel of Thomas*, 61, is typical here. However, some rethinking of the Q

notice. This is in spite of the fact that the verbatim identity in Matthew and Luke is itself explained in terms of a literary link, whether their mutual knowledge of Q or Luke's use of Matthew. The oversight is unfortunate given the degree of similarity between *Thomas* and the Synoptics here, and it illustrates the difficulty with ignoring the presence of verbatim agreement between *Thomas* and the Synoptics. While judgments involving retroverted Greek are, of course, provisional, the agreement between *Thomas* and the Synoptics may include the uncommon words φωλεός ("hole") and κατασκήνωσις ("dwelling"), both of which occur only here in the New Testament.[59]

This representative selection of examples illustrates that the Greek underlying the Coptic translation is likely to confirm the impression made by the Oxyrhynchus fragments, that there are frequent and extended verbatim parallels between *Thomas* and the Synoptic Gospels. Of course it is necessary to be cautious about hypothetical *Vorlagen*, but it is worth bearing in mind that, if anything, the Coptic text is likely to be further away from the Synoptic parallels than the Greek underlying it was. In every place where we can at least get a window on the Greek textual witness, via the Oxyrhynchus fragments, the latter are closer to the Synoptics than is the Coptic.[60]

Coming to Terms with Verbatim Agreement

One of the difficulties with coming to terms with the verbatim agreement between *Thomas* and the Synoptics is that there can be unrealistic expectations. The extent of verbatim agreement among the Synoptics prepares our imagination for something that is quite unusual. The bar is simply too high. We are so familiar with the really high proportion of agreement here

---

hypothesis may provide an additional challenge here in that Matthew is the evangelist who shows strong preference for this kind of paired animal imagery; see Michael Goulder, *Luke*, 463; idem, "Is Q a Juggernaut?" *JBL* 115 (1996): 667-81 (680-81). Goulder does not discuss the evidence from *Thomas*, but it is worth adding that most of the animal pairs in *Thomas* (39, serpents and doves, Matt. 10:16; *Thom.* 76, moth and worm, Matt. 6:19; *Thom.* 93, dogs and swine, Matt. 7:6) are shared with the Synoptics. The exceptions are *Thom.* 3 (fish and birds) and 102 (dogs and oxen).

59. Cf. Hawkins, *Horae Synopticae*, 63. φωλεός is absent from the LXX. κατασκήνωσις occurs five times in the LXX but always in the context of the temple and the divine presence.

60. See further below, 59-63.

that we begin to treat it as a norm rather than as an anomaly.[61] In other words, when we look at the extent of verbatim agreement between Matthew and Mark and contrast it with the extent of verbatim agreement between Matthew and *Thomas*, we are naturally disappointed with the latter.[62] DeConick, for example, notes, "The exact verbal agreement, lengthy sequences of words, and secondary features shared between the Triple Tradition versions and the Quelle versions *far* exceed anything we find in the *Gospel of Thomas*,"[63] but it does not follow that *Thomas* is unfamiliar with the Synoptics.[64]

In other words, the reminder about the sheer difference between intra-Synoptic agreement and Synoptic-*Thomas* agreement is a useful one, but the observation all too easily discourages us from taking Synoptic-*Thomas* agreement sufficiently seriously. After all, the evidence of one document's familiarity with another is not a matter of percentages.[65] If twenty percent of a student's essay shows clear signs of plagiarism, it would be no counterargument for the student to complain that the remaining eighty percent of the essay was his or her own work.[66] If there is evidence in *Thomas* of familiarity with one or more of the Synoptics, it is no counterargument that in many other places *Thomas* shows no traces of familiarity. Thus when Patterson is summarizing his case against *Thomas*'s dependence on the

---

61. Cf. Gathercole, "Luke in the *Gospel of Thomas*," 117. On the proper understanding of the high levels of verbatim agreement in the double tradition and how this points to a literary relationship, see John Kloppenborg, "Variation in the Reproduction of the Double Tradition and an Oral Q?" *ETL* 83/1 (2007): 53-80.

62. Patterson contextualizes his discussion of *Thomas*'s relationship to the Synoptics by looking at the agreement in order and content among the Synoptics, a discussion that may generate unrealistic expectations about the degree of verbatim agreement between *Thomas* and the Synoptics; see especially *Gospel of Thomas*, 12-16.

63. DeConick, *Original Gospel*, 23. ("Quelle" is DeConick's characteristic term for Q.) Given the evidence of the Oxyrhynchus papyri, especially the P.Oxy. 1 witness to *Thom.* 26, she may be overstating a little here.

64. DeConick's position, set out in both *Recovering* and *Original Gospel*, is that the older claims about dependence are too simplistic and that one can only fully understand *Thomas* if one appreciates the oral milieu of the work's evolution and development.

65. This is the serious weakness in Eta Linnemann's arguments against literary dependence in the Synoptic Gospels, *Is There a Synoptic Problem? Rethinking the Literary Dependence of the First Three Gospels* (Grand Rapids: Baker, 1992). Linnemann gathers together a range of percentages of agreement among the Synoptics and regards the figures as low, as if absence of agreement in some places takes away from the presence of agreement in other places.

66. See further on this point below, 54-56.

Synoptics, he acknowledges the argument that *Thomas* sometimes parallels Synoptic redaction and adds that "there are indeed several places where this appears to be true";[67] but he goes on to comment: "But taken together, these instances do not suggest any consistent pattern of borrowing. And they are far outnumbered by the many sayings that show no knowledge at all of their synoptic counterparts, and in many cases appear to come from a stage in the tradition that is more primitive."[68]

In order for *Thomas*'s familiarity with the Synoptics to be established, one only requires knowledge of the Synoptics in certain places. It does not need to be a "consistent pattern." And even if more primitive traditions are contained in *Thomas*, this is relevant only to the issue of *Thomas*'s knowledge of oral traditions, and is not directly relevant to the question of literary priority. It is important here, as elsewhere in discussions of intra-Gospel relationships, to avoid confusing literary priority and the age of traditions.[69]

This general problem is exacerbated by the fact that there is a tendency in *Thomas* scholarship to set up the debate as one of whether *Thomas* is totally dependent on the Synoptics. When DeConick summarizes issues in *Thomas* studies, she characterizes one viewpoint as arguing that *Thomas* "was a late Gnostic gospel entirely dependent on the canonical Gospels,"[70] a viewpoint that would be impossible to defend given that half of *Thomas* is unparalleled in the Synoptics. Indeed, those who argue that *Thomas* is familiar with the Synoptics usually add that this only takes us so far in explaining the document. Klyne Snodgrass, for example, argues that "it is dependent on the canonical Gospels for *some* of its material," adding, "That *Thomas* is dependent in some sayings does not mean that it is dependent in all its sayings";[71] and similar statements are commonplace.[72]

On the whole, the issue of verbatim agreement between *Thomas* and the Synoptics is simply not discussed in the literature, so the key evidence for a direct link between the texts can go unnoticed. Although it is a strong method to look for clear cases of Synoptic redaction in *Thomas*, those cases do not always appear in texts exhibiting large-scale verbatim agreement, and texts like *Thom.* 26 can be neglected.

If we are insufficiently impressed with verbatim agreements of up to

---

67. Patterson, *Fifth Gospel*, 66.
68. Ibid., 67.
69. See further my *Case Against Q*, 65.
70. April DeConick, "The Gospel of Thomas," *ExpT* 118 (2007): 469-79 (469).
71. Snodgrass, "Gospel of Thomas," 19.
72. Note in particular Tuckett's helpful comments in "Thomas and the Synoptics," 156.

thirteen words in ancient texts like this, it might be worth closing with an analogy from contemporary writing that demonstrates knowledge of one text by another in a relatively short sequence of words. We began the chapter with James Robinson's often told story of the discovery of the Nag Hammadi documents. The story is repeated in a drastically abbreviated version by the New Testament scholar who has done more than any other to stress the importance of orality, Werner Kelber:[73]

James Robinson*	Werner Kelber
The date <u>of the discovery</u> of the Nag Hammadi codices can be established by two <u>murders</u> — not altogether uncommon happenings <u>in</u> the <u>blood feuds</u> still found in <u>rural Egypt</u>! . . . . . . They fell upon Ahmad Isma'il pitilessly. Abu al-Majd, then a teenager, brags that he struck the first blow straight to the head. After having <u>hacked</u> Ahmad Isma'il <u>to pieces limb by limb,</u> they <u>cut out</u> his <u>heart and consumed</u> it among them — <u>the ultimate act of blood revenge.</u>	The general area <u>of the discovery</u> is deeply <u>rural</u> and virtually untouched by urban, <u>Egyptian</u> culture. Peasants in this part of the world live in a preliterate society, forever involved <u>in</u> <u>blood feuds</u> among each other and against neighboring villages, and not averse to taking the law into their own hands. Members of the family who made the discovery were before and afterwards victims of brutal <u>murders</u>. They were <u>hacked</u> <u>to pieces limb by limb,</u> their <u>hearts</u> <u>cut out</u> <u>and consumed</u> by the murderers — <u>the ultimate act of blood revenge.</u> It is now admitted that considerable damage and losses occurred as the manuscripts were divided up by the Islamic natives who did not recognize their true significance. . . .
*Robinson, "Discovery," 209. There are multiple versions of the story, but this is the one that Kelber refers to ("Gnosis," 42).	

Kelber's account has only a limited number of words in common with Robinson's, but even if Kelber had not provided the reader with the source

73. Werner H. Kelber, "Gnosis and the Origins of Christianity," in Kenneth Keulman, ed., *Critical Moments in Religious History* (Macon, GA: Mercer University Press, 1983), 41-58 (42). Kelber's redaction of Robinson has introduced some errors into his version in a way analogous to Matthew's redaction of Mark and *Thomas's* redaction of the Synoptics, e.g., the members of the family who made the discovery were not just "victims of brutal murders" but also murderers themselves.

of his information,[74] we would be able to tell that he was reliant on Robinson because of the phrase, "the ultimate act of blood revenge." The phrase is very uncommon, and I have been unable to find it anywhere other than in accounts about the discovery of the Nag Hammadi codices, and only after 1979.[75] It would be special pleading to suggest that Kelber could have gone out to al-Qasr and interviewed the same people Robinson interviewed in the 1970s, and happened to characterize events using the identical phrase.[76] No, this is an example of a direct link between texts, reflected in a six-word verbatim agreement.

Although it is an important step in the case for *Thomas*'s familiarity with the Synoptic Gospels, noticing the presence of verbatim agreement only takes one so far. Verbatim agreement of the kind seen in texts like *Thom.* 26 illustrates that there is a direct link between *Thomas* and the Synoptics. It does not, in itself, say anything about the direction of the link. The next key step is to ask whether there are examples of Synoptic redactional features that show up in *Thomas*. Are there signs of Matthew's or Luke's hands in the material that *Thomas* shares with them? The next four chapters are devoted to illustrating that these signs are present, and that the evidence suggests that *Thomas* was indeed familiar with the Synoptics.

74. See above.

75. The earliest is Pagels, *Gnostic Gospels*, xiv (but quoting Robinson). In some versions, the exact phrase is used, as in the Kelber version above. Sometimes, even when one word is changed, the debt to Robinson remains clear, e.g., "the quintessential act of blood vengeance," Marvin Meyer, *The Gnostic Discoveries: The Impact of the Nag Hammadi Library* (San Francisco: HarperSanFrancisco, 2006), 18; or "the extreme act of blood vengeance," Ehrman, *Lost Christianities*, 52.

76. Indeed, it is possible to get an idea of what a variant oral account looks like. Muhammad 'Ali was interviewed for a British television documentary in 1987, *The Gnostics*. His account has some features in common with Robinson's, but it is radically different in other respects. The documentary itself is now difficult to find, but see Churton, *Gnostics*. On the point in question here, Churton reports 'Ali as saying, "I took my knife and cut out his heart and ate most of his pieces" (11). At best, there are individual vocabulary items in common, but there are no lengthy sequences of words.

CHAPTER 3

Diagnostic Shards

Introduction

The extent of verbatim agreement between *Thomas* and the Synoptics has been insufficiently explored in previous studies, though several striking examples suggest direct lines connecting the Synoptic Gospels to *Thomas*. But this only takes us part of the way. What is required is some indication of which way the lines should be drawn. When we work on the Synoptic Problem, establishing some kind of literary link between the Synoptics is only the first step. The next step is to look for evidence of one text's familiarity with another. Here there is an accepted method: the search for distinctive, redactional features of one text appearing in another. And so here the key question is whether *Thomas* features distinctive, redactional features from the Synoptic Gospels.

There have been several good arguments for *Thomas*'s knowledge of the Synoptics utilizing this straightforward method. The investigator isolates a feature that is clearly redactional in a given Gospel and then shows how *Thomas* parallels that very redactional feature. Under such circumstances, it follows that *Thomas* is likely to have derived the feature from that Gospel and not from its source.[1] The theory itself is little disputed.[2] Indeed, ad-

---

1. Harvey K. McArthur, "The Gospel According to Thomas," in Harvey K. McArthur, ed., *New Testament Sidelights: Essays in Honor of Alexander Converse Purdy* (Hartford: Hartford Seminary Foundation Press, 1960), 43-77 (61, 65, 68); Snodgrass, "Gospel of Thomas," 25-26; Tuckett, "Thomas and the Synoptics," 140-45 *et passim*; Schrage, *Verhältnis*, 4 *et passim*; Fieger, *Das Thomasevangelium*, 6-7 *et passim*. Meier, *Marginal Jew*, 1:123-39, especially 137-38, makes this one of the major grounds for seeing *Thomas* as secondary to the Synoptics.

2. Andrew Gregory, "Prior or Posterior? *The Gospel of the Ebionites* and the Gospel of

vocates of *Thomas*'s independence tend to agree that if a sufficient number of strong examples of Synoptic redaction could be found in *Thomas*, this would indicate *Thomas*'s familiarity with the Synoptics.

The First Beatitude (Matt. 5:3 // Luke 6:20 // *Thom.* 54)

The difficulty is that evidence of the Synoptic evangelists' redaction is often said to be absent from *Thomas*. John Dominic Crossan, in stressing the importance of proper methodology in the discussion, draws attention to a parallel that for him clearly illustrates *Thomas*'s independence of the Synoptics, the first beatitude:[3]

Matt. 5:3	Luke 6:20	*Thom.* 54
μακάριοι οἱ πτωχοὶ τῷ πνεύματι ὅτι αὐτῶν ἐστιν ἡ βασιλεία τῶν οὐρανῶν	μακάριοι οἱ πτωχοί ὅτι ὑμετέρα ἐστὶν ἡ βασιλεία τοῦ θεοῦ	ⲡⲉⲭⲉ ⲓⲥ ⲭⲉ ϩⲛ̄ⲙⲁⲕⲁⲣⲓⲟⲥ ⲛⲉ ⲛ̄ϩⲏⲕⲉ ⲭⲉ ⲧⲱⲧⲛ̄ ⲧⲉ ⲧⲙⲛ̄ⲧⲉⲣⲟ ⲛ̄ⲙⲡⲏⲩⲉ
Blessed are the poor in spirit, for theirs is the kingdom of the heavens	Blessed are the poor, for yours is the kingdom of God	Blessed are the poor, for yours is the kingdom of the heavens

Crossan explains how the parallel points clearly to *Thomas*'s independence from the Synoptics:

> One example may again suffice. The first beatitude in Luke 6:20b has "Blessed are you poor, for yours is the kingdom of God," but in Matt 5:3, "Blessed are the poor in spirit, for theirs is the kingdom of heaven." Scholars had long considered that "in spirit" was a personal, redactional addition by Matthew himself. Now in *Gos. Thom.* 54 we have, "Blessed are the poor, for yours is the Kingdom of Heaven." Precisely what is missing is the proposed editorial addition of Matthew. But what if one objects

---

Luke," *NTS* 51 (2005): 344-60 (348), associates this "widely recognized criterion" with Helmut Koester, *Synoptische Überlieferung bei den Apostolischen Vätern* (TU 65; Berlin: Akademie, 1957), 3; idem, "Written Gospels or Oral Tradition?" *JBL* 113 (1994): 293-97.

3. Crossan, *Four Other Gospels*, 35-37; cf. idem, *Birth of Christianity*, 117-18.

that *Thomas* has simply copied Luke here? That will not work. One would have at least to argue that *Thomas* (a) took the third person "the poor" from Matthew, then (b) the second person "yours" from Luke, and (c) returned to Matthew for the final "Kingdom of Heaven." It might be simpler to suggest that Thomas was mentally unstable.[4]

The rhetoric is powerful but the argument is weak. *Thomas*'s version is in fact very similar to Luke's version, and there is little trouble in imagining *Thomas* having taken over the beatitude largely from Luke. There is a good case for suggesting that *Thomas* was repeating the Lukan version, adding a reminiscence of the Matthean "kingdom of the heavens" at the end.

The problem arises in Crossan's description of the data. His contrast between Luke's "you poor" against *Thomas*'s "the poor" is an error, presumably introduced by comparing the RSV of Luke, which translates μακάριοι οἱ πτωχοί as "Blessed are you poor," with Thomas Lambdin's translation of *Thomas*, which translates ⲞⲨⲘⲀⲔⲀⲢⲒⲞⲤ ⲚⲈ ⲚϨⲎⲔⲈ as "Blessed are the poor."[5] There is in fact no difference here between Luke and *Thomas*. Both Bethge and Greeven provide the only plausible Greek retroversion, and it is identical with Luke, with the exception only of τῶν οὐρανῶν ("of the heavens") at the end, hence μακάριοι οἱ πτωχοί ὅτι ὑμετέρα ἐστὶν ἡ βασιλεία τῶν οὐρανῶν ("Blessed are the poor, for yours is the kingdom of the heavens").

In other words, *Thom.* 54 differs only in using "kingdom of *the heavens*" instead of "kingdom of *God*." For this last phrase, it is indeed the case that *Thomas* shows knowledge of one of Matthew's most distinctive phrases,[6] but Crossan's suggestion that a kind of implausible criss-cross copying would have been involved is an unimaginative caricature, not least given that mixed versions of Synoptic sayings are a common feature of Gospel quotations from the second century onward.[7]

---

4. Crossan, *Four Other Gospels*, 37.

5. Craig Evans, *Fabricating Jesus*, 75-76, criticizes Crossan on the same point, but unnecessarily explains the parallels in terms of *Thomas*'s dependence on a Syriac Matthew, not noticing that the contrast between Luke and *Thomas* in "Blessed are you poor" and "Blessed are the poor" is apparent and not real. Charles L. Quarles, "The Use of the *Gospel of Thomas* in the Research on the Historical Jesus of John Dominic Crossan," *CBQ* 69 (2007): 517-36, also has a convoluted explanation. He says that "οἱ πτωχοί in Luke is likely vocative" (522) and that "the awkward shift" in *Thomas* is "best explained as a product of mixed dependence in which the third person is borrowed from Matthew and the second person is borrowed from Luke" (522). But οἱ πτωχοί cannot be vocative here, and *Thomas* is very close to Luke.

6. See below, 66-69.

7. Cf. Quarles, "Use of the *Gospel of Thomas*," 519, draws attention to the differently

It is true, of course, that *Thomas* lacks Matthew's qualification "in spirit," but all this shows is *Thomas*'s preference for the simpler Lukan version over the more obscure Matthean phrase. Even if Crossan is right that "in spirit" is a Matthean redactional element,[8] its absence from *Thomas* says nothing at all about *Thomas*'s independence. In other words, there are no grounds here for insisting on *Thomas*'s independence, still less for doubting the author's mental stability.[9]

Searching for Synoptic Redaction

Arguments like Crossan's are not strong, but his perspective is shared by others who have argued for *Thomas*'s independence. According to scholars like John Sieber[10] and Stephen Patterson,[11] apparent examples of Synoptic redaction in *Thomas* can be explained in a variety of different ways: appeal to oral tradition, coincidence, and textual assimilation.[12] Before we look at

---

mixed form (Matthew's αὐτῶν for Luke's ὑμετέρα) in Polycarp, *Phil.* 2.3, μακάριοι οἱ πτωχοί . . . ὅτι αὐτῶν ἐστὶν ἡ βασιλεία τοῦ θεοῦ, "If Polycarp could mix texts in this fashion, the author of *Thomas* could have done so as well without any suspicion of mental instability."

8. See my *Case Against Q*, chapter 7, for the argument that this beatitude is best understood as Luke's redactional reworking of Matthew, subsequently copied by *Thomas*. Luke's Jesus characteristically begins his sermon with a blessing on "the poor" (cf. 4:16-30); he engages in eschatological reversal involving the rich (cf. 1:52-53; 16:19-31); and the disciples, who have "left everything" to follow Jesus (5:11R, 28R), are the ones being addressed (6:20). Of course if Luke is responsible for this redactional reformulation of Matthew, *Thomas*'s version clearly shows his knowledge of Luke. In this context, however, I am simply attempting to show the weakness of Crossan's argument for *Thomas*'s independence of Matthew and Luke, not to argue against Q.

9. Patterson, *Gospel of Thomas and Jesus*, 42-44, argues: "When one looks for more positive evidence that Thomas represents an independent tradition, the tradition history of the beatitudes provides some helpful clues" (43), but his tradition history takes for granted the existence of Q rather than arguing for it. He notes, for example, that "not one of those [beatitudes] added by Matthew turns up in Thomas" and that "there are no Thomas parallels to Luke's woes, the one thing that could possibly link Thomas to Luke's text" (43), statements that assume that the four beatitudes in Luke 6:20-23 are the original Q beatitudes, expanded with extra beatitudes by Matthew in Matt. 5:2-12 and by Luke with woes (6:24-26) in Luke 6:20-26.

10. Sieber, "Redactional Analysis."

11. Patterson, *Gospel of Thomas and Jesus*.

12. The situation with the minor agreements between Matthew and Luke against Mark in discussions of the Synoptic Problem is analogous. It has often been pointed out that those who hold to the independence of Matthew and Luke have a "divide and conquer" approach

specific examples of Synoptic redaction in *Thomas* in chapters 4–6, it will be worth pausing to reflect on some of the perceived difficulties with the case, one of which is that those who argue against *Thomas*'s familiarity with the Synoptics tend to assume that cases of familiarity have to look like the Synoptics because they are enticed by the especially close relationship between the Synoptics themselves.

In discussing the question of *Thomas*'s relationship to the Synoptics, Patterson works by comparison with the Synoptic Problem, rightly suggesting that the Synoptic data demand a theory of a literary relationship.[13] His point is that the parallels in content and order between *Thomas* and the Synoptics are not like the parallels in content and order among the Synoptics. The distance between *Thomas* and the Synoptics is more like the distance between John and the Synoptics.

There are, of course, significant points of contact between the two areas of study, but it is important to remember the points of divergence too. In particular, the data set for comparison between *Thomas* and the Synoptics is smaller than the data set for comparison between the Synoptics. In other words, the extent of overlap between Matthew, Mark, and Luke is so much greater than the extent of overlap between those three Gospels and *Thomas*, that one would expect the number of examples of Synoptic redaction in *Thomas* to be much smaller than the number of examples of Markan redaction in Matthew, Matthean redaction in Luke, and so on.

Moreover, the genre difference between the Synoptic Gospels and the *Gospel of Thomas* reduces the number of possible examples of Synoptic redaction in *Thomas*. As a sayings gospel, *Thomas* only parallels the sayings in the narrative gospels. This is not a trivial point. Our ability to detect Synoptic redaction is at its best in the kind of narrative segues that are very common in the Synoptics but practically absent from *Thomas*.[14]

---

that diminishes the overall impact of the minor agreements as evidence for Luke's knowledge of Matthew. See further my *Case Against Q*, chapter 8, especially 163-65.

13. Patterson, *Gospel of Thomas and Jesus*, 12-16. Like many New Testament scholars, Patterson refracts the data that give rise to the Synoptic Problem through its most popular solution, the Two-Source Theory. Nevertheless, he is right that the data he isolates (parallel order and content) do demand a literary solution to the problem. His suggestion that the differences between John and the Synoptics rule out "literary dependence" (14), on the other hand, may be a little overstated.

14. Cf. Snodgrass, "Gospel of Thomas," 26: "The difficulty with the redactional elements is that *Thomas* does not have narrative material or compositional seams, the places where we would expect to find the largest concentrations of the evangelists' own wording." The same is also true with respect to John and the Synoptics; the sheer difference in the crafting of the

Further, the attempt to isolate parallels that feature the redactional stamp of one evangelist on another's work will often inevitably involve minutiae.[15] By definition, something that is distinctive of one writer is less likely to appear when another writer takes it over. All too often, the redactional stamp in question will be something that at first appears minor. We should not be ashamed of this. Crimes are sometimes solved with the DNA extracted from a single hair left on the victim's clothing.

Moreover, not every element in an evangelist's redaction will be loaded with theological interest or significance. When we teach redaction criticism, we focus — inevitably — on the major, theologically interesting differences between the Gospels, like δικαιοσύνη (righteousness) in Matthew,[16] but such famous redactional themes will not necessarily be the ones that are picked up in *Thomas*.[17] One of the difficulties with Sieber's study of the question is just this, that he looks for redactional traits that are invested with theological weight and plays down the more mundane but nevertheless diagnostic Synoptic redactional elements that appear in *Thomas*.[18]

The Plagiarist's Charter

There is a related point. Arguments against *Thomas*'s familiarity with the Synoptics sometimes set a standard that would allow plagiarists to go unpunished. It is sometimes said that the absence of agreement in parts of certain Synoptic-*Thomas* parallels indicates *Thomas*'s ignorance of the Syn-

---

narrative makes it difficult to spot parallel narrative segues. Yet even here the agreement at Matt. 26:46 // Mark 14:42 // John 14:31, ἐγείρεσθε ἄγωμεν, "Arise, let us leave," may be an indicator of a direct link between the texts. So too in *Thomas*, a careful look occasionally reveals knowledge of Synoptic narrative framing, e.g., *Thom.* 79; see chapter 6 below.

15. Sieber, "Redactional Analysis," 17, suggests: "In order to call a reading a redactional trace, one must be able to attribute that reading to a particular evangelist's theological intent"; but this sets the bar too high. Not all evidence of redaction is connected with "theological intent." Authors regularly leave much more subtle clues about their style.

16. Tuckett's example, "Thomas and the Synoptics," 141.

17. Nevertheless, *Thomas* does feature Matthew's preferred redactional term "kingdom of heaven" on three occasions (20, 54, 114), the first two in parallel with Matthean redaction of Mark, on which see further below, 66-69. So too Luke's interest in hearing God's will and doing it (*Thom.* 79a // Luke 11:27-28; see further below, chapter 6).

18. Cf. Tuckett, "Thomas and the Synoptics," 141, "Sieber tended to ignore the smaller, theologically less significant, details in the gospels. But it is recognized by most that the evangelists' redactional activity was not confined to such theological 'bombshells' as δικαιοσύνη!"

optic saying as a whole. The difficulty with this line of argument can be illustrated from teachers' experiences of plagiarism in student work. While from time to time unwise students plagiarize an entire essay from the Internet, it is far more common for students to plagiarize only parts of essays. When the students in question are accused of plagiarism, it is no excuse for them to point to the amount of material that they have not taken over. No reasonable disciplinary body would accept the lack of copying in parts of the paper as an excuse for the copying in other parts of the paper, or as evidence that the copied parts are not copied.[19] Nor is this just the case in relation to student plagiarism. The relevant legal rule is clear: "No plagiarist can excuse the wrong by showing how much of his work he did not pirate."[20]

On a related topic, when discussing the occurrence of "Pharisees and scribes" (Ⲙ̅ⲪⲀⲢⲒⲤⲀⲒⲞⲤ ⲘⲚ̅ ⲚⲄ̅ⲢⲀⲘⲘⲀⲦⲈⲨⲤ) in *Thom.* 39 // Matt. 23:13, Dennis Ingolfsland offers a helpful analogy. Patterson here suggests that the "Pharisees and scribes" pairing is due to textual assimilation to Matthew, adding, "If Thomas were intentionally borrowing this *topos* from Matthew one would expect to see it incorporated into Thomas' own text more frequently."[21] Ingolfsland replies:

> Imagine that a writer copied, with slight alterations, a paragraph from Patterson's book and that Patterson charges that writer with plagiarism. As evidence, Patterson cites the fact that not only does the accused plagiarizer's work agree substantially with Patterson's book, but the writer included the phrase "gnosticizing proclivities" which is a characteristic phrase of Patterson's, occurring not less than seven times in one short chapter (chapter eight) of Patterson's book. The judge rules in the plagiarizer's favor, however, saying that if the writer had really been copying

---

19. It is of course true that punishments may differ in severity in relation to the degree of plagiarism in a given paper, e.g., the online plagiarism detection service turnitin states, "If even a small part of a work is found to have been plagiarized, it is still considered a copyright violation. However, the amount that was copied probably will have a bearing on the severity of the punishment. A work that is almost entirely plagiarized will almost certainly incur greater penalties than a work that only includes a small amount of plagiarized material," "Plagiarism FAQs," Plagiarism dot org, http://www.plagiarism.org/plag_article_plagiarism_faq .html, accessed 15 June 2011.

20. Sheldon v. Metro-Goldwyn Pictures Corp., 81 F.2d 49, 56 (2d Cir.). I am grateful to Stephen Carlson for the legal source here.

21. Patterson, *Gospel of Thomas*, 36.

from Patterson, "we would expect to see the phrase more frequently" in the plagiarizer's work. It is doubtful that Patterson would be convinced.[22]

Examples of what I label "the plagiarist's charter" have already been encountered in the discussion of verbatim agreement between *Thomas* and the Synoptics[23] and further examples will be discussed in chapters 4 and 5.

*　　*　　*

It is, then, a mirage to imagine that the examples of Synoptic redaction in *Thomas* are too few or too weak. We should make sure that we do not allow ourselves to be spoiled by the Synoptics. It is a mistake to think of the Synoptic interrelations as the norm, as the benchmark against which to measure all other cases of source usage, as is the case also in the issue of the extent of verbatim agreement.[24]

In other words, the search for Synoptic redactional features in *Thomas* is a search for indicators, for signs, that *Thomas* is familiar with the Synoptic Gospels themselves. These indicators are actually quite common in *Thomas*, but it is easy to play them down if one begins with unrealistic expectations. To use an analogy from archaeology, what we are looking for are *diagnostic shards*.[25] In an archaeological dig, not every find offers equally useful evidence for identifying the materials; even fewer finds provide helpful dating evidence. We should not fret, then, when particular parallels do not show obvious signs of Synoptic redaction. That is exactly what we ought to expect, and the situation is the same with other pairs of parallel texts where one is the source for the other, including often between the Synoptic Gospels. As Christopher Tuckett points out,

> it is almost inevitable that, *if* Th is dependent on our gospels (at however many stages removed) for his synoptic-type material, not every saying will conveniently contain a parallel to a redactional element in the syn-

22. Dennis Ingolfsland, "The Gospel of Thomas and the Synoptic Gospels," online article, http://dennis-ingolfsland.blogspot.com/2009/04/gospel-of-thomas-and-synoptic-gospels.html, accessed 15 June 2011.

23. See above, 36 and 38.

24. See chapter 2 above, especially 44-46.

25. I am grateful to Ken Olson for the analogy. See Jonathan Reed, *The HarperCollins Visual Guide to the New Testament: What Archaeology Reveals about the First Christians* (New York: HarperCollins, 2007), 19-20.

optic gospels. It is far more likely that sometimes Th will parallel only
traditional elements.[26]

There is, of course, a danger that the attempt to moderate unrealistic expectations might be taken as an apology for paucity of evidence. It is
worth stating clearly, therefore, that the thesis argued here is that the presence of Synoptic redactional material in *Thomas* is frequent and significant.
It is actually far greater than one ought to expect given the size of the data
set and the nature of the material. The evidence is sufficient to establish
Thomasine familiarity with the Synoptic Gospels.

Before beginning to look at examples of Synoptic redaction in *Thomas*,
however, we need to address one further potential complication, because
for some scholars the presence of Synoptic redaction in *Thomas* will not
settle the issue. Clear examples of Synoptic redaction in *Thomas* might, it is
argued, simply draw attention to the possibility of *Thomas*'s harmonization
to the Synoptics in the process of its textual history.

Textual Assimilation?

If it becomes clear that some Synoptic redactional features are present in
Thomas, could it be that this is explicable on the theory that *Thomas* is,
essentially, autonomous? Could the work itself have emerged in isolation
from the Synoptic Gospels but then become corrupted through textual assimilation, as it was copied by scribes familiar with the Synoptics? When
Patterson concedes the presence of several Synoptic redactional elements
in *Thomas*, this is how he explains the situation. For him, they point not
to direct knowledge of the Synoptics but instead to scribal harmonization.
Patterson argues that the set of such examples is "very small" (32, 39, 45.3,
104.1, 104.3), and that this makes it unlikely that *Thomas* depends on the
Synoptics. He explains:

> It is impossible that Nag Hammadi Codex 2, and the many copies of
> Thomas which stand between our extant Thomas manuscripts and the
> original, were immune to the almost universal phenomenon of scribal
> error, especially that of harmonization. That the present text of Thomas
> has such text-critical commonplaces is to be expected; it is only a matter
> of identifying where they occur. Since the text as a whole does not rely

26. Tuckett, "Thomas and the Synoptics," 157.

upon the synoptic tradition, it is reasonable to assign the handful of instances in which influence from a synoptic text is likely, to the phenomenon of textual assimilation.[27]

Patterson's point deserves to be taken seriously, and it should not be sidestepped in a bid to keep the contours of the debate as simple as possible. The issue of the relationships among ancient texts is often complex, and our explanatory models all too often create the impression that complicated interrelationships, in which there were hundreds of points of contact and divergence between texts and traditions, can be reduced to simple, unidirectional diagrams with only two or three dots and arrows.[28] Indeed, the situation is especially complicated with respect to *Thomas* and the Synoptics, where the one group of texts (the Synoptics) has thousands of textual witnesses and another (*Thomas*) has only four, three of them fragmentary and the other in Coptic. Who knows how our picture would change if we had a clearer textual history for *Thomas*?[29]

However, Patterson's appeal to the possibility of scribal harmonization carries with it a problem that is seldom acknowledged. Like all appeals to absent evidence, the absent evidence might actually resolve itself in the opposite direction from that desired by the advocate. In other words, it needs to be acknowledged that if we had more textual evidence, it might provide more examples of Synoptic redaction in *Thomas* and not fewer. The gaps in the data set might, if filled, provide serious counterevidence for Patterson's theory. The question we need to ask is whether there is any reason to imagine that the absent data would

27. Patterson, *Gospel of Thomas and Jesus*, 93. See similarly S. Davies, "Thomas, Gospel of," in David Noel Freedman, Allen C. Myers, and Astrid B. Beck, eds., *Eerdmans Dictionary of the Bible* (Grand Rapids: Eerdmans, 2000), 1303-4 (1303); John S. Kloppenborg Verbin, "The Life and Sayings of Jesus," in Mark Allan Powell, ed., *The New Testament Today* (Louisville: Westminster John Knox, 1999), 10-30 (12).

28. See John S. Kloppenborg Verbin, *Excavating Q: The History and Setting of the Sayings Gospel* (Minneapolis: Fortress, 2000), 50-54, for some useful reflections on what we are doing when we model Synoptic relationships, especially 51, "It is impossible to factor into our models the many imponderables that may have contributed to the composition of the gospels, for this would have the effect of destroying the explanatory power of the model. . . . Hypotheses are heuristic models intended to aid comprehension and discovery; they do not replicate reality."

29. See David Parker, *The Living Texts of the Gospels* (Cambridge: Cambridge University Press, 1997), 103-23, for a discussion of the problems (and possibilities) generated by allowing textual criticism to interact properly with study of the Synoptic Problem.

support the theory of an autonomous *Thomas*, and here there are additional problems.

Patterson's argument is based on a general appeal concerning scribal harmonization in early Christian texts, and it is certainly true that there are many examples of harmonization in these texts.[30] But it would be a mistake to regard the phenomenon as universal and irresistible. Some texts harmonize more than others. We should not assume that the scribe of Coptic *Thomas* harmonizes to the Gospels.[31] But is there any way to be more certain? Is it simply a matter of dealing with assumptions? Happily, we are not in the dark on this issue, and there is a way to get some help.

Patterson's five examples of Synoptic redaction in *Thomas* are all in Coptic *Thomas*. It is worth asking, therefore, whether, with the limited textual evidence we have, the Coptic appears to show greater signs than the Oxyrhynchus fragments of proximity to the Synoptic Gospels. Is it a text that aligns itself with the harmonization theory or not?[32] On repeated occasions, the Coptic text of *Thomas* is further removed from the text of the Synoptics than are the Oxyrhynchus fragments. Several of the examples discussed in chapter 2 above are cases in point; for example, *Thom.* 26 (P.Oxy. 1.1-4) exhibits a thirteen-word verbatim agreement with Matt. 7:5 // Luke 6:42, where the structure of the Greek differs from the structure of the Coptic.[33]

Similarly, in *Thom.* 4.2-3 the Greek (P.Oxy. 654.25-26) is again closer to the Synoptics than the Coptic, with an entire extra clause:

---

30. For a useful discussion of harmonization and the Synoptic Problem, see Gordon Fee, "Modern Textual Criticism and the Synoptic Problem: On the Problem of Harmonization in the Gospels," in Eldon Jay Epp and Gordon D. Fee, *Studies in the Theory and Method of New Testament Textual Criticism* (Grand Rapids: Eerdmans, 1993), 174-82.

31. Examples of Coptic *Thomas*'s harmonization to Coptic New Testament texts are seldom persuasive and apparent agreements against the Greek are usually the natural result of the translation process. Sieber, "Redactional Analysis," 78-79, followed by DeConick, *Original Gospel*, 264-65, suggests that logion 93 is a case where the scribe of Coptic *Thomas* has been influenced by the wording of Sahidic Matthew (cf. Schrage, *Verhältnis*, 179-81), but the links are unimpressive.

32. Cf. Andrew Gregory, *The Reception of Luke-Acts in the Period before Irenaeus: Looking for Luke in the Second Century* (WUNT 2/169; Tübingen: Mohr, 2003), 157. Gregory notes the problem that the Oxyrhynchus fragments pose for Patterson's harmonization hypothesis.

33. See above, 30-33. The Greek retroversions from the Coptic make this point effectively; e.g., see Plisch, *Gospel of Thomas*, 91, on this saying.

Mark 10:31*	*Thom.* 4.2-3 (P.Oxy. 654)	*Thom.* 4.2-3 (Coptic)
<u>πολλοὶ δὲ ἔσονται</u> πρῶτοι ἔσχατοι καὶ [οἱ] ἔσχατοι πρῶτοι.	ὅτι πολλοὶ ἔσονται π[ρῶτοι ἔσχατοι καὶ]** οἱ ἔσχατοι πρῶτοι.	ⲭⲉ ⲟⲩⲛ̄ ϩⲁϩ ⲛ̄ϣⲟⲣⲡ ⲛⲁⲣ̄ ϩⲁⲉ
And many who are first will be last and [the] last first.	For many who are f[irst will be last and] the last first.	For many who are first will be last.

* See also Matt. 19:30, which is almost identical to Mark here; cf. also Matt. 20:16 // Luke 13:30, which are also similar but lack the construction with πολλοί.

**On the reconstruction with καί (Grenfell and Hunt; Attridge), see above, 37 n. 36.

Once again, the Coptic clearly does not show any signs of harmonization to the Synoptics. Quite the contrary.

The clearest example, though, is *Thom.* 36, which provides extensive parallel content to the Synoptics that is absent from the Coptic. (See the table on pp. 62-63.)

This Oxyrhynchus fragment witnesses to a text type that is radically closer to the Synoptics than is the Coptic text. The brief version in Coptic *Thomas* parallels only Matt. 6:25 // Luke 12:22, whereas the Greek fragment provides a fuller version of that verse, which is much closer to the Synoptics, and then it has additional parallels to Matt. 6:27 // Luke 12:25[34] and Matt. 6:28 // Luke 12:27. Indeed, the latter parallel, far from being an irrelevant or accidental harmonization to the Synoptics, is now a celebrated example of an early variation of a Jesus saying in Greek, with οὐ ξαίνειν ("do not card") appearing in Greek *Thomas* in contrast to αὐξάνειν ("grow") appearing in Matthew and Luke.[35] The Greek fragment here represents a stage of transmission that is more primitive than the Coptic, and the latter appears to be

34. See previous note.

35. οὐ ξαίνουσιν also appears in Matt. 6:28 ℵ[vid]. James M. Robinson and Christoph Heil argue that a scribal error in Q led to the reading witnessed by Matthew and Luke. They have published multiple versions of the argument, seven of which are reproduced in James M. Robinson (ed. Christoph Heil and Joseph Verheyden), *The Sayings Gospel Q: Collected Essays* (BETL 189; Leuven: Leuven University Press, 2005), 713-886. Robinson's and Heil's thesis is unnecessarily complex. Matt. 6:28 ℵ[vid] is actually irrelevant to their case since they are not arguing that οὐ ξαίνουσιν was the original reading in Matthew. A range of possibilities exists, one of which is that both Greek *Thomas* and the scribe of Matt. 6:28 ℵ[vid] made the same emendation (or "error") by changing οὐ ξαίνειν to αὐξάνειν. Here, as often, the appeal to Q complicates rather than clarifies.

an abbreviation.[36] The Oxyrhynchus Greek fragment is close enough to the texts of Matthew and Luke to make clear that the Coptic text is a long way from harmonizing, but at the same time it is not so close to Matthew and Luke as to be under suspicion from harmonization itself. What we have here is clear counterevidence to the thesis of scribal harmonization in Coptic *Thomas*. The latter is further removed from the Synoptics than are the earlier Greek fragments.

We should, of course, be careful to avoid the assumption that the Oxyrhynchus fragments approximate the Greek text that was the *Vorlage* for the Coptic translation. It is easy to be seduced by the fact that the fragments are closer in date to and in the same language as the Synoptic Gospels and so to imagine that we are necessarily looking at something very similar to the text the Coptic translator saw.[37] Nevertheless, we have to work with extant evidence rather than absent data, and while caution is necessary, it is worth underlining that the extant textual evidence does not support the hypothesis of scribal harmonization in Coptic *Thomas*. In other words, the interesting theoretical possibility of a harmonizing Coptic *Thomas* is not supported by the actual textual evidence. Appeal to absent textual evidence only serves to emphasize the possibility that a fuller model would show more and not fewer examples of Synoptic redaction in *Thomas*. On balance, then, it is important to take the presence of Synoptic redaction in *Thomas* seriously.

*   *   *

36. M. Marcovich, "Textual Criticism on the Gospel of Thomas," *JTS* 20 (1969): 53-74 (70), sees this as "a clear example of a *drastic* cutting of the original text of the *GTh* by the redactor of [the] C[optic] . . . . in his zeal to bring *logion* 36 logically as close as possible to the following *logion* 37." Similarly, DeConick, *Original Gospel*, 149, "The longer version provided by the Greek appears to be earlier than the Coptic truncation"; Patterson, *Gospel of Thomas*, 76 n. 298, writes, "It is also possible there has been some residual influence from the synoptic text on the Oxyrhynchus version of Thomas, which, for whatever reason, fails to show up in the Nag Hammadi version." Plisch, *Gospel of Thomas*, 106, is less certain: "The brevity of the Coptic text of the saying is quite typical of the Gospel of Thomas, but the long version of the Greek text is rather unusual." But both are characteristically much shorter than the Synoptic parallels. It may be that we should reckon with a trajectory whereby the scribes of Coptic *Thomas* continue along the abbreviating route of early Greek *Thomas*. For a thesis that requires a harmonizing tendency in Nag Hammadi *Thomas*, Patterson's "for whatever reason" here is problematic.

37. Moreover, it is important to remember also that the scribe of the NH II text of *Thomas* is unlikely to be the same person who translated the text from Greek. Our Coptic text may be several texts removed from the first translation into Coptic.

Matt. 6:25-30	Luke 12:22-28	Thom. 36 (P.Oxy. 655)	Thom. 36 (NH II)
25 Διὰ τοῦτο λέγω ὑμῖν, μὴ μεριμνᾶτε	22 Εἶπεν δὲ πρὸς τοὺς μαθητάς [αὐτοῦ], Διὰ τοῦτο λέγω ὑμῖν, μὴ μεριμνᾶτε	[λέγει Ἰ(ησοῦ)ς· μὴ μεριμνᾶτε α]πὸ πρωῒ ἕ[ως ὀψέ, μήτ]ε ἀφ᾽ ἑσπ[έρας ἕως π]ρωῖ, μήτε	ΠΕϪΕ ΙC̄ ΜⲚϬΙ ΡΟΟΥϢ ϪΙ(Ν) ϨΤΟΟΥΕ ϢⲀ ΡΟΥϨΕ ⲀΥϢ ϪΙΝ
τῇ ψυχῇ ὑμῶν τί φάγητε [ἢ τί πίητε], μηδὲ τῷ σώματι ὑμῶν τί ἐνδύσησθε: οὐχὶ ἡ ψυχὴ πλεῖόν ἐστιν τῆς τροφῆς καὶ τὸ σῶμα τοῦ ἐνδύματος; ... 27 τίς δὲ ἐξ ὑμῶν μεριμνῶν δύναται προσθεῖναι ἐπὶ τὴν ἡλικίαν αὐτοῦ πῆχυν ἕνα; 28 καὶ περὶ ἐνδύματος τί μεριμνᾶτε; καταμάθετε τὰ κρίνα τοῦ ἀγροῦ πῶς αὐξάνουσιν: οὐ κοπιῶσιν οὐδὲ νήθουσιν: 29 λέγω δὲ ὑμῖν ὅτι οὐδὲ Σολομὼν ἐν πάσῃ τῇ δόξῃ αὐτοῦ περιεβάλετο ὡς ἓν τούτων. 30 εἰ δὲ τὸν χόρτον τοῦ ἀγροῦ σήμερον ὄντα καὶ αὔριον εἰς κλίβανον βαλλόμενον ὁ θεὸς οὕτως ἀμφιέννυσιν, οὐ πολλῷ μᾶλλον ὑμᾶς, ὀλιγόπιστοι;	τῇ ψυχῇ τί φάγητε, μηδὲ τῷ σώματι τί ἐνδύσησθε. 23 ἡ γὰρ ψυχὴ πλεῖόν ἐστιν τῆς τροφῆς καὶ τὸ σῶμα τοῦ ἐνδύματος. ... 25 τίς δὲ ἐξ ὑμῶν μεριμνῶν δύναται ἐπὶ τὴν ἡλικίαν αὐτοῦ προσθεῖναι πῆχυν; 26 εἰ οὖν οὐδὲ ἐλάχιστον δύνασθε, τί περὶ τῶν λοιπῶν μεριμνᾶτε; 27 κατανοήσατε τὰ κρίνα πῶς αὐξάνει: οὐ κοπιᾷ οὐδὲ νήθει: λέγω δὲ ὑμῖν, οὐδὲ Σολομὼν ἐν πάσῃ τῇ δόξῃ αὐτοῦ περιεβάλετο ὡς ἓν τούτων. 28 εἰ δὲ ἐν ἀγρῷ τὸν χόρτον ὄντα σήμερον καὶ αὔριον εἰς κλίβανον βαλλόμενον ὁ θεὸς οὕτως ἀμφιέζει, πόσῳ μᾶλλον ὑμᾶς, ὀλιγόπιστοι.	[τῇ τροφῇ ὑ]μῶν τί φά[γητε, μήτε] τῇ στ[ολῇ ὑμῶν] τί ἐνδύ[ση]σθε. [πολ]λῷ κρεί[σσον]ές ἐ[στε] τῶν κρί[νων, ἅτι[να ο]ὐ ξα[ί]νει οὐδὲ ν[ήθ]ει. μ[ηδ]ὲν ἔχοντ[α ἔ]νδ[υ]μα, τί ἐν[δεῖτε] καὶ ὑμεῖς; τίς ἂν προσθ<εί>η ἐπὶ τὴν εἰλικίαν ὑμῶν; αὐτὸ[ς δ]ώσει ὑμεῖν τὸ ἔνδυμα ὑμῶν.	ϨΙΡΟΥϨΕ ϢⲀ ϨΤΟΟΥΕ ϪΕ ΟΥ ΠΕ<Τ>ΕΤⲚ ⲀΤⲀⲀϤ ϨΙⲰΤ ΤΗΥΤⲚ̄.

Matt. 6:25-30	Luke 12:22-28	Thom. 36 (P.Oxy. 655)	Thom. 36 (NH II)
Therefore I tell you, do not worry about your life, what you will eat or what you will drink, or about your body, what you will wear. Is not life more than food, and the body more than clothing? . . . 27 And can any of you by worrying add a single hour to your span of life? 28 And why do you worry about clothing? Consider the lilies of the field, how they grow: they neither toil nor spin, 29 yet I tell you, even Solomon in all his glory was not clothed like one of these. 30 But if God so clothes the grass of the field, which is alive today and tomorrow is thrown into the oven, will he not much more clothe you — you of little faith?	He said to his disciples, "Therefore I tell you, do not worry about your life, what you will eat, or about your body, what you will wear. 23 For life is more than food, and the body more than clothing. . . . 25 And can any of you by worrying add a single hour to your span of life? 26 If then you are not able to do so small a thing as that, why do you worry about the rest? 27 Consider the lilies, how they grow: they neither toil nor spin; yet I tell you, even Solomon in all his glory was not clothed like one of these. 28 But if God so clothes the grass of the field, which is alive today and tomorrow is thrown into the oven, how much more will he clothe you — you of little faith!	[Jesus says, "Do not be anxious] from morning [until evening and] from evening [until] morning, neither [about] your [food] and what [you will] eat, [nor] about [your clothing] and what you [will] wear. [You are far] better than the [lilies] which [neither] card nor [spin]. As for you, when you have no garment, what [will you put on]? Who might add to your stature?* He will give you your garment."	Jesus says, "Do not be anxious from morning until evening and from evening until morning about what you will wear."

*For this sentence, cf. Matt. 6:27 // Luke 12:25, προσθεῖναι ἐπὶ τὴν ἡλικίαν αὐτοῦ πῆχυν ἕνα, which is sometimes translated "to add one cubit to his height" (cf. KJV; NIV margin).

Given the number of good examples of Synoptic redaction in *Thomas*, it will be worth taking a little time to discuss them. Chapter 4 will focus on examples from Matthew, chapter 5 on examples from Luke, and chapter 6 on one particularly strong example from Luke that requires some additional space. Most of these examples have been noticed in the literature before, and strong cases have been made. I am bringing them forward again here not because previous cases have been inadequate but because they have been ignored or underestimated. I will try to explain why the counterarguments are unpersuasive and in several cases I will offer some fresh arguments and evidence.

In setting out the evidence for *Thomas*'s familiarity with the Synoptics in each of the following cases, I will add a synopsis of the relevant evidence from the Synoptics and *Thomas*. It is one of the major shortcomings of discussions of *Thomas*'s relationship with the Synoptics that no synopsis of *Thomas* and the Synoptics is available,[38] so that scholars are not able to see quickly and straightforwardly the evidence in favor of familiarity. Even the more meticulous scholars who set out the evidence from each of the Gospels fail to present this evidence in a two-, three-, or four-column synopsis in order to help their readers to see how the texts are related.[39] It may be that this lack of good visual arrangement of the data has itself contributed

38. An early example of good practice here is McArthur, "Gospel According to Thomas," 57-65, though his synopses are in English and are not word-aligned. Hans-Gebhard Bethge prepared "Appendix 1: Evangelium Thomae copticum," which helpfully appears in the context of the most widely used Synopsis of the Gospels (Aland, ed., *Synopsis Quattuor Evangeliorum*), but no vertically aligned synopsis of *Thomas* and the Gospels is provided. *Thomas* is added to Robinson et al., *Critical Edition of Q*, but the synopsis is only available for passages where *Thomas* parallels double tradition material. A recent example of good practice is Gathercole, "Luke in the *Gospel of Thomas*." John Dominic Crossan's popular *Sayings Parallels: A Workbook for the Jesus Tradition* (Philadelphia: Fortress, 1986), is a useful English-language collection of sayings parallels organized by form, but there is no line alignment, let alone word alignment.

39. DeConick, for example, helpfully sets out all the evidence from *Thomas*, Coptic and Greek, with parallels both from the Synoptics and other literature, throughout her commentary (*Original Gospel*, 44-298), but she does not place them in vertically aligned synopsis format. DeConick's appendix listing "Verbal Similarities Between *Thomas* and the Synoptics" in English translation, with agreements underlined (*Original Gospel*, 299-316), is a step forward, but it is in two columns, with *Thomas* on the left and the Synoptics on the right, with no word alignment or line alignment of the kind necessary for the relationships between the texts to be clearly visualized. One of the difficulties with the contrasting English translations used by DeConick is that *Thomas* is given in gender-inclusive language, "If a blind person leads a blind person . . ." and the Synoptics in androcentric language, "If a blind man leads a blind man . . ." (304, etc.).

to the view that *Thomas* is independent of the Synoptics. Thus the relationship among the Synoptics, which everyone agrees is a literary relationship, is illustrated and confirmed when one consults the synopsis. The relationship of the Synoptics to *Thomas*, rarely illustrated in a vertical synopsis, remains a matter of confusion to many who are unacquainted with the data and who are unable to visualize the material mentally.[40]

40. The potential for an electronic synopsis of Thomas is helpfully illustrated by John Marshall, Five Gospel Parallels (1996-2001), http://www.utoronto.ca/religion/synopsis/. This uses frames technology to lay out a simple synopsis in English, with parallel columns for the canonical Gospels and Thomas. It illustrates that something more sophisticated, in Greek and Coptic, ought to be achievable.

CHAPTER 4

Matthean Redaction in *Thomas*

Since the discovery of the *Gospel of Thomas*, several scholars have drawn attention to places in the text that mirror Synoptic redactional elements. Such diagnostic shards provide the signs that *Thomas* was familiar with the Synoptic Gospels and that the work was not independent. Several of these occur in parallels with the Gospel of Matthew and still more occur in parallels with the Gospel of Luke. The *Thomas*/Luke parallels will be the focus of chapters 5 and 6. In this chapter, several examples of Matthean redaction appearing in *Thomas* will suggest *Thomas*'s familiarity with Matthew.

The Kingdom of Heaven (*Thom.* 20, 54)

Even the beginner in biblical studies knows that "the kingdom of heaven," or more accurately "kingdom of the heavens" (ἡ βασιλεία τῶν οὐρανῶν), is one of Matthew's most characteristic expressions. One would struggle to find anything more clearly and distinctively Matthean. It occurs thirty-two times in his Gospel and never in Mark, John,[1] or Luke–Acts. It appears frequently in Matthew's redactional reworkings of Mark.[2] If we cannot attribute this phrase to Matthew's hand, then we cannot attribute any phrase to Matthew's hand.

The term "kingdom of the heavens" occurs three times in the *Gospel of Thomas*,[3] on two occasions in parallel with Matthew:

1. With the exception of a weakly attested variant in John 3:5.

2. Matt. 3:2; 4:17 R; 5:3 QD; 5:10 QD; 5:19 QD (2x); 5:20; 7:21 QD; 8:11 QD; 10:7 QD; 11:11 QD; 11:12 QD; 13:11 R; 13:24; 13:31 R; 13:33 QD; 13:44, 45, 47, 52; 16:19; 18:1 R; 18:3 R; 18:4 R; 18:23; 19:12, 14; 19:23 R; 20:1; 22:2; 23:13 QD; 25:1.

3. The third occurrence is 114, which has no parallel in the Synoptics. See n. 18 below.

Matt. 5:3	**Luke 6:20**	***Thom.* 54**
μακάριοι οἱ πτωχοὶ τῷ πνεύματι ὅτι αὐτῶν ἐστιν ἡ βασιλεία <u>τῶν οὐρανῶν</u>	μακάριοι οἱ πτωχοί ὅτι ὑμετέρα ἐστὶν ἡ βασιλεία τοῦ θεοῦ	ⲡⲉϫⲉ ⲓ̅ⲥ̅ ϫⲉ ϩⲛ̅ⲙⲁⲕⲁⲣⲓⲟⲥ ⲛⲉ ⲛϩⲏⲕⲉ ϫⲉ ⲧⲱⲧⲛ̅ ⲧⲉ ⲧⲙⲛ̅ⲧⲉⲣⲟ <u>ⲛⲙ̅ⲡⲏⲩⲉ</u>
Blessed are the poor in spirit, for theirs is the kingdom <u>of the heavens</u>.	Blessed are the poor, for yours is the kingdom of God.	Blessed are the poor, for yours is the kingdom <u>of the heavens</u>.

Matt. 13:31	**Mark 4:30-31**	**Luke 13:18-19**	***Thom.* 20**
Ἄλλην παραβολὴν παρέθηκεν αὐτοῖς λέγων, Ὁμοία ἐστὶν ἡ βασιλεία <u>τῶν</u> <u>οὐρανῶν</u> κόκκῳ σινάπεως. . . .	Καὶ ἔλεγεν, Πῶς ὁμοιώσωμεν τὴν βασιλείαν τοῦ θεοῦ, ἢ ἐν τίνι αὐτὴν παραβολῇ θῶμεν; ὡς κόκκῳ σινάπεως. . . .	Ἔλεγεν οὖν, Τίνι ὁμοία ἐστὶν ἡ βασιλεία τοῦ θεοῦ, καὶ τίνι ὁμοιώσω αὐτήν; ὁμοία ἐστὶν κόκκῳ σινάπεως. . . .	ⲡⲉϫⲉ ⲙ̅ⲙⲁⲑⲏⲧⲏⲥ ⲛ̅ ⲓ̅ⲥ̅ ϫⲉ ϫⲟⲟⲥ ⲉⲣⲟⲛ ϫⲉ ⲧⲙⲛ̅ⲧⲉⲣⲟ <u>ⲛⲙ̅ⲡⲏⲩⲉ</u> ⲉⲥⲧⲛ̅ⲧⲱⲛ ⲉⲛⲓⲙ. ⲡⲉϫⲁϥ ⲛⲁⲩ ϫⲉ ⲉⲥⲧⲛ̅ⲧⲱⲛ ⲁⲩⲃⲗ̅ⲃⲓⲗⲉ ⲛ̅ ϣⲗ̅ⲧⲁⲙ. . . .
He put another parable before them, saying, "The kingdom <u>of the heavens</u> is like a grain of mustard seed. . . ."	And he said, "How shall we compare the kingdom of God, or in what parable shall we put it? Like a grain of mustard seed. . . ."	Therefore he said, "To what is the kingdom of God like, and to what shall I compare it? It is like a grain of mustard seed. . . ."	The disciples said to Jesus, "Tell us what the kingdom <u>of</u> <u>the heavens</u> is like." He said to them, "It is like a grain of mustard seed. . . ."

In both Matt. 5:3[4] and 13:31,[5] the phrase "kingdom of the heavens" is reasonably seen to come from the evangelist's hand. On each of these oc-

4. On the Two-Source Theory, Matthew is redacting Q in Matt. 5:3, and the wording of Q 6:20 is reconstructed as "kingdom of God" by the IQP. On the Farrer theory, we do not have access to Matthew's source material here, but there is no reason to doubt that it is the evangelist who is contributing this phrase given his established redactional usage elsewhere. For further comments on *Thomas*'s use of the beatitude in Matt. 5:3 // Luke 6:20, see above, 50-52.

5. On the Two-Source Theory, the Mustard Seed parable is a Mark-Q overlap passage

casions, *Thomas*'s parallel to the Synoptics appears to have been influenced by the redactional phrase that is so distinctive of Matthew.[6]

Stephen Patterson is unimpressed by the occurrence of this phrase in *Thom.* 20 and 54, and he says that "Thomas avoids reference to 'God' no less assiduously than Matthew, and never refers to 'God's kingdom.'"[7] But this is a mistake born out of the Coptic priority fallacy, which treats the Coptic witness to the *Gospel of Thomas* as if it is the only witness.[8] It is true that the term "kingdom of God" is absent from Coptic *Thomas,* but it is present in P.Oxy. 1.4-8 (*Thom.* 27)[9] and probably also P.Oxy. 654.15-16 (*Thom.* 3).[10] Even if it were true, Patterson is assuming the standard but dubious notion that the use of "kingdom of the heavens" is due to avoidance of the divine name, so that the phrase can be "attributed to common Jewish roots."[11]

The general failure to see the strikingly Matthean nature of "the kingdom of the heavens" in *Thomas* may result from the tendency to underestimate just how unusual the term is among early Jewish and early Christian works. As Jonathan Pennington notes, "kingdom of heaven is found only in literature which postdates Matthew."[12] It is not in the Old Testament or in the Dead Sea Scrolls; it is not in the Apocrypha or Pseudepigrapha. Among

---

and the term "kingdom of the heavens" is Matthew's redactional addition to Mark and Q, both of which had "kingdom of God." On the Farrer theory too, the term is redactional, an element in Matthew's revision of Mark. The term "kingdom of the heavens" is used repeatedly in Matt. 13 (see n. 2 above).

6. Surprisingly, it is rare to see this example of Matthean redaction in *Thomas* discussed in the literature. But see Schrage, *Verhältnis,* 62 (*Thom.* 20) and 118-19 (*Thom.* 54); cf. 31. Similarly Fieger, *Thomasevangelium,* 91, "Dies kann somit ein Zeichen der Abhängigkeit des ThEv von Mt sein" (*Thom.* 20). See further Jens Schröter, "Die Herausforderung einer theologischen Interpretation des *Thomasevangeliums,*" in Jörg Frey, Enno Ezard Popkes, and Jens Schröter, *Das Thomasevangelium. Entstehung — Rezeption — Theologie* (BZNW 157; Berlin: de Gruyter, 2008), 435-59 (448-50).

7. Patterson, *Gospel of Thomas,* 28, in discussion of *Thom.* 20. Cf. Sieber, "Redactional Analysis," 163-65. Quarles, "Use of the *Gospel of Thomas,*" also engages in the Coptic priority fallacy here: "Thomas never uses the phrase 'kingdom of God'" (522).

8. See further Chapter 2 above.

9. DeConick, *Original Gospel,* 129, suggests that the term "of God" is "a scribal addition in the Greek," but with only two references to "kingdom" in the Oxyrhynchus fragments, here and in *Thom.* 3, it is impossible to say what the tendencies of the Greek scribes of *Thomas* might have been.

10. See above, 35.

11. Patterson, *Gospel of Thomas,* 28.

12. Jonathan T. Pennington, *Heaven and Earth in the Gospel of Matthew* (NovTSup 126; Leiden: Brill, 2007), 3.

Christian works, it only begins to appear in the mid-second century, in Justin Martyr, the *Pseudo-Clementines,* and elsewhere. It is absent from the works we know to have come from the earliest period, like Paul's Epistles, which always use the term "kingdom of God."[13]

Moreover, the tendency to see the term as an attempt at offering a reverential circumlocution for the divine name, always questionable given Matthew's frequent use elsewhere of θεός ("God"), is increasingly seen now to be dubious.[14] The term "kingdom of the heavens" is invested with importance for Matthew, symbolizing a theology in which heaven and earth are in tension and seeking eschatological resolution.[15] The disciples are to pray for this (6:10), they are given authority that whatever they bind or loose on earth will be bound or loosed in heaven (16:19; 18:18), and the "kingdom of the heavens" language is best understood in line with this thought and not as a mere phrasal variation.[16]

Furthermore, if *Thomas* was trying to avoid the term "kingdom of God," there were plenty of options available other than the distinctive Matthean phrase, whether "kingdom" alone or "kingdom of the Father,"[17] both of which are common in *Thomas.*[18]

---

13. Rom. 14:17; 1 Cor. 4:20; 6:9, 10; 15:50; Gal. 5:21; Col. 4:11; 2 Thess. 1:5. Cf. 1 Cor. 15:24, "the kingdom"; 1 Thess. 2:12, "the God who calls you to his own kingdom and glory"; Eph. 5:5, "kingdom of Christ and God"; Rev. 12:10, "kingdom of our God."

14. See in particular Pennington, *Heaven and Earth;* on the phrase see also Robert Foster, "Why on Earth Use 'Kingdom of Heaven'? Matthew's Terminology Revisited," *NTS* 48 (2002): 487-99.

15. So Pennington, *Heaven and Earth.*

16. It is also worth noticing the unusual nature of the plural *heavens;* see Pennington, *Heaven and Earth,* 3, 5, *et passim.*

17. For a helpful study of "kingdom" language in *Thomas,* see Pheme Perkins, "The Rejected Jesus and the Kingdom Sayings," in Charles W. Hedrick, ed., *The Historical Jesus and the Rejected Gospels* (*Semeia* 44; Atlanta: Society of Biblical Literature, 1988), 79-94, though she begins with: "Absence of the expression 'Kingdom of God' may reflect the absence of the term 'God' from the Gospel of Thomas generally. It occurs only in log. 100" (83). This is another instance of the Coptic priority fallacy (discussing the Coptic text as if it is the only witness to *Thomas*).

18. This leaves unanswered the occurrence of "kingdom of the heavens" also in *Thom.* 114, which has no Matthean parallel, but this may simply show that the distinctively Matthean locution had made sufficient impact on the author that he used it on this extra occasion, in spite of his general preference for other "kingdom" terms. The point is that the distinctive, pervasive nature of the phrase in Matthew and its presence in two parallel sayings in *Thomas* are impressive. Justin Martyr is further along the same trajectory, paralleling several of Matthew's "kingdom of the heavens" sayings but also adding "kingdom of the heavens" on his own (*1 Apol.* 15, when quoting Matt. 5:29 // Matt. 18:9).

Matt. 15:11 // *Thom.* 14, Out of the Mouth

Matt. 15:10-11	Mark 7:14-15	*Thom.* 14.5
Καὶ προσκαλεσάμενος τὸν ὄχλον εἶπεν αὐτοῖς, Ἀκούετε καὶ συνίετε· οὐ τὸ εἰσερχόμενον εἰς <u>τὸ στόμα</u> κοινοῖ τὸν ἄνθρωπον, ἀλλὰ τὸ ἐκπορευόμενον ἐκ <u>τοῦ στόματος</u> τοῦτο κοινοῖ τὸν ἄνθρωπον.	Καὶ προσκαλεσάμενος πάλιν τὸν ὄχλον ἔλεγεν αὐτοῖς, Ἀκούσατέ μου πάντες καὶ σύνετε· οὐδέν ἐστιν ἔξωθεν τοῦ ἀνθρώπου εἰσπορευόμενον εἰς αὐτὸν ὃ δύναται κοινῶσαι αὐτόν, ἀλλὰ τὰ ἐκ τοῦ ἀνθρώπου ἐκπορευόμενά ἐστιν τὰ κοινοῦντα τὸν ἄνθρωπον.	ΠΕΤΝΑΒШΚ ΓΑΡ ΕϨΟΥΝ ϨΝ ΤΕΤ͞ΝΤΑΠΡΟ ϤΝΑΧШϨΜ ΤΗΥΤ͞Ν ΑΝ ΑΛΛΑ ΠΕΤ͞ΝΝΗΥ ΕΒΟΛ ϨΝ ΤΕΤ͞ΝΤΑΠΡΟ Ν͞ΤΟϤ ΠΕΤΝΑΧΑϨΜ ΤΗΥΤ͞Ν.
And he called the people to him and said to them, "Hear and understand: not what goes into <u>the mouth</u> defiles a person, but what comes out of <u>the mouth</u>, this defiles a person."	And he called the people to him again, and said to them, "Hear me, all of you, and understand: there is nothing outside a person that by going into them can defile them; but the things that come out of a person are what defile them."	For what goes into <u>your mouth</u> will not defile you, but what comes out of <u>your mouth</u>— it is that which will defile you."

Whereas the previous example is a case of a striking Mattheanism finding its way into different contexts in *Thomas*, this example is a little different. It is, nevertheless, straightforward in its simplicity,[19] at least for those who hold to Markan priority.[20] Matthew redacts Mark by adding "into the mouth . . . out of the mouth," and *Thomas* parallels this redactional addition. The parallels form part of the pericope Matt. 15:1-20, commonly and correctly

19. See already in McArthur, "Gospel According to Thomas," 61; idem, "Dependence," 286.

20. Risto Uro, "*Thomas* and the Oral Gospel Tradition," 23-26, argues effectively that "Matt. 15.11 is a Matthean reformulation based on Mark 7.15" (26).

taken to be Matthew's redactional reworking of Mark 7:1-23. The texts are close to one another, and little in Matthew's pericope does not make sense as Matthew's characteristic reworking of Mark. In other words, there is no reason to imagine that he takes over the gloss "into the mouth" from an independent tradition. He makes the same gloss twice again in this passage (Matt. 15:17 // Mark 7:18 and Matt. 15:18 // Mark 7:20), and it is a word that occurs frequently in Matthew.[21] He is simply engaging in characteristic Matthean clarification of Mark, and *Thomas* takes over the gloss.[22]

Those arguing for an independent *Thomas* suggest either that Matthew is redacting Mark in line with an independent source,[23] or that both Matthew and *Thomas* are independently attempting to clarify the saying.[24] The difficulty with the former is that it is unnecessary to postulate independent sources for what is simply a clarifying addition.[25] The more economical explanation is that Matthew has reworked Mark in characteristic fashion and *Thomas* is showing his knowledge of that redaction. The latter explanation, from coincidental redaction, has the advantage of conceding that *Thomas*, like Matthew, is secondary to Mark; but it is problematic in that Matthew has a known tendency to make these kinds of clarificatory additions to Mark. *Thomas*, by contrast, is regularly more obscure than the Synoptic evangelists.[26]

---

21. στόμα ("mouth") is found frequently in Matthew and Luke, who often have the word where parallels lack it: Matt. 4:4 LXX QD; 5:2 QD; 12:34 QC; 13:35 LXX M; 15:11 R (2x); 15:17 R; 15:18 R; 17:27 M; 18:16 LXX M; 21:16 LXX R; Luke 1:64, 70; 4:22; 6:45 QC; 11:54 QD; 19:22 QD; 21:15 R; 21:24 R; 22:71 R.

22. There is another possible sign of *Thomas* carrying over Matthean redaction here. Bethge retroverts the Coptic ⲚⲦⲞϤ ⲠⲈⲦⲚⲀⲬⲀϨⲘ̄ ⲦⲎⲨⲦⲚ̄ ("it is that which will defile you") to τοῦτο κοινώσει ὑμᾶς (contrast Greeven: ἔσται τὸ κοινοῦν ὑμᾶς). This kind of resumptive οὗτος is found elsewhere in Matthew's redaction of Mark, e.g., Matt. 13:19, 20, 23.

23. Sieber, "Redactional Analysis," 192-93; Koester, *Ancient Christian Gospels*, 111.

24. Patterson, *Gospel of Thomas*: 25 n. 33, "The subject matter is, after all, 'eating'; that both specify what goes into the 'mouth' could easily be ascribed to an independent effort by both authors to clarify the saying."

25. See also James D. G. Dunn, "Jesus and Ritual Purity: A Study of the Tradition-History of Mark 7.15," in F. Refoulé, ed., *À cause de l'Évangile: Études sur les Synoptiques et les Actes offertes au P. Jacques Dupont* (LD 123; Paris: Cerf, 1985), 251-76; repr. in James D. G. Dunn, *Jesus, Paul and the Law* (London: SPCK, 1990), 37-60. Dunn suggests that both Matthew and *Thomas* know a variant Q version of the logion not attested in Luke.

26. Note also the intrusive presence of "Heal the sick among them" in *Thom.* 14.4. Grant and Freedman, *Secret Sayings*, 106, comment on the anomalous nature of this element: "This command has nothing whatever to do with the subject he is discussing, and it breaks the continuity of his thought into pieces. Why did he include it? Because it is found in Luke

The previous two examples feature items that at first appear to be relatively minor in *Thomas*, a distinctive phrase ("kingdom of the heavens") and a Matthean redactional addition to Mark ("out of the mouth"). I suggested in chapter 3 that it is important not to play down these kinds of diagnostic shards and that it is in the nature of the case that a lot of the evidence in given parallels will appear to be minor. Other examples of Matthean redaction in *Thomas* are similar in nature. When "the Pharisees and the scribes" appear in *Thom.* 39 (ⲘⲪⲀⲢⲒⲤⲀⲒⲞⲤ ⲘⲚ ⲚⲄⲢⲀⲘⲘⲀⲦⲈⲨⲤ), the reader who knows the Synoptic Gospels might not be particularly impressed with so familiar a pairing of antagonists. But the appearance of the pairing is usually taken as a sign of Matthew's redaction in the parallel (Matt. 23:13 // Luke 11:53) not least because the pairing is characteristic of the evangelist (Matt. 5:20; 12:38; 15:1);[27] and, we might add, it is the way he has set up his version of the discourse where it appears, with the Pharisees and scribes occupying the place of importance at the outset (Matt. 23:2), and repeated six times in the discourse (23:13, 14, 15, 23, 25, 27).[28] In spite of its relatively minor appearance, it is enough to suggest to Patterson that there must have been some influence from Matthew in the textual tradition of *Thomas*,[29] even if not in the original composition.[30]

10:9, directly after the words about eating what is set before you." DeConick, *Original Gospel*, 89-90, is unconvinced. Like almost all the Synoptic parallels it is one of her "kernel sayings." However, the "heal the sick" command is anomalous not only here in logion 14, but also in *Thomas* as a whole. Nowhere else does *Thomas* show any interest in Jesus' or his disciples' healing activity. Rather, it looks like a little Synoptic fragment, picked up by *Thomas* from Luke 10:9.

27. Thus the IQP regards the pairing as Matthean redaction and tentatively reconstructs with Luke's νομικοί. Contrast Koester, *Ancient Christian Gospels*, 92, who reconstructs with "Pharisees and scribes," suggesting also that "Thomas preserves the original form of this saying." For a critique see Christopher M. Tuckett, "Q and Thomas: Evidence of a Primitive 'Wisdom Gospel'? A Response to H. Koester," *ETL* 67 (1991): 346-60 (354).

28. Examples like this are suggestive rather than conclusive. Thomas has the pairing in reverse order, "Pharisees and scribes" rather than "scribes and Pharisees." And while most Q theorists see the "scribes and Pharisees" here as Matthew's own addition to the Q verse attested also in Luke 11:53, Q skeptics are generally less sanguine about their ability to reconstruct Matthew's source material here. Moreover, the pairing is found on one clear occasion in Mark, at 7:5 (cf. also Mark 2:16, "scribes of the Pharisees"; and 7:1); so, unlike "kingdom of the heavens," it is not so clearly a *distinctive* Matthean phrasing.

29. Patterson, *Gospel of Thomas*, 36, notes that these are "typically Matthaean opponents" but suggests that the absence of the pairing elsewhere in *Thomas* tells against "systematic use of Matthew in the composition of the Thomas collection." To borrow a phrase from Farrer, this is "a plea against apparent evidence." When looking for Synoptic redaction in *Thomas*, it

Nevertheless, without wishing to have unrealistic expectations, it would be encouraging also to see something in *Thomas* that exhibits Matthean influence at the pericope level and not just the phrasal level. As it happens, there is something like this, but it is often missed in the literature — the parable of the Wheat and the Tares.

The Wheat and the Tares (Matt. 13:24-30 // *Thom.* 57)

The parable of the Wheat and the Tares provides a particularly telling example of a Synoptic parable that is taken over secondarily in *Thomas*. Although the possibility of *Thomas*'s use of Matthew is sometimes discussed in the literature,[31] one important element, the apparent parallel with Mark's Seed Growing Secretly, is rarely mentioned,[32] so it is worth taking a moment to lay out the case. Matthew's parable appears to be his redactional expansion of Mark's parable of the Seed Growing Secretly (Mark 4:26-29).[33] Here are the three pericopae in parallel:

---

is in the nature of the case that the evangelists' characteristic expressions will occur only occasionally. If they were to occur more frequently, they would get attributed to common early tradition (as Patterson does with "kingdom of heaven," above). For more on the issue of harmonization, see above, 56-63; and on this example see above, 55-56. Reinhard Nordsieck, *Das Thomas-Evangelium: Einleitung; Zur Frage des historischen Jesus; Kommentierung aller 114 Logien* (3rd ed.; Neukirchen-Vluyn: Neukirchener Verlag, 2006), 168-69, attempts to play down the importance of the parallel between Matthew and *Thomas* and argues for independence.

30. Comparison with the Greek witness is not much help. P.Oxy. 655 is really fragmentary in this saying, and nothing remains of lines 39-40 where the key phrase would have occurred. Nevertheless, Fitzmyer, "Oxyrhynchus Logoi," 413, reconstructs the text with οἱ φαρισαῖοι καὶ οἱ γραμματεῖς, for which there is certainly enough space.

31. See further below, n. 43.

32. Neither Patterson, *Gospel of Thomas*, 45-46, nor DeConick, *Original Gospel*, 193-95, for example, mentions the Seed Growing Secretly in this connection. It is not even listed among DeConick's "literature parallels" (194-95).

33. Michael Goulder, *Midrash and Lection in Matthew* (London: SPCK, 1974), 367, traces the view to H. J. Holtzmann, *Handkommentar zum Neuen Testament* (3rd ed.; Tübingen: Mohr, 1901), 248. See R. H. Gundry, *Matthew: A Commentary on His Handbook for a Mixed Church Under Persecution* (Grand Rapids: Eerdmans, 1994), 261-65, for a persuasive case that "Matthew composed this parable by conflating the parables of the sower and the seed growing by itself and by adding a bit of John the Baptist's preaching. His constructing the parable rules out extracanonical derivation of the version in *Gos. Thom.* 57" (265). See too Donald Senior, *Matthew* (Abingdon New Testament Commentaries; Nashville: Abingdon, 1998), 152-54.

Mark 4:26-29	Matt. 13:24-30	*Thom.* 57
καὶ ἔλεγεν, οὕτως ἐστὶν ἡ βασιλεία τοῦ θεοῦ ὡς ἄνθρωπος βάλῃ τὸν σπόρον ἐπὶ τῆς γῆς 27 καὶ καθεύδῃ καὶ ἐγείρηται νύκτα καὶ ἡμέραν καὶ ὁ σπόρος βλαστᾷ καὶ μηκύνηται ὡς οὐκ οἶδεν αὐτός. 28 αὐτομάτη ἡ γῆ καρποφορεῖ πρῶτον χόρτον εἶτα στάχυν εἶτα πλήρης σῖτον ἐν τῷ στάχυϊ. 29 ὅταν δὲ παραδοῖ ὁ καρπός εὐθὺς ἀποστέλλει τὸ δρέπανον ὅτι παρέστηκεν ὁ θερισμός.	ἄλλην παραβολὴν παρέθηκεν αὐτοῖς λέγων, ὡμοιώθη ἡ βασιλεία τῶν οὐρανῶν ἀνθρώπῳ σπείραντι καλὸν σπέρμα ἐν τῷ ἀγρῷ αὐτοῦ. 25 ἐν δὲ τῷ καθεύδειν τοὺς ἀνθρώπους ἦλθεν αὐτοῦ ὁ ἐχθρὸς καὶ ἐπέσπειρεν ζιζάνια ἀνὰ μέσον τοῦ σίτου καὶ ἀπῆλθεν. 26 ὅτε δὲ ἐβλάστησεν ὁ χόρτος καὶ καρπὸν ἐποίησεν τότε ἐφάνη καὶ τὰ ζιζάνια. 27 προσελθόντες δὲ οἱ δοῦλοι τοῦ οἰκοδεσπότου εἶπον αὐτῷ, κύριε, οὐχὶ καλὸν σπέρμα ἔσπειρας ἐν τῷ σῷ ἀγρῷ; πόθεν οὖν ἔχει ζιζάνια; 28 ὁ δὲ ἔφη αὐτοῖς, ἐχθρὸς ἄνθρωπος τοῦτο ἐποίησεν. οἱ δὲ δοῦλοι λέγουσιν αὐτῷ, θέλεις οὖν ἀπελθόντες συλλέξωμεν αὐτά; 29 ὁ δέ φησιν, οὔ, μήποτε συλλέγοντες τὰ ζιζάνια ἐκριζώσητε ἅμα αὐτοῖς τὸν σῖτον. 30 ἄφετε συναυξάνεσθαι ἀμφότερα ἕως τοῦ θερισμοῦ καὶ ἐν καιρῷ τοῦ θερισμοῦ ἐρῶ τοῖς θερισταῖς, συλλέξατε πρῶτον τὰ ζιζάνια καὶ δήσατε αὐτὰ εἰς δέσμας πρὸς τὸ κατακαῦσαι αὐτά, τὸν δὲ σῖτον συναγάγετε εἰς τὴν ἀποθήκην μου.	ΠΕΧΕ ΙC ΧΕ ΤΜΝΤΕΡΟ ΜΠΕΙШΤ ΕCΤΝΤШ(Ν) ΑΥΡШΜΕ ΕΥΝΤΑϤ ΜΜΑΥ ΝΝΟΥϬΡΟϬ ΕΝ[ΑΝΟ] ΥϤ ΑΠΕϤΧΑΧΕ ΕΙ ΝΤΟΥШΗ ΑϤCΙΤΕ ΝΟΥΖΙΖΑΝΙ[Ο]Ν ΕΧΝ ΠΕϬΡΟ[Ϭ Ε]ΤΝΑΝΟΥϤ ΜΠΕ ΠΡШΜΕ ΚΟΟΥ ΕϨШΛΕ ΜΠΖΙΖΑΝΙΟΝ ΠΕΧΑϤ ΝΑΥ ΧΕ ΜΗΠШC ΝΤΕΤΝΒШΚ ΧΕ ΕΝΑϨШΛΕ ΜΠΖΙΖΑΝΙΟ(Ν) ΝΤΕΤΝϨШΛΕ ΜΠCΟΥΟ ΝΜΜΑϤ ϨΜ ΦΟΟΥ ΓΑΡ ΜΠШϨC ΝΖΙΖΑΝΙΟΝ ΝΑΟΥШΝϨ ΕΒΟΛ CΕϨΟΛΟΥ ΝCΕΡΟΚϨΟΥ.

Mark 4:26-29	Matt. 13:24-30	*Thom.* 57
26 And he was saying, "The kingdom of God is like a man who casts seed upon the soil; 27 and he goes to bed at night	24 Another parable he put before them, saying, "The kingdom of the heavens may be compared to a man who sowed good seed in his field; 25 but while the people were sleeping, his enemy came and sowed weeds among the wheat, and went away. 26 So when the plants came up and bore grain, then the weeds appeared also. 27 And the servants of the householder came and said to him, 'Sir, did you not sow good seed in your field? How then has it weeds?' 28 He said to them,	Jesus says, "The kingdom of the Father is like a man who had [good] seed. His enemy came by night and sowed weeds among the good seed.
and gets up by day, and the seed sprouts and grows — how, he himself does not know. 28 The soil produces crops by itself; first the blade, then the head, then the mature grain in the head. 29 But when the crop permits, he immediately puts in the sickle, because the harvest has come."	'An enemy has done this.' The servants said to him, 'Then do you want us to go and gather them?' 29 But he said, 'No; lest in gathering the weeds you root up the wheat along with them. 30 Let both grow together until the harvest; and at harvest time I will tell the reapers, Gather the weeds first and bind them in bundles to be burned, but gather the wheat into my barn.'"	The man did not allow them to pull up the weeds; he said to them, 'I am afraid that you will go intending to pull up the weeds and pull up the wheat along with them.' For on the day of the harvest the weeds will be plainly visible, and they will be pulled up and burned."

There are several reasons for seeing Matthew's parable as his redactional expansion of Mark's Seed Growing Secretly:[34]

34. Cf. Charles W. F. Smith, "The Mixed State of the Church in Matthew's Gospel," *JBL* 82 (1963): 149-68 (150-53). C. H. Dodd set the standard for the rejection of the notion that the Wheat and the Tares and the Seed Growing Secretly are parallel, *Parables of the Kingdom* (rev. ed.; New York: Scribner, 1961), 137. Klyne R. Snodgrass, *Stories with Intent: A Comprehensive*

1. Parallel Order. Matthew's Wheat and Tares appears in the same place in Matthew as the Seed Growing Secretly appears in Mark, immediately before the parable of the Mustard Seed (Matt. 13:31-32 // Mark 4:30-32), and just after the interpretation of the Sower (Matt. 13:18-23 // Mark 4:13-20).[35] In terms of placement, this is Matthew's parallel to Mark's parable.

2. The Lack of Matthean Omissions of Markan Material. It is worth bearing in mind, moreover, that few pieces of Mark have no parallel in Matthew. All of them are odd Markan narrative pericopae (Mark 7:32-36: Deaf Mute; Mark 8:22-26: Blind Man of Bethsaida; Mark 14:51-52: Man Runs Away Naked).[36] Indeed, this would be the only Markan parable not to appear in Matthew. It is reasonable to conceptualize the Wheat and the Tares as in some sense Matthew's version of Mark's Seed Growing Secretly.

3. Parallel Content. Matthew's parable shares the same skeleton as Mark's parable, and they have several motifs in common.[37] In both stories, a man sows a seed, the seed grows while he sleeps, and then there is a harvest. The words in common are βασιλεία (kingdom), ἄνθρωπος (person), καθεύδω (to sleep), βλαστάνω (to sprout, grow), χόρτος (grass), σῖτος (wheat), καρπός (fruit), θερισμός (harvest). Some of these words are common and it would be easy to play down their importance. But βλαστάνω is rare in the Gospels. It occurs only here, in parallel, in Mark 4:27 and Matt. 13:26.[38] And it is a mistake to overlook the importance of clusters of common words, especially when the words in question are all connected with key moments in the plot.[39] It is not as if the only words in common are "and," "but," and "therefore."

Guide to the Parables of Jesus (Grand Rapids: Eerdmans, 2008), 199-200, also resists the idea that the Wheat and the Tares is Matthew's redactional reworking of the Seed Growing Secretly, though he thinks that *Thom.* 57 is dependent on Matt. 13:24-30 (195-96, 200).

35. Mark 4:21-25 intervenes in Mark, but the material here has all already been used by Matthew (5:15; 10:26; 7:2; 13:12).

36. See my *Case Against Q*, 32-34.

37. Dodd, *Parables*, 137, simply denies that the parable is Matthew's elaboration of Mark's Seed Growing Secretly: "This does not seem to me in the least probable. The Matthaean parable stands on its own feet." For a thorough attempt to refute the idea that Matthew's Wheat and the Tares is derived from Mark's Seed Growing Secretly, see Ramesh Khatry, "The Authenticity of the Parable of the Wheat and the Tares and Its Interpretation" (PhD diss., Westminster College, 1991).

38. The only two other occurrences in the New Testament are at Heb. 9:4 and Jas. 5:18. Cf. Goulder, *Midrash*, 368, "καθεύδω, βλαστάνω, and χόρτος are neither common words nor inevitable in a harvest parable."

39. See further David R. Catchpole, "John the Baptist, Jesus and the Parable of the Tares," *SJT* 31 (1978): 557-70; and for counterargument, Khatry, "Authenticity," 20-22.

The Matthean parable is, of course, significantly longer than the Markan one, and it has a key new element, the introduction of an enemy sowing weeds among the wheat, elements that point to Matthean redaction of Mark.

4. Matthean Imagery and Thought in the Additional Material. The fresh elements in the parable feature characteristically Matthean imagery and thought, and they align so well with the interpretation provided by Matthew in 13:36-43 that it seems likely that it is Matthew himself who redacted the Markan parable to produce the Matthean allegory:[40]

- **The Enemy**: The protagonist has an "enemy" (ἐχθρός, 13:25, 28), identified as the devil (διάβολος) in the interpretation (13:39). It is a major feature of Matthew's thought that the enemy, the evil one, the devil stands in opposition to Jesus/the Son of Man and that his influence continues until the eschaton, when the great separation will take place (25:41).
- **Wheat/weeds contrast**: As well as introducing the character of the enemy, Matthew introduces the kind of stark, black-and-white contrast that characterizes his Gospel's imagery and thought, first introduced in John the Baptist's speech (Matt. 3:10, 12 // Luke 3:9, 17), but found also in the parable of the Sheep and Goats (Matt. 25:31-46) and elsewhere. There are no shades; the ten virgins are either wise or foolish (Matt. 25:1-13); the fish are either good or bad (Matt. 13:48).
- **Separation at the eschaton**: The separation between good and evil comes at the eschaton, often expressed in harvest imagery in Matthew, as here. Wheat and chaff are separated, the wheat to the barn and the chaff to be burned (Matt. 3:12); the good and bad fish are separated, "the wicked from among the righteous" (Matt. 13:48-49); and the separation of good and bad sets up the context for the parable of the Sheep and the Goats, "He will separate them from one another, as the shepherd separates the sheep from the goats" (25:32). Agricultural and harvest imagery do appear to be congenial to *Thomas* (*Thom.* 21, 45, 57, 73), but the motif of apocalyptic separation is not, and is found only here.[41]
- **Eternal Fire**: After the separation has taken place, the key image for the

40. See Goulder, *Midrash*, 367-69.

41. Cf. *Thom.* 111.1-2, "Jesus says, 'The heavens will roll up, and the earth before you. And whoever is living from the Living One will not see death,'" which suggests a division between the in-group and the out-group, alongside cosmic imagery. However, as usual in *Thomas*, it is death rather than judgment that separates. See further below, 186-87.

punishment of the wicked is eternal, unquenchable fire, on repeated occasions (Matt. 3:10, 12; 7:19; 13:50, "into the furnace of fire"; 25:41, where the goats go to "the eternal fire prepared for the devil and his angels"). It is a view of hell that coheres with its description as a place of "weeping and gnashing of teeth" (Matt. 8:12 // Luke 13:28; Matt. 13:42, 50; 22:13; 24:51; 25:30).

- **Waiting until the eschaton**: A large part of the Wheat and the Tares is given over to the issue of waiting to uproot the tares until the harvest. The importance of waiting is a repeated theme in Jesus' parables in Matthew, perhaps because the delay of the parousia had become a key concern by the time Matthew was writing. The theme is particularly marked in Matt. 24–25, "My master is not coming for a long time" (24:48); "the bridegroom was delaying" (25:5); "after a long time the master of those slaves came" (25:19). This theme, of good behavior in the interim in the face of the sudden return of the Lord, is key to Matthew's ethics.

Matthew seems to have creatively expanded the Markan parable, retaining the skeleton structure but adding elements that transform the parable into a typical Matthean allegory of good and evil, the devil, a mixed present world, separation, and future judgment, aligning it with Matthean imagery and themes found often elsewhere.

If Matthew has redacted the Markan Seed Growing Secretly to create the parable of the Wheat and the Tares, then *Thomas*'s familiarity with the parable has to be traced to Matthew. In other words, there is no earlier form of the parable on which *Thomas* could be drawing except, of course, the Seed Growing Secretly, which he also knows (*Thom.* 21.10).[42]

If the parable of the Wheat and the Tares is Matthew's redactional creation, it is worth asking whether there are other ways in which *Thomas* demonstrates its familiarity with Matthew here. A further element that apparently shows *Thomas*'s secondary nature here is the parable's "missing middle," and its resulting lack of an antecedent for ⲚⲀⲨ ("them") in *Thom.* 57.3, ⲠⲈϪⲀϤ ⲚⲀⲨ, "he said to them, . . ." which Wolfgang Schrage took to

42. That the contemporary interpreter is able to see Matthew's Wheat and Tares parable as his expansion of Mark's Seed Growing Secretly does not, of course, mean that *Thomas* was able to do the same. That *Thomas* has a parallel to Mark's Seed Growing Secretly, one of the few pieces of special Markan material, is itself a striking phenomenon in the case for *Thomas*'s knowledge of the Synoptics (see above, 21). See further below, 80 n. 49.

be a sign of *Thomas*'s familiarity with Matthew.[43] This characteristic feature of *Thomas*'s use of source material will be treated in detail below (chapter 7).

Those inclined to see *Thomas* as independent of the Synoptics have never, to my knowledge, discussed the difficulty that arises when Matthew's Wheat and Tares is seen as a redactional expansion of Mark's Seed Growing Secretly. This is a good example of the difficulty sometimes faced in discussions of *Thomas* and the Synoptics, where issues that are well known in discussions of inter-Synoptic relations have not yet trickled down to discussions of Synoptic-*Thomas* relations. Nevertheless, those inclined toward an independent *Thomas* usually note the presence of some features in *Thomas*'s version that are uncongenial, and it is claimed that *Thomas* witnesses to an alternative version of the parable.[44]

It is not just the missing antecedent in the missing middle of the parable, however, that points to the secondary and dependent nature of *Thomas*'s version. Even Helmut Koester, a champion of an independent, non-apocalyptic *Thomas*, admits that the burning of the weeds at the harvest time is "possibly a reference to the last judgment."[45] Indeed, this is as good an example as any of a foreign element in *Thomas*, an apocalyptic, allegorical Synoptic residue.[46]

In summary, the presence of this parable in *Thomas* provides strong grounds for seeing *Thomas*'s familiarity with Matthew. Matthew's parable is best understood as his redactional re-creation of Mark's Seed Growing Secretly, appearing at the same point in the narrative, with a similar

---

43. Schrage, *Verhältnis*, 124-26. The point is largely conceded by those arguing for Thomasine independence, but alongside the suggestion that *Thomas* is familiar with a hypothetical alternative version; see J. Sieber, "Redactional Analysis," 168-69; Patterson, *Gospel of Thomas*, 46. Cf. DeConick, *Original Gospel*, 194, who suggests that "both versions of the parable represent later developments of an earlier form no longer extant." See also R. McL. Wilson, *Studies*, 91.

44. See previous note.

45. Koester, *Ancient Christian Gospels*, 103.

46. In contrast, for example, to the claim of Ron Cameron, "Parable and Interpretation in the Gospel of Thomas," *Foundations & Facets Forum* 2/2 (1986): 3-39 (19 and 34). Cf. Funk and Hoover, *Five Gospels*, 505: "Although the version in Thomas lacks the appended allegorical interpretation, there is a distant echo of the final apocalyptic judgment made explicit in Matthew. This note is alien to Thomas, so it must have been introduced into the Christian tradition at an early date, probably by the first followers of Jesus who had been disciples of John the Baptist." It is striking to see how the theory of *Thomas*'s independence can lead to this kind of convoluted solution, when the theory of familiarity with Matthew's version with its distinctive emphases is both more economical and more plausible.

structure, and featuring much of the same vocabulary, including one word (βλαστάνω, "to grow") found only here. The elements that are not paralleled in Mark are so pervasively Matthean in thought, word, and image that postulation of an additional Matthew-like *Vorlage* is unnecessary. And the parable does not sit particularly well in *Thomas*, not least given the residue of apocalyptic imagery that *Thomas* usually takes care to avoid.[47]

The curiosity is why *Thomas* includes the parable at all. It is worth noting an apparent fondness for the parables of Matt. 13, every one of which is paralleled in *Thomas* (*Thom.* 8 // Matt. 13:47-50, Wise Fisherman; *Thom.* 9 // Matt. 13:3-8, Sower; *Thom.* 20 // Matt. 13:31-32, Mustard Seed; *Thom.* 76 // Matt. 13:45-46, Pearl; *Thom.* 96 // Matt. 13:33, Leaven).[48] It is a familiarity that extends also to Mark 4, with a parallel to Mark's Seed Growing Secretly (*Thom.* 21 // Mark 4:29)[49] and parallels to the wording of Mark's version of the Mustard Seed (Mark 4:30-32), examples that may point to Thomasine knowledge also of Mark.[50] If indeed *Thomas* shows his familiarity with the Synoptic Gospels in this material, it is clear that he has a particular fondness for agricultural imagery but that he dislikes the allegorical explanations of the parables in the Synoptics (Matt. 13:18-23 // Mark 4:13-20 // Luke 8:11-15, interpretation of the Sower; Matt. 13:36-43, interpretation of the Wheat and Tares; Matt. 13:49-50, interpretation of the Dragnet), and these are dropped. Unlike the Synoptics, *Thomas* does not have Jesus expounding the meaning of the parables to those in his circle (Mark 4:10-12 and par.); it is the one who interprets the secret sayings who finds life (Incipit).

---

47. Cf. John W. Marshall, "The *Gospel of Thomas* and the Cynic Jesus," in William E. Arnal and Michel Desjardins, eds., *Whose Historical Jesus?* (Studies in Christianity and Judaism 7; Waterloo, Ont.: Wilfrid Laurier University Press, 1997), 37-60, "The intense eschatology of this kingdom saying is at odds with the tendency within *Thomas* to picture the kingdom without catastrophic eschatology" (55), though Marshall works with an independent *Thomas* model.

48. Cf. McArthur, "Dependence," 287, "Again, if the Gospel of Thomas was completely independent of Matthew is it not a curious coincidence that it includes all seven of the Parables of the Kingdom found in Mt 13? (see Logia 8, 9, 20, 57, 76, 96)."

49. *Thomas*'s parallel to Mark's Seed Growing Secretly probably shows that like many modern New Testament scholars, the author of *Thomas* thought of Matthew's Wheat and the Tares not as an expanded version of Mark's parable, but as independent of it. The presence of parallels to both in *Thomas* in no way detracts from the case for Matthew's redactional expansion of the Markan parable. It does, however, suggest that *Thomas* may well have been familiar with Mark as well as Matthew. See further above, 21, and 78 n. 42.

50. On the evidence for *Thomas*'s Mustard Seed showing familiarity with Mark's version of the parable, see Tuckett, "Thomas and the Synoptics," 149-53.

Conclusion

The agreed method for detecting signs of *Thomas*'s familiarity with the Synoptic Gospels is the presence of Synoptic redactional elements in *Thomas*. Several clear cases of Matthean redaction appear in *Thomas*. Three cases are worth special attention. First, "the kingdom of the heavens," one of the evangelist's most distinctive, pervasive, and famous usages, though frequently underestimated, appears twice in *Thomas* in parallels with Matthew (*Thom.* 20, 54). Second, in a passage where Matthew is dependent on Mark (Matt. 15:11 // Mark 7:15), the evangelist's redactional rewording, "into the mouth" and "out of the mouth," appears in *Thomas*'s parallel (*Thom.* 14). Third, Matthew's thoroughly characteristic imagery, thought, and language in the parable of the Wheat and the Tares (Matt. 13:24-30) finds its way into *Thomas*'s secondary version (*Thom.* 57).

Thomas's familiarity with Matthew's Gospel, though, only takes us part of the way. In looking at the extent of the verbatim agreement between *Thomas* and the Synoptics in chapter 2, we noticed several clear cases where *Thomas* was close also to Luke's Gospel. It is important, therefore, also to look at the possibility that *Thomas* parallels Lukan redactional features.

CHAPTER 5

Lukan Redaction in *Thomas*

Thomas's familiarity with Matthew is strongly suggested by several cases where Matthean redaction appears in the *Gospel of Thomas*. The same is true of Luke in *Thomas*. There are clear examples of the hand of the third evangelist appearing in material where *Thomas* parallels Luke. These make up the major subject of this chapter. The first example is similar to the parallel between Matt. 15:11 and *Thom.* 14.5. There Matthew's modification of Mark appeared in the Thomasine parallel. Here Luke, in triple tradition material, modifies his Markan source and *Thomas* shows familiarity with the Lukan version.[1]

Mark 4:22 // Luke 8:17 // *Thom.* 5 (P. Oxy. 654.29-31)

Mark 4:22	Luke 8:17	*Thom.* 5 (P.Oxy. 654.29-31)
οὐ γάρ ἐστιν κρυπτὸν ἐὰν μὴ ἵνα φανερωθῇ, οὐδὲ ἐγένετο ἀπόκρυφον ἀλλ᾽ ἵνα ἔλθῃ εἰς φανερόν.	<u>οὐ γάρ ἐστιν κρυπτὸν ὃ οὐ φανερὸν γενήσεται,</u> οὐδὲ ἀπόκρυφον ὃ οὐ μὴ γνωσθῇ καὶ εἰς φανερὸν ἔλθῃ.	[<u>οὐ γάρ ἐσ]τιν κρυπτὸν ὃ οὐ φανε[ρὸν γενήσεται]</u>, καὶ τεθαμμένον ὃ ο[ὐκ ἐγερθήσεται]

---

1. As in the previous chapter and throughout, I am assuming Markan priority, for which I have argued elsewhere (see above, 19 n. 54, for references).

Mark 4:22	Luke 8:17	*Thom.* 5 (P.Oxy. 654.29-31)
For there is nothing hidden except to be manifested, nor is anything hidden except to come to light.	For nothing is hidden that will not be made manifest, nor is anything secret that will not become known and come to light.	For nothing is hidden that will not be made manifest, nor buried that will not be raised.

One of the values of this example is that it features in P.Oxy. 654.[2] Although the Greek witness here is fragmentary, the impressive eight-word verbatim agreement with Luke has already sparked interest.[3] What is further striking here is that the agreement occurs with material that is an element in Luke's redactional rephrasing of Mark.[4] Where Mark uses the aorist passive subjunctive of φανερόω (to manifest) in the clause ἐὰν μὴ ἵνα φανερωθῇ (except to be manifested), Luke rephrases with the relative pronoun, a negative, the future middle of γίνομαι (to make) and the adjective φανερός (manifest).[5] This kind of rephrasing might seem trivial, but the very triviality of the differences draws attention to a key point. It is the kind of rephrasing that is best explained on the grounds of Luke's own literary style — there is no need to appeal to a substantive, variant oral tradition to explain Luke's literary rewriting. It is a matter of style and not of substance. Luke has rephrased Mark, and *Thomas* parallels this Lukan rephrasing.

Those who argue against *Thomas*'s familiarity with the Synoptics are generally on the back foot here. Patterson invokes Q (Matt. 10:26b // Luke 12:2b), suggesting that it is evidence for the circulation of a variant form of the saying, a form that may have influenced the Lukan redaction in 8:17.[6] But the double tradition version of the saying simply draws attention to the fact that it is pos-

2. Tuckett, "Thomas and the Synoptics," 145, mistakenly attributes it to P.Oxy. 1 but rightly stresses that "the existence of the verbal agreement in Greek must have some force here" (146).

3. Above, 38.

4. On this example see McArthur, "Dependence," 287; Tuckett, "Thomas and the Synoptics," 145-46; Schrage, "Evangelienzitate," 259-60; and Gathercole, "Luke in the *Gospel of Thomas*," 125. See also the discussion in John S. Kloppenborg, *The Tenants in the Vineyard* (WUNT 195; Tübingen: Mohr Siebeck, 2006), 244-46.

5. This kind of construction is actually rare in the Gospels. Luke uses a similarly constructed clause, relative pronoun + negative + future middle indicative, in 21:15, ἐγὼ γὰρ δώσω ὑμῖν στόμα καὶ σοφίαν ᾗ οὐ δυνήσονται ἀντιστῆναι ἢ ἀντειπεῖν ἅπαντες οἱ ἀντικείμενοι ὑμῖν.

6. Patterson, *Gospel of Thomas*, 21-22; his ὃ οὐ φανερὸν γενήσεται (21) should read ὃ οὐ φανερὸν γενήσεται.

sible to word aphorisms like this differently; Matt. 10:26 and Luke 12:2 both have a relative pronoun[7] but otherwise do not have each of the Lukan modifications found in 8:17.[8] DeConick asks, "Is this phrase enough to *prove* Lukan dependence especially when the rest of L[ogion] 5.2 is wildly divergent from Luke 8.17, particularly the final clause of the passage which is not known in the Thomasine parallel?"[9] But this is another instance of the plagiarist's charter.[10] Evidence of divergence from Luke in parts of *Thom.* 5[11] does not rule out evidence of dependence on Luke in the parallel at hand that features verbatim agreement.[12]

Mark 6:4 // Luke 4:24 // *Thom.* 31 (P.Oxy. 1.36-41)

Mark 6:4	Luke 4:24	*Thom.* 31 (P.Oxy. 1.36-41)
καὶ ἔλεγεν αὐτοῖς ὁ Ἰησοῦς ὅτι Οὐκ ἔστιν προφήτης ἄτιμος εἰ μὴ ἐν τῇ πατρίδι αὐτοῦ καὶ ἐν τοῖς συγγενεῦσιν αὐτοῦ καὶ ἐν τῇ οἰκίᾳ αὐτοῦ.	εἶπεν δέ, Ἀμὴν λέγω ὑμῖν ὅτι οὐδεὶς προφήτης <u>δεκτός</u> ἐστιν ἐν τῇ πατρίδι αὐτοῦ.	λέγει Ἰ(ησοῦς)· οὐκ ἔστιν <u>δεκτὸς</u> προφήτης ἐν τῇ π(ατ)ρίδι αὐτοῦ, οὐδὲ ἰατρὸς ποιεῖ θεραπείας εἰς τοὺς γινώσκοντας αὐτόν.*
And Jesus was saying to them, "A prophet is not without honor except in his home country and among his relatives and in his house."	And he said, "Amen, I say to you that no prophet is <u>accepted</u> in his home country."	Jesus says, "A prophet is not <u>accepted</u> in his home country, nor does a physician perform healings for those who know him."

*This reconstruction of the Greek is from J.-É. Ménard, *L'Évangile selon Thomas* (NHS 5; Leiden: Brill, 1975), 127.

7. Greeven reads the relative pronoun in Mark 4:22 too (and also τι before κρυπτόν), οὐ γάρ ἐστιν <u>τι</u> κρυπτὸν <u>ὃ</u> ἐὰν μὴ ἵνα φανερωθῇ.

8. The variant form of the saying in *Thomas* 6 also does not alter the case for *Thomas*'s knowledge of the Lukan redactional wording in Luke 8:17.

9. DeConick, *Original Gospel*, 61.

10. See above, 54-56.

11. For the interesting parallel to the second half of the saying as witnessed by P.Oxy. 654, see the Oxyrhynchus burial shroud presented in H.-Ch. Puech, "Un logion de Jésus sur bandelette funéraire," *RHR* 147 (1955): 126-29.

12. Nordsieck concedes the likelihood of *Thomas*'s familiarity with Luke, at least via oral tradition, even if not directly, *Thomas-Evangelium*, 45-46.

The word δεκτός (accepted)[13] is used here in *Thom.* 31 (P.Oxy. 1.36-41) in the saying, "A prophet is not accepted (δεκτός) in his home country." This is striking because it is the word that is used in Luke's redactional reformulation (Luke 4:24) of Mark, who has ἄτιμος (Mark 6:4 // Matt. 13:57). On the premise of Markan priority, Luke is rewording his Markan source in the light of his (Luke's) recent quotation of Isa. 58:5 earlier in the same passage (Luke 4:19), where δεκτός is also used.

As Snodgrass points out,[14] the word is uncommon in the New Testament. It occurs only here (Luke 4:19, 24) in the Gospel tradition.[15] It is Lukan redaction of Mark, appearing here in *Thomas*. Apparently, the example satisfies the desired criterion with little fuss. Indeed, several of those who argue for *Thomas*'s familiarity with the Synoptics highlight the case,[16] a case that is appealing in its simplicity because it is straightforward to see Luke's redaction of Mark, a redaction that appears here in *Thomas*, and which is available in one of the Greek fragments, P.Oxy. 1, so that no retroversion from the Coptic is necessary.[17]

Life is rarely so simple, however, and the literature contains several arguments for *Thomas*'s independence, as when Sieber argues that Luke was familiar with a pre-Markan version of the logion, and that he chose this over

---

13. The Coptic here in NH 87, 5-6 is ϢΗΠ, which corresponds to ϢΗΠ in the Coptic of Luke 4:24, in contrast to ϹΗϢ for ἄτιμος at Mark 6:4 // Matt. 13:57. See also Schrage, *Verhältnis*, 75; and Fieger, *Thomasevangelium*, 117-18.

14. Snodgrass, "Gospel of Thomas," 31-32. DeConick, *Original Gospel*, 140, misreads Snodgrass's argument as appealing to "a *hapax legomenon*, appearing nowhere else in the Gospels," but the word δεκτός appears twice here in Luke, in 4:19 and 24, and this is the key issue in the argument made by Snodgrass and others.

15. See also Acts 10:35; 2 Cor. 6:2, which quotes Isa. 49:8; and Phil. 4:18.

16. Schrage, *Verhältnis*, 75-77; H. Schürmann, "Das Thomasevangelium und das lukanische Sondergut," *BZ* 7 (1963): 236-60 (237-38); repr. in H. Schürmann, *Traditionsgeschichtliche Untersuchungen zu den synoptischen Evangelien* (Düsseldorf: Patmos-Verlag, 1968), 228-47; McArthur, "Gospel According to Thomas," 68-69; Snodgrass, "Gospel of Thomas," 31-32; Fieger, *Thomasevangelium*, 117-18; Tuckett, "Thomas and the Synoptics," 143, but with more caution; Gathercole, "Luke in the *Gospel of Thomas*," 126.

17. Cf. W. J. Lyons, "A Prophet Is Rejected in His Home Town (Mark 6.4 and Parallels): A Study in the Methodological (In)Consistency of the Jesus Seminar," *JSHJ* 6 (2008): 59-84, "By altering the Markan saying so that the word δεκτός ('acceptable') is repeated within a context of rejection only five verses later, Luke has created a deeply ironic echo, foregrounding the notion of what is or is not acceptable for his ensuing account of Jesus' ministry. Since the word δεκτός possesses a positive connotation, the conditional construction that was necessary for Mark's negative term ἄτιμος ('without honour') was rendered redundant. The Lukan saying was thus simplified into an absolute sentence" (71).

Mark's version because he had happened to use the word δεκτός recently, in his quotation of Isa. 58:5.[18] But this convoluted explanation is hardly more plausible than the simpler alternative, that Luke has redacted Mark[19] and that *Thomas* shows his knowledge of that redaction. It is only the presence of the parallel in *Thomas* and the attempt to establish its independence of the Synoptics that generates arguments of the kind supported by Sieber. The argument for independence is then bolstered by an appeal to Bultmann,[20] whose form-critical analysis here works on the basis of the problematic notion that brief apophthegmata like that found in *Thom.* 31 necessarily precede narrative, a form-critical "canon" that does not stand up to scrutiny.[21]

In short, then, both *Thom.* 5 and *Thom.* 31 provide good examples of Luke's redaction of Mark appearing in the Thomasine parallels, pointing to *Thomas*'s familiarity with the Gospel of Luke. These examples are all the stronger for featuring in two of the Greek witnesses of *Thomas*, P.Oxy. 1 and 654, where there are no issues about translation or retroversion. Given the limited extent of the Oxyrhynchus fragments, and the limited set of triple tradition parallel examples among them, it is necessary also to look at examples of Lukan redaction appearing in Coptic *Thomas,* including this example from the Lukan special material.

---

18. Sieber, "Redactional Analysis," 22-23. See also Helmut Koester, "*GNOMAI DIAPHO-ROI*: The Origin and Nature of Diversification in the History of Early Christianity," *HTR* 58 (1965): 279-318; repr. in Robinson and Koester, *Trajectories,* 114-57 (129-31); Patterson, *Gospel of Thomas,* 31-32; DeConick, *Original Gospel,* 140-41. Zöckler, *Jesu Lehren,* 43-44, invokes Bultmann and Wendling against Schrage (see n. 20 below) but remarkably discusses only the Markan parallel and does not mention Luke.

19. For the case that Luke 4:16-30 *in toto* is Luke's redaction of Mark 6:1-6, and is not based on independent traditional material, see Goulder, *Luke,* 299-310.

20. All those mentioned in n. 18 cite Bultmann, *History of the Synoptic Tradition,* 31-32, with approval, itself dependent here on Emil Wendling, *Die Entstehung des Marcus-Evangeliums: Philologische Untersuchungen* (Tübingen: Mohr, 1908), 53-56. But Bultmann's thesis is not economical. He recognizes that Luke constructs 4:16-30 on the pattern of Mark 6:1-6, but then adds that he uses the "παραβολή which had been handed down in another context" (32). Martin Dibelius, *From Tradition to Gospel* (ET; London: Ivor Nicholson and Watson, 1934), is more cautious, "I no longer believe that the whole passage had been developed out of this saying" (110). Another element at work here is the apparently prophetic nature of Bultmann's form-critical analysis: he only had the Oxyrhynchus fragments to work with. But there is nothing impressive about the apparent foresight. Those arguing for Thomasine independence are indebted to Robinson and Koester's *Trajectories* model, which develops out of Bultmann's legacy.

21. On the problems with the kind of form-critical analysis that assumes that the tradition begins with compact sayings and expands to larger narrative units, see below, 145-50.

Rich Fool (Luke 12:15-21 // *Thom.* 63)

Thomas's parable of the Rich Fool features several Lukan elements. These elements are often played down in the literature, and the case for *Thomas* having derived its version from Luke is underestimated. As usual, it helps to view *Thomas* in synopsis in order to see the similarities and differences as clearly as possible:

Luke 12:15-21	*Thom.* 63
12:15 εἶπεν δὲ πρὸς αὐτούς· ὁρᾶτε καὶ φυλάσσεσθε ἀπὸ πάσης πλεονεξίας, ὅτι οὐκ ἐν τῷ περισσεύειν τινὶ ἡ ζωὴ αὐτοῦ ἐστιν ἐκ τῶν ὑπαρχόντων αὐτῷ. 16 εἶπεν δὲ παραβολὴν πρὸς αὐτοὺς λέγων· ἀνθρώπου τινὸς πλουσίου εὐφόρησεν ἡ χώρα. 17 καὶ <u>διελογίζετο ἐν ἑαυτῷ</u> λέγων· τί ποιήσω, ὅτι οὐκ ἔχω ποῦ συνάξω τοὺς καρπούς μου; 18 καὶ εἶπεν. τοῦτο ποιήσω, καθελῶ μου τὰς ἀποθήκας καὶ μείζονας οἰκοδομήσω καὶ συνάξω ἐκεῖ πάντα τὸν σῖτον καὶ τὰ ἀγαθά μου. 19 καὶ ἐρῶ τῇ ψυχῇ μου· ψυχή, ἔχεις πολλὰ ἀγαθὰ κείμενα εἰς ἔτη πολλά· ἀναπαύου, φάγε, πίε, εὐφραίνου. 20 εἶπεν δὲ αὐτῷ ὁ θεός· ἄφρων, ταύτῃ τῇ νυκτὶ τὴν ψυχήν σου ἀπαιτοῦσιν ἀπὸ σοῦ· ἃ δὲ ἡτοίμασας, τίνι ἔσται; 21 οὕτως ὁ θησαυρίζων ἑαυτῷ καὶ μὴ εἰς θεὸν πλουτῶν.	ΠΕΧΕ ⲒⲤ ΧΕ ΝΕⲨⲚ ΟⲨΡⲰΜΕ ⲘⲠⲖΟⲨⲤΙΟⲤ ΕⲨⲚΤΑϤ ⲘΜΑⲨ Ⲛ2Α2 ⲚⲬΡΗΜΑ ΠΕΧΑϤ ΧΕ ϯΝΑΡΧΡⲰ ⲚΝΑΧΡΗΜΑ ΧΕΚΑⲀⲤ ΕΕΙΝΑΧΟ ⲚΤΑⲰ[2]Ⲥ2 ⲚΤΑΤⲰϬΕ ⲚΤΑΜΟⲨ2 ⲚΝΑΕ2ⲰΡ ⲚΚΑΡΠΟⲤ ϢΙΝΑ ΧΕ ⲚⲒⲢ̄ ϬΡⲰ2 ⲀⲖⲀⲀⲨ <u>ΝΑΕΙ ΝΕΝΕϤΜΕΕⲨΕ ΕΡΟΟⲨ 2Ⲙ ΠΕϤ2ΗΤ</u> ⲀⲨⲰ 2Ⲛ ΤΟⲨϢΗ ΕΤⲘΜΑⲨ ⲀϤΜΟⲨ ΠΕΤΕⲨⲘ ΜΑΧΕ ⲘΜΟϤ ΜΑΡΕϤⲤⲰΤⲘ

Luke 12:15-21	*Thom.* 63
15 Then he said to them, "Watch out! Be on your guard against all kinds of greed; a man's life does not consist in the abundance of his possessions." 16 And he told them this parable: "The ground of a certain rich man produced a good crop. 17 He <u>thought to himself</u>, 'What shall I do? I have no place to store my crops.' 18 Then he said, 'This is what I will do. I will tear down my barns and build bigger ones, and there I will store all my grain and my goods. 19 And I will say to myself, "You have plenty of good things laid up for many years. Take life easy; eat, drink, and be merry."' 20 But God said to him, 'You fool! This very night your life will be demanded from you. Then who will get what you have prepared for yourself?' 21 This is how it will be with anyone who stores up things for himself but is not rich toward God."	Jesus said: "There was a rich man who had many possessions. He said: 'I will use my wealth to sow my field, to plant, to fill my barn with harvest, so that need will not touch me.' Such were the things that he <u>thought in his heart</u>. But during that night, he died. Whoever has ears to hear, let them hear!"

The Lukan nature of the parable is clear from several features, all of which are shared by *Thomas*:

1. Example Story

There are four "example stories" among the Gospel parables. None is in Matthew; none is in Mark. All four appear in Luke, and just one of them, the Rich Fool, has a parallel in *Thomas*:

- The Good Samaritan (Luke 10:25-37)
- The Rich Fool (Luke 12:15-21 // *Thom.* 63)
- The Rich Man and Lazarus (Luke 16:19-31)
- The Pharisee and the Tax Collector (Luke 18:9-14)

These *Beispielerzählungen* or "illustration stories" have been recognized as unique in the parable tradition since Jülicher.[22] It is a self-explanatory category, defined by B. B. Scott as a story that has "no figurative element but offers an example of correct behavior or of negative behavior to avoid."[23] Unlike other parables, this one has a straightforward moral designed to be drawn directly from the narration itself, the point being that the accumulation of wealth is futile given the unpredictable arrival of death.

The example story is a Lukan trademark, and it is continuous with other features typical of his approach to parables, which have more developed, three-dimensional human characters, with a marked ethical, hortatory dimension. Somewhat surprisingly, literature on *Thomas* rarely notices that the Rich Fool is an example story, a symptom of the common difficulty of Thomas experts and Synoptic experts not talking to one another.

2. Rich, Poor, and Eschatological Reversal
One of the pervasive themes of Luke's Gospel is eschatological reversal, especially involving rich and poor. It is in the signature pieces of the Magnificat (1:46-55), the Beatitudes and Woes (6:20-26), and the parable of Dives and Lazarus (16:19-31). The rule, for Luke, is that the poor will be rewarded and the rich will receive nothing — the roles will be reversed.[24] This parable plays into that scenario, with the rich man unable to enjoy his wealth. Although *Thomas* too has its fair share of anti-rich sentiment (see below), this is the only occasion where fate intervenes to level the scores, in contrast with Luke.

3. Interior Monologue
Interior monologue, or soliloquy, is a regular feature of Luke's parables. His characters frequently give the reader insight into their motivations through soliloquy, the Prodigal Son in 15:17-19, the Unjust Steward in 16:3-4, the Un-

---

22. A. Jülicher, *Die Gleichnisreden Jesu* (2nd ed.; 2 vols.; Tübingen: Mohr [Siebeck], 1910), 1:112-25 and 585-641. Tucker (see n. 23) notes that the distinction actually predates Jülicher.

23. B. B. Scott, *Hear Then the Parable: A Commentary on the Parables of Jesus* (Minneapolis: Fortress, 1989), 29. The major discussion of example stories is found in Jeffrey T. Tucker, *Example Stories: Perspectives on Four Parables in the Gospel of Luke* (JSNTSup 162; Sheffield: Sheffield Academic Press, 1998). Tucker wishes to erase the classification but I am not persuaded; see my review it in *RRT* 6 (1999): 387-88. See further my *Goulder and the Gospels: An Examination of a New Paradigm* (JSNTSup 133; Sheffield: Sheffield Academic Press, 1996), 213-16.

24. See further my *Case Against Q*, 136-38.

just Judge in 18:4b-5.[25] There is just one example outside Luke, in the Tenants in the Vineyard (Mark 12:6 // Matt. 21:37 // Luke 20:13), where Luke enhances the soliloquy he takes over from Mark. Moreover, Luke's soliloquies have a distinctive form: the characters reflect on their circumstances, sometimes with τί ποιήσω (What shall I do?), and they follow on with a statement about what they will do.[26]

Thomas, by contrast, only has interior monologue in parallel with the Synoptics, here in the Rich Fool, and briefly in the Tenants in the Vineyard.[27] Of course, one might say that this is not a Lukanism taken over by *Thomas.* One could argue that Luke has enhanced the soliloquy here, in the parable of the Rich Fool, to make it conform more closely to his parable soliloquies elsewhere, so that an earlier version of the parable might have looked more like the version in *Thomas.* Careful attention to the synopsis of Luke and *Thomas,* however, makes this unlikely. Luke sets up the soliloquy in characteristic fashion, καὶ διελογίζετο ἐν ἑαυτῷ λέγων ("and he debated in himself, saying . . . ," Luke 12:17). This is missing in *Thomas*'s recasting of the parable. It has just the typically terse Thomasine ΠЄΧΑϤ ΧЄ ("he said . . ."), which leaves open the possibility that the man is saying this aloud to an audience. But then the author appears to betray his knowledge of the earlier element in the Lukan narrative, in a manner analogous to Synoptic editorial fatigue, when he writes ΝΑЄΙ ΝЄΝЄϤΜЄЄΥЄ ЄΡΟΟΥ 2Μ̄ ΠЄϤ2ΗΤ ("such were the things he was thinking in his heart"). As with his recasting of the parable of the Wheat and the Tares, the phenomenon of the missing middle rears its head.[28] Here, as there, *Thomas* drops the middle part of a story only to betray his knowledge of it in the subsequent material, inadvertently showing the reader his familiarity with the Synoptics. In cases like this, the author of *Thomas* appears to be a much less sophisticated storyteller than the Synoptic authors, especially Luke.[29]

25. Notice also the Pharisee's and the tax collector's prayers in 18:9-14.

26. See my *Goulder and the Gospels,* 169-71, for further detail.

27. Here too *Thomas* shows his familiarity with the Lukan version of the parable. *Thomas*'s ΜЄϢΑΚ ("perhaps") parallels Luke's ἴσως ("perhaps," Luke 20:13) in the vineyard owner's soliloquy; this occurs only here in the New Testament, and ΜЄϢΑΚ occurs only in this passage, twice, in *Thomas*; cf. Schrage, *Verhältnis,* 140.

28. See below, 111-12.

29. The interior monologue is seldom discussed in literature about the relationship between *Thomas* and Luke. A rare exception is Philip Sellew, "Interior Monologue as a Narrative Device in the Parables of Luke," *JBL* 111 (1992): 239-53, who helpfully describes interior monologue as "a signature device of Luke the author" (251). He does not, however, see *Thomas* as dependent on Luke for the device here because he works with the autonomous *Thomas* model.

There is a good case, then, for seeing features that characterize the hand of Luke getting carried over into *Thomas*, the very form of the parable as an "example story," eschatological reversal involving rich and poor, and the use of interior monologue. However, *Thomas*'s Rich Fool is often regarded as clearly independent from Luke. For Patterson, it is "all but impossible" that *Thomas* derived his version of the parable from Luke 12:16-21.[30] He suggests that the Lukan version of this parable features major embellishments. The wealth of the man and the size of the harvest are stressed (12:18-19); the divine scolding is explicit (12:20); Luke has a "generalizing conclusion" lacking in *Thomas*; and the framing of the unit is Lukan, with additional material introducing the parable (12:13-14 // *Thom.* 72) and a different speech following on from it (Luke 12:22-31 // Matt. 6:25-34; cf. *Thom.* 36). *Thomas*, Patterson says, has none of these features. Where he has parallels to the material Luke uses to frame this unit (*Thom.* 72 and 36), these appear in different parts of his collection. *Thomas* itself has secondary features, he says, but they are different from Luke's. Thus *Thomas* appears to be ignorant of Luke's specific version of this parable. Patterson concludes that he has derived it from a separate tradition history.[31]

This is not the most fruitful way to find out whether *Thomas* knows Luke. The absence of certain alleged secondary elements in *Thomas* need not indicate *Thomas*'s ignorance of Luke. It might simply show that *Thomas* chose not to use certain elements in Luke, especially as most of the elements listed by Patterson are about the narrative framing of the parable in Luke and not about the parable itself. *Thomas* rarely has the same narrative frame as any Synoptic pericope, and it is unsurprising that the sayings gospel is consistent in lacking that narrative frame here.

Moreover, a good case can be made for *Thomas*'s knowledge of the Lukan framing of the parable, which he has transferred to another context:

---

30. Patterson, *Gospel of Thomas*, 48.

31. Ibid., 47-48. Similarly Plisch, *Gospel of Thomas*, 155, "This logion seems simpler and more archaic compared to . . . Luke 12:16-21. The Thomas version is certainly not derived from Luke's version of the narrative, which contains several secondary elements." Riley, "Influence of Thomas Christianity," contends that this parallel provides evidence of Thomasine redaction appearing in Luke, since μεριστής (divider, arbitrator) is more congenial to *Thomas* than to Luke. His contention that the word is new and awkward in Luke is unnecessary; it comes quite naturally from μερίσασθαι in Luke 12:13. And μεριστής is not a "title for Jesus or a title for Jesus to deny" in Luke (231); it is simply part of a characteristically Lukan narrative setup. That the term is congenial to *Thomas* is probably the reason for *Thomas*'s use of it and interest in it.

Luke 12:13-14	*Thom.* 72
εἶπεν δέ τις ἐκ τοῦ ὄχλου αὐτῷ· διδάσκαλε, εἰπὲ τῷ ἀδελφῷ μου μερίσασθαι μετ᾽ ἐμοῦ τὴν κληρονομίαν. 14 ὁ δὲ εἶπεν αὐτῷ· ἄνθρωπε, τίς με κατέστησεν κριτὴν ἤ μεριστὴν ἐφ᾽ ὑμᾶς;	[ⲡⲉ]ϫⲉ ⲟⲩⲣ[ⲱⲙ]ⲉ ⲛⲁϥ ϫⲉ ϫⲟⲟⲥ ⲛ̅ⲛⲁⲥⲛⲏⲩ ϣⲓⲛⲁ ⲉⲩⲛⲁⲡⲱϣⲉ ⲛ̅ⲛ̅ϩⲛⲁⲁⲩ ⲙ̅ⲡⲁⲉⲓⲱⲧ ⲛ̅ⲙⲙⲁⲉⲓ ⲡⲉϫⲁϥ ⲛⲁϥ ϫⲉ ⲱ ⲡⲣⲱⲙⲉ ⲛⲓⲙ ⲡⲉ ⲛ̅ⲧⲁϩⲁⲁⲧ ⲛ̅ⲣⲉϥⲡⲱϣⲉ ⲁϥⲕⲟⲧϥ̅ ⲁⲛⲉϥⲙⲁⲑⲏⲧⲏⲥ ⲡⲉϫⲁϥ ⲛⲁⲩ ϫⲉ ⲙⲏ ⲉⲉⲓϣⲟⲟⲡ ⲛ̅ⲣⲉϥⲡⲱϣⲉ
And someone from the crowd said to him, "Teacher, tell my brother to divide the inheritance with me." But he said to him, "<u>Man</u>, who appointed me as judge or arbitrator over you?"	A man said to him, "Tell my brothers to divide my father's possessions with me." He said to him, "<u>O man</u>, who has made me a divider?" He turned to his disciples and said, "I am not a divider, am I?"

The texts are very close to one another, and μεριστής (divider, arbitrator) appears only here, in Luke 12:14, in the New Testament.[32] The corresponding ⲡⲱϣⲉ appears only here in *Thomas*.[33] The material is transformed in *Thomas* from Luke's introductory foil comment to a freestanding logion, recrafted to support *Thomas*'s oft-repeated theme of singularity and division, where it provides a fine excuse for *Thomas* to add a concluding saying, "I am not a divider, am I?" much more congenial to *Thomas*'s interests than it would be in its Lukan context before the parable of the Rich Fool.[34]

Reminders of its origin in Luke are evident not only in the Lukan introductory foil from an anonymous member of the crowd introduced by

32. On the text-critical issues here, see the authoritative article by Tjitze Baarda, "Luke 12.13-14: Text and Transmission from Marcion to Augustine," in J. Helderman and S. J. Noorda, eds., *Early Transmission of Words of Jesus: Thomas, Tatian and the Text of the New Testament* (Amsterdam: VU Boekhandel and Uitgeverij, 1983), 117-72, which concludes that the original reading in Luke 12:14 is κριτὴν ἤ μεριστήν (131).

33. Three times in *Thom.* 72, but nowhere else in *Thomas*. Both Bethge and Greeven retrovert to μεριστής. See also ⲡⲏϣ (divide) in *Thom.* 61. It is worth remembering Snodgrass's comments ("Gospel of Thomas," 26) about the hapax legomena as signs of *Thomas*'s familiarity with Luke. Snodgrass is not here inclined to press the occurrence of this one since it is in L material ("Gospel of Thomas," 35). The point can be nuanced, though, by separating the discussion into two stages — first, the evidence of a direct link between the texts (cf. chapter 2 above); and second, the evidence of Lukan redaction in *Thomas*.

34. The case for Luke's knowledge of *Thom.* 72 is made in Riley, "Influence of Thomas Christianity"; and refuted in Gathercole, "Luke in the *Gospel of Thomas*," 139-41.

τις (cf. 9:57; 11:27; 13:23; 14:15),[35] but also in the use of the vocative ἄνθρωπε (O, man), used three times elsewhere by Luke (5:20; 22:58, 60), each time in redactional additions to Mark,[36] and here paralleled in *Thomas* (ⲱ ⲠⲢⲰⲘⲈ).[37] Furthermore, the motif of brothers asking about their inheritance has a distinctly Lukan ring. Luke's parable of the Prodigal Son (15:11-32) has a similar setting, with two brothers and an inheritance up for grabs. The adoption and development of a similar idea here may well be due to the evangelist.[38]

The only elements in Patterson's list that are not related to Luke's narrative frame are the additional details about the wealth of the man, the size of the harvest (Luke 12:18-19), and the explicit divine rebuke (12:20). These differences are not surprising. The lack of detail here is typical of the tendency toward greater brevity in his parables. In other words, it is a symptom of his typical redactional tendency rather than a witness to form-critically derived greater primitivity.[39] And it is difficult to imagine *Thomas* including divine speech of the kind that occurs here in Luke (with θεός, 12:20).[40] Not only do we never hear God's voice in *Thomas*; we rarely hear about God (θεός) at all, and when the character does occur, the context is negative (*Thom.* 100).[41]

The difficulty with Patterson's argument, though, is that it proceeds on the basis of the differences between *Thomas* and Luke. The case for *Thomas's* familiarity with Luke proceeds rather from an analysis of the similarities

---

35. See further on this Lukanism below, 100-102.

36. Cf. Snodgrass, "Gospel of Thomas," 35; Baarda, "Luke 12.13-14," 160.

37. The usage is not, however, alien in *Thomas*. ⲠⲢⲰⲘⲈ occurs again in Salome's address to Jesus in *Thom.* 61. On the minor difference between Coptic *Thomas* and Luke here, see Baarda, "Luke 12.13-14," 159, "One should not stress the small incongruity between (ⲱ ⲠⲢⲰⲘⲈ) [*sic*] and Luke (ἄνθρωπε alone). In keeping with Koine usage, the use of the vocative particle ὦ is not frequent in the New Testament." (The word *"Thomas'"* should be supplied after "between.")

38. For the case that the framing is a Lukan creation, see Goulder, *Luke*, 535-36, but already suggested in A. Loisy, *L'Evangile selon Luc* (Paris: E. Nourry, 1924), 344-45. For Schürmann, "Thomasevangelium," 243-44, *Thomas* is dependent on Luke, but Luke is here dependent on Q.

39. See further below, 145-50.

40. God appears as a character only in other Lukan parables, Luke 18:1-8 (Unjust Judge), "there was a judge who neither feared God nor had respect for people. . . . 'Though I have no fear of God and no respect for anyone'" (vv. 2 and 4; cf. v. 7); and Luke 18:9-14 (Pharisee and Tax Collector), "God, I thank you. . . . God, be merciful to me" (vv. 11 and 13).

41. Note also the occurrence of "kingdom of God" in *Thom.* 27 (P.Oxy. 1) and possibly in *Thom.* 3 (P.Oxy. 654); see further above, 35.

between the two texts, and noting the distinctively Lukan nature of the common features. The parable of the Rich Fool is strikingly Lukan, and a good case can be made that Luke is the source of *Thomas*'s knowledge of the parable.

Given the Lukan nature of the parable, it is worth asking why it might have appealed to *Thomas*. What were the features that might have made this example story stand out to *Thomas* where others of Luke's example stories did not? It is always important to ask these questions since it is clear that, on the assumption of *Thomas*'s familiarity with the Synoptics, he has a large number of parables to choose from, and there are many apparent rejects. Here it is easy to imagine what might have attracted *Thomas* to the parable. It has a negative attitude to worldly wealth, and this wealth is associated with death. Hostility to wealth is found throughout *Thomas*, perhaps most clearly in 110, "Whoever finds the world and becomes rich, let them renounce the world." Death is a major theme in the *Gospel of Thomas*.[42] Unlike Mark and Matthew, in Luke and *Thomas* natural death appears in parables, Dives and Lazarus (Luke 16:19-31) and the Hidden Treasure (*Thom*. 109), a point that may reflect the later dates of Luke and *Thomas* when compared with Mark and Matthew, which only have violent or eschatological deaths.

No doubt *Thomas* found in this story a narrative that illustrated the importance of seeking Jesus while there is still the chance to do so, expressed clearly in the typically Thomasine saying 59, which occurs only shortly before the parable of the Rich Fool, "Take heed of the Living One while you are alive, lest you die and seek to see him and be unable to do so." Here, in logion 63, is a man who does not take heed of the Living One while he is alive, instead falling prey to the corrupting worldly wealth that *Thomas* so despises. It is not surprising that *Thomas* found this story congenial, in spite of the fact that its form and storytelling techniques are not Thomasine staples.

It is straightforward to see why Luke's other three example stories would not have appealed to *Thomas*. None is congenial. Luke 16:19-31 (Dives and Lazarus) is all about the afterlife, Abraham's bosom and Hades, with which *Thomas* is unconcerned, and still less the climax of the story about resurrection from the dead and listening to Moses and the prophets, about which

---

42. See further below, 186-87. Death and dying appears in a variety of ways in *Thomas*: avoiding experiencing death (*Thom*. 1, 18, 19, 85, 111); death and corpses (*Thom*. 11); death robbing one of the chance to seek the living one (*Thom*. 59); one dying, one living (*Thom*. 61); one's images not dying (*Thom*. 84); man with the treasure field dies (*Thom*. 109).

Thomas has nothing positive to say.[43] The Pharisee and the Tax Collector (Luke 18:9-14) tells a story about two men at prayer in the temple; *Thomas* has no positive references to the temple or to prayer or to God,[44] the key motifs in this parable. The Good Samaritan (Luke 10:25-37) would also have been uncongenial to *Thomas,* with its grounding in key Old Testament texts like Deut. 6:5 and Lev. 19:18, and still further with its ethic of helping the stranger, which is foreign to *Thomas.*[45]

Factors like these make *Thomas's* familiarity with Luke's Rich Fool much more likely than is usually assumed. The difficulty, though, when analyzing Thomasine parallels with L material is that there are no other extant versions with which to compare *Thomas.* For those who are inclined toward a conservative perspective on L, it might always be claimed that the *Thomas* version independently witnesses to a version of the parable independent of Luke. DeConick, for instance, thinks of it as "a fine example of an independent oral multiform."[46] Like Patterson and others, though, she does not comment on or account for the pervasively Lukan elements like the example story and the rich man's soliloquy. Others have missed the Lukan nature of the parable because it sometimes gets treated as a Q parable, in spite of its lack of parallel in Matthew,[47] a classification that can throw people off the scent. An origin in Q also fails to account for the Lukan cast of the parable.

If there is a pre-Lukan source for the Rich Fool, though, one does not have to look far. Sirach 11:17-19 has a short parable that may well have influenced Luke:[48]

---

43. See further below, 187-91.

44. For the temple, there is only *Thom.* 71, on which see below, 167-68. For *Thomas* and God, see above, 93. For *Thomas* and prayer, note especially *Thom.* 14, "if you pray, you will be condemned"; and cf. *Thom.* 104.

45. Perhaps too, "Be passers-by" in *Thom.* 42 rather contradicts the parable of the Good Samaritan, where the ones who passed by are the villains of the piece. The only place where *Thomas* implies contact with outsiders is in *Thom.* 14, "When you go into any land and walk about in the districts, if they receive you, eat what they will set before you, and heal the sick among them"; but even here the all-important prerequisite is, "if they receive you."

46. DeConick, *Original Gospel,* 208.

47. Koester, *Ancient Christian Gospels,* 97-98, for example, deals with this parable as part of his discussion of *Thomas's* parallels with Q, without even noting the lack of a Matthean parallel. The pericope does not make it into *The Critical Edition of Q,* 324-25.

48. I am grateful to Stevan Davies for drawing my attention to this parallel, which is rarely noted in the literature on *Thomas.*

17 The Lord's gift remains with the devout, and his favor brings lasting success. 18 One becomes rich through diligence and self-denial, and the reward allotted to him is this: 19 when he says, "I have found rest, and now I shall feast on my goods!" he does not know how long it will be until he leaves them to others and dies. (NRSV)

Given Luke's apparent familiarity with Ben Sira elsewhere in his Gospel,[49] and *Thomas*'s apparent ignorance of Ben Sira, it is more likely that the story is mediated to *Thomas* via Luke than that he has independently adapted it, particularly given the Lukan nature of several of the elements common to Luke and *Thomas*.[50]

Conclusion

Several parallels between *Thomas* and Luke show clear signs of Lukan redaction and suggest *Thomas*'s familiarity with the third Gospel. Luke's rewording of a triple tradition passage (Luke 8:17) appears verbatim in one of the Greek witnesses of *Thomas*, at *Thom.* 5. Similarly, in *Thom.* 31 another of the Greek witnesses features Luke's own redactional rewording of another triple tradition passage (Luke 4:24). A further example occurs in the L material, where several distinctively Lukan elements in the Rich Fool parable (Luke 12:15-21) appear in the parallel in *Thom.* 63. These diagnostic shards point to *Thomas*'s familiarity with Luke's Gospel. But there is one example that is stronger than any of these, and it deserves a chapter of its own.

49. NA[26] lists the following parallels: Sir. 1:30, cf. Acts 13:10; Sir. 4:31, cf. Acts 20:35; Sir. 10:14, cf. Luke 1:52; Sir. 11:19, cf. Luke 10:19; Sir. 19:26, cf. Acts 12:10; Sir. 24:32, cf. Acts 2:39; Sir. 28:7, cf. Acts 17:30; Sir. 28:18, cf. Luke 21:24; Sir. 35:12, cf. Acts 10:34; Sir. 35:22, cf. Luke 18:7; Sir. 36:7, cf. Acts 2:11; Sir. 48:5, cf. Luke 7:22; Sir. 48:10, cf. Luke 1:17; 9:8; Sir. 48:12, cf. Acts 2:4; Sir. 48:21, cf. Acts 12:23; Sir. 50:20, cf. Luke 24:20; Sir. 50:22, cf. Luke 24:53; Sir. 51:1, cf. Matt. 11:25 // Luke 10:21. Luke 10:19 in that list is an error for Luke 12:19 (correct in the margin of the latter).

50. Snodgrass does not see any "direct dependence" on the Ben Sira passage, but he discusses it in terms of "Jesus' familiarity with literature such as Sirach" (*Stories with Intent*, 397).

CHAPTER 6

A Special Case: *Thomas* 79 and Luke

One saying in *Thomas* proves so strikingly Lukan that it deserves separate treatment. *Thomas* 79 features language, setting, imagery, and theology that are so at home in Luke that the term "diagnostic shards" risks understating the case for *Thomas's* familiarity with Luke. Moreover, while the parallel has occasionally been noticed in the scholarship, its potential for pointing to *Thomas's* relationship with Luke has generally been underestimated.

As usual, it is helpful to begin with a synopsis of the passages. *Thomas* 79 has parallels to two passages in Luke, 11:27-28 and 23:29. The latter is an element in Luke's Passion Narrative, and a little extra Lukan context will be helpful.

Luke 11:27-28; 23:27-31	*Thom.* 79
Ἐγένετο δὲ ἐν τῷ λέγειν αὐτὸν ταῦτα ἐπάρασά τις φωνὴν γυνὴ ἐκ τοῦ ὄχλου εἶπεν αὐτῷ· Μακαρία ἡ κοιλία ἡ βαστάσασά σε καὶ μαστοὶ οὓς ἐθήλασας· 28 αὐτὸς δὲ εἶπεν· Μενοῦν μακάριοι οἱ ἀκούοντες τὸν λόγον τοῦ θεοῦ καὶ φυλάσσοντες.	ΠЄϪЄ ΟΥϹϨΙΜ[Є] ΝΑϥ ϨΜ ΠΜΗϢЄ ϪЄ ΝЄЄΙΑΤ[Ϲ] [Ν̄]ΘϨΗ Ν̄ΤΑϨϥΙ ϨΑΡΟΚ ΑΥⲰ Ν̄ΚΙ[Β]Є ЄΝΤΑϨ ϹΑΝΟΥϢΚ ΠЄϪΑϥ ΝΑ[Ϲ] ϪЄ ΝЄЄΙΑΤΟΥ Ν̄ΝЄΝΤΑϨϹⲰΤΜ̄ ΑΠⲖΟΓΟϹ Μ̄ΠЄΙⲰΤ ΑΥΑΡЄϨ ЄΡΟϥ ϨΝ̄ ΟΥΜЄ

Luke 11:27-28; 23:27-31	*Thom.* 79
23:27 Ἠκολούθει δὲ αὐτῷ πολὺ πλῆθος τοῦ λαοῦ καὶ γυναικῶν αἳ ἐκόπτοντο καὶ ἐθρήνουν αὐτόν. 28 στραφεὶς δὲ πρὸς αὐτὰς ὁ Ἰησοῦς εἶπεν· Θυγατέρες Ἰερουσαλήμ, μὴ κλαίετε ἐπ' ἐμέ· πλὴν ἐφ' ἑαυτὰς κλαίετε καὶ ἐπὶ τὰ τέκνα ὑμῶν, 29 ὅτι ἰδοὺ ἔρχονται ἡμέραι ἐν αἷς ἐροῦσιν, Μακάριαι αἱ στεῖραι καὶ αἱ κοιλίαι αἳ οὐκ ἐγέννησαν καὶ μαστοὶ οἳ οὐκ ἔθρεψαν. 30 τότε ἄρξονται λέγειν τοῖς ὄρεσιν· Πέσετε ἐφ' ἡμᾶς, καὶ τοῖς βουνοῖς, Καλύψατε ἡμᾶς· 31 ὅτι εἰ ἐν τῷ ὑγρῷ ξύλῳ ταῦτα ποιοῦσιν, ἐν τῷ ξηρῷ τί γένηται;	ΟΥⲚ ⳒⲚⲌⲞⲞⲨ ⲄⲀⲢ ⲚⲀϢⲰⲠⲈ ⲚⲦⲈⲦⲚ̄ϪⲞⲞⲤ ϪⲈ ⲚⲈⲈⲒⲀ ⲦⲤ̄ Ⲛ̄ⲐⳈ ⲦⲀⲈⲒ ⲈⲦⲈ Ⲙ̄ⲠⲤⲰ ⲀⲨⲰ Ⲛ̄ⲔⲒⲂⲈ ⲚⲀⲈⲒ ⲈⲘⲠⲞⲨ† ⲈⲢⲰⲦⲈ.
11:27 And it came to pass while he was saying these things that a certain woman from the crowd raised her voice and said to him, "Blessed are the womb that bore you and the breasts that you sucked!" 28 But he said, "Blessed rather are those who hear the word of God and keep it!"	A woman in the crowd said to him, "Blessed are the womb that bore you and the breasts that nourished you." He said to her, "Blessed are those who have heard the word of the Father and have truly kept it.
23:27 And following him was a large crowd of the people, and of women who were mourning and lamenting him. 28 But Jesus, turning to them, said, "Daughters of Jerusalem, stop weeping for me, but weep for yourselves and for your children. 29 For behold, the days are coming when they will say, 'Blessed are the barren, and the wombs that never bore, and the breasts that never nursed.' 30 Then they will begin to say to the mountains, 'Fall on us,' and to the hills, 'Cover us.' 31 For if they do these things when the tree is green, what will happen when it is dry?"	For there will be days when you will say, 'Blessed is the womb that has not conceived and the breasts that have not given milk.'"

In the first half of *Thom.* 79, the parallel with Luke 11:27-28 is very close. The only differences of substance are the absence in *Thomas* of an equivalent to Luke's ἐπάρασά . . . φωνήν (raised her voice)[1] and the absence in *Thomas* of any equivalent to Luke's μενοῦν (rather). The only element present in *Thomas*'s version that is lacking in Luke is ϨⲚ ⲞⲨⲘⲈ (truly, in truth).[2]

Other variations are at best minor: ⲚⲔⲒⲂⲈ ⲈⲚⲦⲀϨ ⲤⲀⲚⲞⲨⲰⲔ (the breasts that nourished you) for μαστοὶ οὓς ἐθήλασας (breasts that you sucked), ⲚⲚⲈⲚⲦⲀϨⲤⲰⲦⲘ ([those] who have heard) for οἱ ἀκούοντες (those who hear), and ⲘⲠⲈⲒⲰⲦ (of the father) for τοῦ θεοῦ (of God). The indefinite article (ⲞⲨ) in ⲞⲨⲤϨⲒⲘⲈ (a woman) might be regarded as equivalent to Luke's indefinite pronoun in τις γυνή (a certain woman).[3]

The two texts are very close, and most of the variations are of the kind that translation of a Greek original would explain. If we were looking at this degree of agreement among the Synoptics, we would incline toward literary relationship of some kind. There is so little variation here that the idea of *Thomas*'s independence from Luke is problematic.[4]

The Lukan Nature of Luke 11:27-28

Similarity between the texts is, however, only the first step in making a case for *Thomas*'s familiarity with Luke. It is necessary to proceed to the key question of the presence of Lukan features in the text in question. It is

---

1. ἐπαίρω is characteristic of Luke (here, 6:20; 16:23; 18:13; 21:28; 24:50; Acts 1:9; 2:14; 14:11; 22:22; 27:40).

2. Cf. Plisch, *Gospel of Thomas*, 186, "The enhancing adverb 'truly' could have been added by the *Gospel of Thomas*."

3. Cf. Greeven's retroversion of *Thom.* 79 into Greek, which begins, Εἶπεν αὐτῷ τις γυνὴ ἐκ τοῦ ὄχλου, which is very close to Luke 11:27. Greeven's full retroversion for the first half of *Thom.* 79 is: Εἶπεν αὐτῷ τις γυνὴ ἐκ τοῦ ὄχλου· μακαρία ἡ κοιλία ἡ βαστάσασά σε καὶ οἱ μαστοὶ οἱ θρέψαντές σε. Εἶπεν αὐτῇ· μακάριοι οἱ ἀκούσαντες τὸν λόγον τοῦ πατρὸς (καὶ) φυλάξαντες αὐτὸν ἐπ' ἀληθείας. Bethge's retroversion is quite similar but reverses the position of τις and γυνή and has ἀληθῶς ἐφύλαξαν αὐτόν rather than φυλάξαντες αὐτὸν ἐπ' ἀληθείας.

4. The possibility that *Thomas* and Luke are both dependent on Q or earlier versions of Q (hinted, for example, by Koester, *Ancient Christian Gospels*, 152-53) is here a moot point. The IQP's Critical Text does not include Luke 11:27-28, but in any case my argument in this chapter is that *Thomas* shows knowledge of Luke in the form in which we have it, and that this version is heavily redacted by Luke. Thus, even if one wants to postulate an origin in Q, the version familiar to *Thomas* will be Luke's, not Q's.

surprising that this parallel has evaded serious attention in the discussion of the relationship between *Thomas* and the Synoptics.[5] One of the major factors here may be its status, like the Rich Fool (Luke 12:16-21 // *Thom*. 63, above), as Special Lukan material.[6] It is, of course, much more straight-forward to observe Lukan redaction when there are parallels in Mark and Matthew, but redaction criticism does not need to be suspended whenever the reader turns to material found only in one Gospel. Here there is a text with a distinctively Lukan character, shot through with features that are typical of his writing. And the parallel features in *Thomas* are in some ways anomalous.[7] Let us first take the Lukan features in turn. In each case we will look at the feature to see whether it is in some way unusual or anomalous in *Thomas*.

Foil Questions and Comments from Anonymous Individuals

There are several examples in Luke of foil questions or comments from anonymous individuals that lead up to Jesus' sayings, five of them with τις (someone, a certain person):

9:57: καὶ πορευομένων αὐτῶν ἐν τῇ ὁδῷ εἶπέν <u>τις</u> πρὸς αὐτόν· Ἀκολουθήσω σοι ὅπου ἐὰν ἀπέρχῃ . . . (contrast Matt. 8:19, εἷς γραμματεύς).

As they were going along the road, <u>a certain person</u> said to him, "I will follow you wherever you go . . ." (contrast Matt. 8:19, "a scribe").

11:27: Ἐγένετο δὲ ἐν τῷ λέγειν αὐτὸν ταῦτα ἐπάρασά <u>τις</u> φωνὴν <u>γυνὴ</u> ἐκ

---

5. But see Snodgrass, "Gospel of Thomas," 36-37; and Schrage, *Verhältnis*, 164-68. Schrage makes much of the change to second person plural in the second half of *Thom*. 79. He suggests that it makes sense only on the understanding that it has in view the address to "Daughters of Jerusalem" in the parallel Luke 23:28-29. Schrage's point is suggestive rather than conclusive since Luke 23:29 does not have a second person plural here; cf. Patterson, *Gospel of Thomas*, 60 n. 217. However, Patterson's comment that "nothing of Luke's redactional hand is to be found" here in *Thomas* (*Gospel of Thomas*, 60) is premature.

6. See, for example, DeConick, *Original Gospel*, 242-43. Somewhat surprisingly, Bovon thinks that the case for *Thomas*'s knowledge of Luke is weaker here than elsewhere in the L material; see F. Bovon, "Sayings Specific to Luke in the *Gospel of Thomas*," in *New Testament and Christian Apocrypha: Collected Studies* (WUNT 2/237; Tübingen: Mohr, 2009), 161-73 (168-69).

7. Schrage, *Verhältnis*, 5, suggests that this is the only place in *Thomas* where one sees an example of the Synoptics' framing (*Rahmennotiz*).

τοῦ ὄχλου εἶπεν αὐτῷ· Μακαρία ἡ κοιλία ἡ βαστάσασά σε καὶ μαστοὶ οὓς ἐθήλασας· . . .

And it came to pass while he was saying these things that a certain wom-an from the crowd raised her voice and said to him. . . .

12:13: Εἶπεν δέ τις ἐκ τοῦ ὄχλου αὐτῷ· Διδάσκαλε, εἰπὲ τῷ ἀδελφῷ μου μερίσασθαι μετ᾽ ἐμοῦ τὴν κληρονομίαν.

And someone from the crowd said to him, "Teacher, tell my brother to divide the inheritance with me" (cf. *Thom.* 72, above).

13:23: εἶπεν δέ τις αὐτῷ· Κύριε, εἰ ὀλίγοι οἱ σῳζόμενοι;

And someone said to him, "Lord, is it a few who will be saved?" (contrast Matt. 7:13).

14:15: Ἀκούσας δέ τις τῶν συνανακειμένων ταῦτα εἶπεν αὐτῷ· Μακάριος ὅστις φάγεται ἄρτον ἐν τῇ βασιλείᾳ τοῦ θεοῦ.

And when a certain one among those reclining with him heard these things, he said to him, "Blessed is the one who will eat bread in the king-dom of God!" (contrast Matt. 22:2 and *Thom.* 64).

Foil comments and questions are common in the Synoptics,[8] and they are found in *Thomas* too (e.g., 91, 99, 100, and 104), but the distinctive feature in the five cases listed above is that these are the only places in the Gospel tradition where teaching is introduced by foil comments from anonymous individuals, always τις (someone, a certain person).[9] This feature appears at least five times in Luke, and it is probably due to his own redaction, especially since, on three of the occasions (9:57; 13:23; 14:15), there is a contrast with Mat-thew.[10] The only times that it appears to occur in *Thomas*, in 72 and 79,[11] it is parallel to Luke.

8. For an analysis, see my *Goulder and the Gospels*, 146-49.

9. Patrick L. Dickerson draws attention to this feature as an aspect of the distinctive Lukan "new character narrative" in "The New Character Narrative in Luke–Acts and the Syn-optic Problem," *JBL* 116/2 (1997): 291-312.

10. For Q skeptics, these will be examples of Lukan redaction of Matthew. For Q theo-rists, these will be examples of Lukan redaction of Q. On each occasion here, the IQP regards the Lukan wording as redactional and not due to Q.

11. See above, 92-93, for *Thom.* 72.

There are other features in common between Luke 11:27 and the foil questions and comments listed above. The woman's remark in Luke 11:27 has a striking similarity to the man's remark in 14:15. On both occasions there is a misplaced macarism on the lips of someone other than Jesus (contrast *Thom.* 64), on both occasions in need of correction by Jesus.[12] Moreover, 11:27 is like 12:13 in that the person asking the foil question or making the comment is someone "from the crowd" (contrast *Thom.* 72), which introduces the next point.

The Crowd

One of the most striking features of this parallel is the occurrence in *Thomas* of the term "the crowd" (ⲠⲘⲎⲎϢⲈ), its sole occurrence in the text. It comes as a surprise at this point in the *Gospel of Thomas*, the first and last time that "the crowd" appears, in massive contrast to Luke's Gospel, where "the crowd" is ubiquitous. Indeed, in the previous saying (*Thom.* 78) it is implied that Jesus and his disciples are not part of the rather large group traveling through Israel that is found in Luke's central section but are, rather, those who have "come out to the countryside."[13]

The presence of the crowd is particularly surprising given *Thomas*'s stress on the "secret" nature of the sayings contained in his book (especially in the Incipit).[14] There is a marked contrast with Luke, where "the crowd/s" are present throughout, especially in the central section (11:14, 27, 29; 12:1, 13, 54; 13:14, 17; 14:25; 18:36). In other words, the crowd is superfluous and out of place here in *Thomas* but coherent, important, and pervasive here in Luke.[15]

---

12. So Goulder, *Luke*, 91, "cloying piety"; cf. my *Goulder and the Gospels*, 146-50.

13. The problem here is compounded by the question of the implied audience in *Thom.* 78 and elsewhere. The most recently mentioned explicit audience was "the disciples" in *Thom.* 72, but it is not clear whether one can speak of an "implied audience" for many of *Thomas*'s sayings given the work's lack of narrative coherence and setting.

14. I am grateful to Andrew Bernhard for this point.

15. Cf. Schrage, *Verhältnis*, 165.

Gynecology

Thomas refers to gynecological details only here in *Thom.* 79, in parallel with Luke's typical usage in 11:27-28 and 23:29.[16] Of all the evangelists, Luke is the one most inclined to use this imagery. Κοιλία (womb) occurs again at Luke 1:15, 41, 42, 44; 2:21; Acts 3:2; and 14:8;[17] and μαστοί (breasts) occurs only in Luke among the (canonical) Gospels, here in 11:27 and 23:29.[18] Indeed, the combination of elements, Jesus' mother, womb, and blessing, occurs also in Luke 1:41-44, clearly closely related to 11:27-28:

> And when Elizabeth heard the greeting of Mary, the babe leaped in her womb; and Elizabeth was filled with the Holy Spirit and she exclaimed with a loud cry: "Blessed are you among women, and blessed is the fruit of your womb! And why is this granted me, that the mother of my Lord should come to me? For behold, when the voice of your greeting came to my ears, the babe in my womb leaped for joy."

This comes in material usually thought to have been carefully crafted by Luke and its similarity in imagery, theme, and vocabulary to 11:27-28 is difficult to miss. It might be objected, of course, that there is some tension between the content of the two passages. Mary is blessed in Luke 1:41-44, but the woman's blessing in 11:27-28 is now supplemented or even corrected by Jesus.[19] But to press this tension would be to miss the point. The parallel cluster of Lukan themes, imagery, and vocabulary is striking and due attention should be paid, as always in Luke, to order. Luke 1:41-44 is the appropriate place for a macarism on "the fruit of your womb," Jesus. In the central section

16. Note that ⲐⲎ occurs also in *Thom.* 69, but here it means "belly." Further, in *Thom.* 22 there is reference to infants "taking milk" or "being suckled." I am grateful to Mike Grondin for this point.

17. κοιλία = womb occurs elsewhere in the Synoptic Gospels only at Matt. 19:12. Other uses of κοιλία (= belly) occur at Matt. 12:40; Matt. 15:17 // Mark 7:19; and in some manuscripts of Luke 15:16.

18. See also Rev. 1:13.

19. It may be that μενοῦν should not be taken in an adversative sense. The corrective "Yea, rather," of the KJV may be preferable given that Luke elsewhere uses οὐχί, λέγω ὑμῖν to express contradiction (12:51; 13:3, 5). Margaret E. Thrall, *Greek Particles in the New Testament: Linguistic and Exegetical Studies* (New Testament Tools and Studies 3; Leiden: Brill, 1962), 34-35, notes too that for affirmation Luke uses ναί (7:26; 10:21; 11:51; 12:5); cf. also C. F. D. Moule, *An Idiom Book of New Testament Greek* (2nd ed.; Cambridge: Cambridge University Press, 1960), 163, "an introduction to a new statement correcting or modifying a foregoing statement."

of Luke, on the other hand, the woman is detracting from what is important, which is to hear the word of God and to do it, arguably the major theme of these chapters and indeed of the whole Gospel, the next key topic.

Hearing the Word of God and Keeping It

Luke 11:28 features phraseology and motifs that are distinctively Lukan. "Hearing the word of God" (ἀκούειν τὸν λόγον τοῦ θεοῦ) is a major preoccupation of Luke and one of the clearest aspects of his agenda.[20] It recurs often and particularly in redactional changes to Mark.[21] In 5:1, for example, Luke writes: "While the people pressed upon him to hear the word of God (ἀκούειν τὸν λόγον τοῦ θεοῦ), he was standing by the lake of Gennesaret . . ." (cf. Mark 1:16-20 // Matt. 4:18-22).

Similarly, Luke accentuates the theme in his version of the interpretation of the Sower (8:11-12): "Now the parable is this: The seed is the word of God (ὁ λόγος τοῦ θεοῦ). The ones along the path are those who have heard . . . (οἱ ἀκούσαντες)" (cf. Mark 4:14-15: "The sower sows the word [ὁ λόγος]. And these are the ones along the path, where the word is sown; when they hear . . . [ὅταν ἀκούωσιν]"; cf. also Matt. 13:18-19).

Most striking, however, is Luke's redaction of the saying at the conclusion of the Mother and Brothers pericope (8:19-21), which he has moved to the conclusion of his parable chapter (8:4-18), where it acts as a comment on it:

---

20. This feature is picked up briefly by Risto Uro, "the words 'hear the word of God and keep it' (cf. Luke 8:21) have a Lukan flavor. The similar expression in *Thomas* may therefore reveal a Lukan redaction" ("Is *Thomas* an Encratite Gospel?" in Risto Uro, ed., *Thomas at the Crossroads: Essays on the Gospel of Thomas* [Studies of the New Testament and Its World; Edinburgh: T & T Clark, 1998], 140-62 [148 n. 29]). See too the slightly different version of the same essay, "Asceticism and Anti-Familial Language in the Gospel of Thomas," in Halvor Moxnes, ed., *Constructing Early Christian Families: Family as Social Reality and Metaphor* (London & New York: Routledge, 1997), 216-34 (221). The feature is usually missed in scholarship on *Thomas*.

21. This is working, of course, on the assumption of Markan priority. For those who do not accept Markan priority, it is worth noting that all the examples also make sense on the assumption that Luke's sole written source was Matthew.

Mark 3:35	Luke 8:21
ὃς [γὰρ] ἂν ποιήσῃ τὸ θέλημα τοῦ θεοῦ, οὗτος ἀδελφός μου καὶ ἀδελφὴ καὶ μήτηρ ἐστίν.	μήτηρ μου καὶ ἀδελφοί μου οὗτοί εἰσιν <u>οἱ τὸν λόγον τοῦ θεοῦ ἀκούοντες</u> καὶ ποιοῦντες.
[For] whoever does the will of God, this one is my brother and sister and mother.	My mother and my brother, these are <u>those who hear the word of God</u> and do it.

This example is all the more interesting because it is closely related to the passage under discussion, Luke 11:27-28. Family ties are in question and Jesus corrects a worldly misapprehension with a spiritual pronouncement. And here, as in his redaction of Mark 3:35, Luke uses his distinctive language of hearing the word of God and doing (ποιέω, 8:21) or keeping (φυλάσσω, 11:28) it.[22]

It might be objected that hearing the word of God and doing it sounds like a cliché, a commonplace in the Hebrew Bible and in early Judaism. Even if this is true, authors choose their clichés in accordance with their interests, and the key point here is that it is indeed a penchant specifically of Luke. The "word of God" (λόγος τοῦ θεοῦ) occurs only once in Matthew and once in Mark (Matt. 15:6 // Mark 7:13), and the usage here is in marked contrast to the usage in Luke. Here it is clearly referring to Scripture and not to the preaching of the gospel, which tends to be the sense in which the term is used by Luke. It is used in this sense not only in Luke in the passages quoted above, but often in Acts (4:31; 6:2, 7; 8:14; 11:1; 12:24; 13:5, 7, 46; 17:13; 18:11). Sometimes one "receives" the word of God (δέδεκται ἡ Σαμάρεια τὸν λόγον τοῦ θεοῦ, Acts 8:14; τὰ ἔθνη ἐδέξαντο τὸν λόγον τοῦ θεοῦ, Acts 11:1) or "hears" it (ἀκοῦσαι τὸν λόγον τοῦ θεοῦ, Acts 13:7). Similarly, the term "the word of the Lord" (ὁ λόγος τοῦ κυρίου) occurs regularly in this connection in Acts (8:25; 13:44, 48, 49; 15:35, 36; 16:32; 19:10), on one occasion (19:10) again with ἀκούειν.

It seems clear that "hearing the word of God and keeping it" has a distinctively Lukan ring, but it is worth noting that both the theme and the language in which it is expressed are not quite at home in *Thomas*. The term "the word" in the singular (ΠΛΟΓΟС) occurs only here in *Thomas*.[23] It fol-

22. φυλάσσω too is characteristic of Luke (Matt. 19:20 // Mark 10:20 // Luke 18:21; Luke 2:8; 8:29; 11:21; here; 12:15; Acts 7:53; 12:4; 16:4; 21:24, 25; 22:20; 23:35; 28:16).

23. The term translated "word" here is ΛΟΓΟС, which is, of course, a Greek loanword. It may be significant that the preferred term in Coptic *Thomas* is ϢΑϪΕ (Incipit, *Thom.* 1, 13

lows, of course, that "word of the Father" is otherwise absent from *Thomas*. But more importantly, the theme is not consonant with one of the key, repeated emphases of *Thomas*, the importance of hearing the words (plural) *of Jesus*. In *Thom.* 19, for example, Jesus says:

> If you become my disciples and listen to my words, these stones will minister to you.

Likewise in *Thom.* 38 Jesus says:

> Many times have you desired to hear these words which I am saying to you, and you have no one else to hear them from.

Again the stress is on listening to Jesus' words, which appear to be exclusive to him, something clear also from *Thom.* 17:

> I shall give you what no eye has seen and what no ear has heard and what no hand has touched and what has never occurred to the human mind.

Nor will even the most casual reader of *Thomas* fail to notice the repeated formula that is familiar from the Synoptics but much more common in *Thomas*:

> Whoever has ears to hear, let them hear! (*Thom.* 8, 21, 24, 63, 65, 96)

The Incipit and the first saying in *Thomas* clearly emphasize this message, on the importance of properly listening to Jesus' sayings:

> These are the secret sayings which the living Jesus spoke and which Didymos Judas Thomas wrote down. And he said, "Whoever finds the interpretation of these sayings will not experience death."[24]

In short, a key theme in *Thomas* is that one finds life by properly listening to the sayings of Jesus.[25] The matter of "hearing the word of the Father and truly keeping it" in *Thom.* 79 is not at home here, and it is not at home

---

[twice], 19, 38; cf. 52). Perhaps Coptic *Thomas*'s Greek *Vorlage* here had λόγος. But note that λόγος (plural) occurs twice in P.Oxy. 654 (Incipit and *Thom.* 1).

24. Cf. also *Thom.* 43: "Who are you, that you should say these things to us?"

25. Cf. Koester, "GNOMAI DIAPHOROI," 139, who rightly notes that the fundamental theological tendency of the *Gospel of Thomas* is "the view that the Jesus who spoke these words was and is the Living One, and thus gives life through his words."

because it has come to *Thomas* from Luke, for whom this is, by contrast, a major and distinctive emphasis.

There Will Be Days

The presence of a distinctively Lukan saying in *Thomas* raises the question of why *Thomas* includes it and how it functions in his book of sayings. The answer touches on *Thomas's* method of working with the Synoptics, and it requires a closer look at the second half of *Thom.* 79 with its parallel in Luke 23:29. Here *Thomas* is again close to Luke, though with greater variation than in the parallel with Luke 11:27-28. The blessing ("Blessed is"/"Blessed are") and the gynecological imagery ("womb" and "breasts") are common to Luke 23:29 and *Thom.* 79, and *Thomas's* familiarity with Luke may also be indicated by the parallel "the days are coming" (ἔρχονται ἡμέραι, Luke) or "there will be days" (ΟΥⲚ ⲀⲚϨⲞⲞΥ . . . ⲚⲀϢⲰⲠⲈ, Coptic *Thomas*) since that expression is characteristically Lukan (cf. Luke 5:35; 17:22; 19:43; 21:6).[26]

The second half of *Thom.* 79 therefore seems to draw closely on Luke 23:29 and shows the reader how *Thomas* uses similar Synoptic content in order to adjust the meaning of a saying. In Luke 11:27-28 all the emphasis goes on Jesus' blessing on those who hear the word of God and keep it. Luke 23:29 is a lament that takes place as Jesus addresses women in the crowd on his way to crucifixion. *Thom.* 79 connects these two sayings from different contexts that use the same imagery, and the connection may show his degree of familiarity with Luke, where the wording and imagery of one saying trigger a memory of another.

In bringing together these two sayings from different contexts in Luke, and with only minimal changes, *Thomas* is able to evoke the ascetic agenda that is a running theme throughout his work. The combined sayings in *Thom.* 79 proceed through successive stages, where first the blessing on Jesus' mother's womb and breasts is replaced by a blessing on those who hear the word of the Father. Then there is the time, now fulfilled in the writer's day, when the true blessing is on the celibate woman, whose womb does not bear children and whose breasts do not nurse them.[27] This woman is like the one for whom

---

26. Cf. Snodgrass, "Gospel of Thomas," 36; Luke 5:35, ἐλεύσονται ἡμέραι, is paralleled in Matt. 9:15 // Mark 2:20, but the other usages are in Luke only. The expression ΟΥⲚ ϨⲚϨⲞⲞΥ ⲚⲀϢⲰⲠⲈ occurs again in Coptic *Thom.* 38.

27. Cf. F. F. Bruce, "The Gospel of Thomas," *Faith and Thought* 92/1 (1961): 3-23, "The first part of this saying, found in Luke xi. 27, originally implies that there is something more

Jesus answers Simon Peter's query in the last saying of *Thomas*. She is like the woman who has achieved the ultimate goal of becoming male (114). So, by juxtaposing two sayings from Luke that are linked in their imagery, *Thomas* is able to serve one of his favorite redactional agendas, notwithstanding the clues he has left behind about the sources of his new construction.

Conclusion

Thomas 79 and Luke 11:27-28 and 23:29 are parallel texts that, when one allows for differences in language, have very similar wording. In several key respects, this wording is distinctively Lukan. The style, thought, and terminology of this passage are common elsewhere in Luke and are paralleled in agreed redactional reworkings of Mark and Matthew (or Q). There is a Lukan foil comment framed with τις, gynecological imagery, and, most importantly, a thoroughly Lukan stress on "hearing the word of God [my Father] and keeping it."[28] Since the same features are, on the whole, anomalous in *Thomas*, the conclusion from the data is that *Thomas* is indeed familiar with Luke's Gospel.[29]

---

wonderful than being the mother of Jesus — namely, doing the will of God. But here this saying is linked to the following one in such a way as to suggest that the bearing of children is contrary to the Father's will, and that those who renounce marriage and family life are to be congratulated. This, of course, completely dehistoricises the second part of the saying, where Jesus in Luke xxiii. 29 is not laying down a permanent principle, but telling the weeping women on the Via Dolorosa that, when the impending distress overtakes Jerusalem, childless women will have something to be thankful for" (14).

28. I leave open the question of whether Luke is responsible for the creation of this passage in toto. In view of the pervasive Lukan nature of these verses, Lukan creation seems quite likely, but accepting this is not necessary to the argument for Thomasine dependence. It might be that Luke had a source in his tradition for these verses and that he redacted the source in characteristic manner, introducing his favorite imagery, thought, and vocabulary. The key point is that *Thomas* shares the distinctively Lukan elements, whether these are due to full Lukan composition or Lukan redaction of traditional material.

29. I am grateful to Stevan Davies for some helpful, critical comments on a much earlier draft of this chapter. I would also like to thank Stephen Carlson, Andrew Bernhard, and Michael Grondin for helpful comments.

CHAPTER 7

The Missing Middle in *Thomas*

Introduction

In chapters 4–6 we looked at places where *Thomas* features parallels to Matthew's and Luke's redactional work. These parallels suggest that the author of *Gospel of Thomas* was familiar with the Synoptic Gospels rather than their sources. Having drawn attention to this key evidence for *Thomas*'s familiarity with the Synoptics, it will be worth taking some time to focus on one of the ways in which the author works with his Synoptic source material. This chapter presents evidence of the way that the author of *Thomas* often redacts the material he takes over from the Synoptics in a phenomenon that I call "the missing middle."

Unlike the Synoptic evangelists, especially Luke, the author of *Thomas* is not a sophisticated storyteller, and sometimes *Thomas* misses key parts of a given story or saying. On several occasions we see the phenomenon of the missing middle, whereby *Thomas* fails to narrate the middle part of a given parable or saying. Sometimes the account presupposes the material that has not been narrated, and the story would be unintelligible to anyone unfamiliar with the Synoptic accounts. There are several examples of the phenomenon.

The Parable of the Wheat and the Tares (*Thom.* 57; Matt. 13:24-30)

Several examples of the missing middle occur in *Thomas*'s parable material. The parable of the Wheat and the Tares[1] repays a careful look:[2]

Matt. 13:24-30	*Thom.* 57
24 Another parable he put before them, saying, "The kingdom of heaven may be compared to a man who sowed good seed in his field; 25 but while the people were sleeping, his enemy came and sowed weeds among the wheat, and went away. 26 So when the plants came up and bore grain, then the weeds appeared also. 27 And the servants of the householder came and said to him, 'Sir, did you not sow good seed in your field? How then does it have weeds?' 28 He said to them, 'An enemy has done this.' The servants said to him, 'Then do you want us to go and gather them?' 29 But he said, 'No; lest in gathering the weeds you root up the wheat along with them. 30 Let both grow together until the harvest; and at harvest time I will tell the reapers, Gather the weeds first and bind them in bundles to be burned, but gather the wheat into my barn.'"	Jesus says, "The kingdom of the Father is like a man who had [good] seed. His enemy came by night and sowed weeds among the good seed. The man did not allow them to pull up the weeds; he said to them, 'I am afraid that you will go intending to pull up the weeds and pull up the wheat along with them.' For on the day of the harvest the weeds will be plainly visible, and they will be pulled up and burned."

The middle of the story is missing in *Thomas*'s version, to the detriment of its narrative flow and logic. The missing middle part of the story, which is present in Matthew (13:26-28), continues the narration, with the weeds coming up and servants introduced who begin a conversation with their master. Setting the passages alongside one another in synopsis (above) illustrates the large white space — the missing middle — where the relevant material is present in Matthew but absent from *Thomas*. When *Thomas* resumes the story, it turns out that his omission of the middle has serious consequences.

1. See above, 73-81, for the case that the parable of the Wheat and the Tares is Matthew's redactional expansion of Mark's Seed Growing Secretly (Mark 4:26-29) and that *Thomas* is familiar with the Matthean version.

2. For Greek and Coptic synopsis of the passage, see above, 74.

He has not introduced the servants, and so he has no antecedent for "them" (ⲘⲠⲈ ⲠⲢⲰⲘⲈ ⲔⲞⲞⲨ . . . ⲠⲈⲬⲀϤ ⲚⲀⲨ, "the man did not allow them . . . he said to them"), rendering this part of the story intelligible only to those already familiar with Matthew. Wolfgang Schrage rightly took this to be a sign of *Thomas*'s familiarity with Matthew.[3] The story is poorly told and *Thomas*'s inconcinnity appears to result from his abbreviation of Matthew's version.

Rich Fool (Luke 12:15-21 // *Thom.* 63)

The parable of the Rich Fool provides another clear example of the phenomenon:[4]

Luke 12:15-21	*Thom.* 63
15 Then he said to them, "Watch out! Be on your guard against all kinds of greed; a man's life does not consist in the abundance of his possessions." 16 And he told them this parable: "The ground of a certain rich man produced a good crop. 17 He <u>thought to himself</u>, 'What shall I do? I have no place to store my crops.' 18 Then he said, 'This is what I will do. I will tear down my barns and build bigger ones, and there I will store all my grain and my goods. 19 And I will say to myself, "You have plenty of good things laid up for many years. Take life easy; eat, drink, and be merry."'	Jesus said: "There was a rich man who had many possessions. He said: 'I will use my wealth to sow my field, to plant, to fill my barn with harvest, so that need will not touch me.'

3. Schrage, *Verhältnis*, 124-26. Hugh Montefiore, "A Comparison of the Parables of the Gospel According to Thomas and of the Synoptic Gospels," in H. E. W. Turner and H. Montefiore, *Thomas and the Evangelists*, Studies in Biblical Theology 35 (London: SCM Press, 1962), 51, sees it as "a striking instance of compression to the point of absurdity." The point is largely conceded by those arguing for Thomasine independence, but alongside the suggestion that *Thomas* is familiar with a hypothetical alternative version; see Sieber, "Redactional Analysis," 168-69; Patterson, *Gospel of Thomas*, 46. Cf. DeConick, *Original Gospel*, 194, who suggests that "both versions of the parable represent later developments of an earlier form no longer extant." However, these ad hoc explanations do not take seriously the feature of the missing middle as a characteristic of *Thomas*'s redaction in narrative material, nor do they discuss the thesis that Matthew, by reworking Mark 4:26-29 (Seed Growing Secretly), is the originator of the parable; see n. 1 above.

4. For Greek and Coptic synopsis of the passage, see above, 87.

Luke 12:15-21	Thom. 63
20 But God said to him, 'You fool! This very night your life will be demanded from you. Then who will get what you have prepared for yourself?' 21 This is how it will be with anyone who stores up things for himself but is not rich toward God."	Such were the things that he thought in his heart. But during that night, he died. Whoever has ears to hear, let them hear!"

Thomas lacks the middle part of Luke's story, 12:18b-19, in which the rich fool is reflecting on his apparent great fortune, in characteristic Lukan fashion,[5] "And I will say to myself, 'You have plenty of good things laid up for many years. Take life easy; eat, drink, and be merry.'" *Thomas's* fool is thinking things in his heart, but the full content of Luke's version provides a much better antecedent than the blander, truncated soliloquy of *Thomas's* version.

Tribute to Caesar (Mark 12:13-17 // *Thom.* 100)

That the missing middle is a characteristic feature of *Thomas's* apparent lack of storytelling ability and not the effect of *Thomas's* closeness to raw, primitive oral traditions of Jesus' parables is confirmed by the fact that the same feature occurs in *Thomas* outside the narrative parables. The Tribute to Caesar story (Matt. 22:15-22 // Mark 12:13-17 // Luke 20:20-26 // *Thom.* 100) provides another example of the phenomenon:

---

5. For a study of Lukan soliloquy in the parable tradition, see my *Goulder and the Gospels*, 169-71; cf. above, 89-91.

Mark 12:13-17	*Thom.* 100
13 Καὶ ἀποστέλλουσιν πρὸς αὐτόν τινας τῶν Φαρισαίων καὶ τῶν Ἡρῳδιανῶν ἵνα αὐτὸν ἀγρεύσωσιν λόγῳ. 14 καὶ ἐλθόντες λέγουσιν αὐτῷ, Διδάσκαλε, οἴδαμεν ὅτι ἀληθὴς εἶ καὶ οὐ μέλει σοι περὶ οὐδενός, οὐ γὰρ βλέπεις εἰς πρόσωπον ἀνθρώπων, ἀλλ᾽ ἐπ᾽ ἀληθείας τὴν ὁδὸν τοῦ θεοῦ διδάσκεις· ἔξεστιν δοῦναι κῆνσον Καίσαρι ἢ οὔ; δῶμεν ἢ μὴ δῶμεν; 15 ὁ δὲ εἰδὼς αὐτῶν τὴν ὑπόκρισιν εἶπεν αὐτοῖς, Τί με πειράζετε; φέρετέ μοι δηνάριον ἵνα ἴδω. 16 οἱ δὲ ἤνεγκαν. καὶ λέγει αὐτοῖς, Τίνος ἡ εἰκὼν αὕτη καὶ ἡ ἐπιγραφή; οἱ δὲ εἶπαν αὐτῷ, Καίσαρος. 17 ὁ δὲ Ἰησοῦς εἶπεν αὐτοῖς, Τὰ Καίσαρος ἀπόδοτε Καίσαρι καὶ τὰ τοῦ θεοῦ τῷ θεῷ. Καὶ ἐξεθαύμαζον ἐπ᾽ αὐτῷ.	ⲀⲨⲦⲤⲈⲂⲈ ⲒⲤ ⲀⲨⲚⲞⲨⲂ ⲀⲨⲰ ⲠⲈⲬⲀⲨ ⲚⲀϤˈ ⲬⲈ ⲚⲈⲦⲎⲠˈ ⲀⲔⲀⲒⲤⲀⲢˈ ⲤⲈϢⲒⲦⲈ ⲘⲘⲞⲚ ⲚⲚϢⲰⲘˈ ⲠⲈⲬⲀϤ ⲚⲀⲨ ⲬⲈ † ⲚⲀ ⲔⲀⲒⲤⲀⲢˈ ⲚⲔⲀⲒⲤⲀⲢ † ⲚⲀ ⲠⲚⲞⲨⲦⲈ ⲘⲠⲚⲞⲨⲦⲈ ⲀⲨⲰ ⲠⲈⲦⲈ ⲠⲰⲈⲒ ⲠⲈ ⲘⲀ ⲦⲚⲚⲀⲈⲒϤ
13 Then they sent to him some Pharisees and some Herodians to trap him in what he said. 14 And they came and said to him, "Teacher, we know that you are sincere, and show deference to no one; for you do not regard people with partiality, but teach the way of God in accordance with truth. Is it lawful to pay taxes to Caesar, or not? 15 Should we pay them, or should we not?" But knowing their hypocrisy, he said to them, "Why are you putting me to the test? Bring me a denarius and let me see it." 16 And they brought one. Then he said to them, "Whose head is this, and whose title?" They answered, "Caesar's." 17 Jesus said to them, "Give to Caesar the things that are Caesar's, and to God the things that are God's." And they were utterly amazed at him.	They showed Jesus a gold coin and said to him, "Caesar's agents are exacting taxes from us." He said to them, "Give to Caesar the things that are Caesar's, give to God the things that are God's, and give to me that which is mine."

Here *Thomas* lacks the middle part of the Synoptic story in which it is revealed that the coin bears Caesar's image (Matt. 22:20-21a // Mark 12:16 //

Luke 20:24).[6] In order for the story to make sense, this exchange is crucial. That the coin has Caesar's image on it provides the catalyst for the shared aphorism, "Give to Caesar the things that are Caesar's. . . ."[7] Without that exchange, the showing of the coin is pointless, a fragment left over from the Synoptic version in which the feature is coherent.[8] *Thomas* appears to have drastically abbreviated the Synoptic story,[9] but the act of abbreviation, in which the key middle section is omitted, has led to the kind of inconcinnity that betrays the redactor's hand.[10]

This rather clumsy feature of *Thomas*'s storytelling may come from the author's familiarity with the Synoptic stories he is retelling. In the rush to retell the familiar story, he does not notice that key parts have been left

6. Gathercole, "Luke in the *Gospel of Thomas*," 135, notes the presence of two minor agreements between *Thomas* and Luke against Mark, which may indicate *Thomas*'s familiarity with the Lukan version of the pericope. For the point at hand, though, the missing middle in *Thomas* can be illustrated in comparison with any of the Synoptic accounts.

7. Note the close agreement here between the Synoptic formulation, Τὰ Καίσαρος ἀπόδοτε Καίσαρι καὶ τὰ τοῦ θεοῦ τῷ θεῷ, and the Thomasine formulation, † Νⲁ ⲕⲁⲓⲥⲁⲣ' ⲛ̄ⲕⲁⲓⲥⲁⲣ † Νⲁ ⲡⲛⲟⲩⲧⲉ ⲙ̄ⲡⲛⲟⲩⲧⲉ, which both Greeven and Bethge retrovert to Greek as ἀπόδοτε τὰ Καίσαρος Καίσαρι. ἀπόδοτε τὰ τοῦ θεοῦ τῷ θεῷ. See further on verbatim agreements above, chapter 2.

8. Cf. Plisch, *Gospel of Thomas*, 219, "In the Thomas version, showing Jesus a gold coin at the beginning of the scene is hardly motivated." Similarly Crossan, *Four Other Gospels*, 77, "The showing of the coin to Jesus has very little point in this account. It is almost like a residue in a Gospel which is predominantly discourse." "Residue" is the right word, though Crossan does not think that *Thomas*'s residue is from the Synoptic narrative.

9. Contrast Patterson, *Gospel of Thomas*, 69, who sees the Synoptic version as "much more highly developed" and *Thomas*'s version as "the simplest form of chreia." This works with the form-critical trajectory from simple to complex, endemic in much *Thomas* scholarship but contradicted by literary analysis of the Synoptic and later texts. Far from being "clearly secondary to the primitive version found in Thomas," the Synoptic version makes good sense as the coherent source from which *Thomas* derives his incoherent one. Cf. Koester, *Ancient Christian Gospels*, 112, for a similar view, though with an illustrative (English) synopsis (with an error in the verse numbers, "Mark 12:14-16").

10. Compare the abbreviation of the story in Justin, *1 Apol.* 17, "for at that time some came to him and asked him if one ought to pay tribute to Caesar; and he answered, 'Tell me, whose image does the coin bear?' And they said, 'Caesar's.' And again he answered them, 'Render therefore to Caesar the things that are Caesar's, and to God the things that are God's.'" As in *Thomas*, the abbreviation leads to inconcinnity, though a different one. Here the question about the image on the coin is asked without the coin first having been produced. As in *Thomas* it is easy to miss the inconcinnity because of our familiarity with the Synoptic story. See further on Justin below, 123-27. Baarda, "Gospel of Thomas," 60, also draws attention to the same abbreviation of the story in Clement, *Extracts of Theodotus*, 86.3; and *Pistis Sophia* III.113.

out. This may be a casualty of writing a sayings gospel rather than a narrative gospel. The Synoptic writers are all, to varying degrees, used to writing mini-narratives in their Gospels, and on the whole they make a good job of it. But *Thomas* is focused on shorter, self-contained sayings, with minimal narrative settings. When it comes to writing a fuller narrative, the author of *Thomas* is not as well practiced as the Synoptic evangelists.

We might ask, though, how we can be clear that this is a feature of *Thomas's* redaction rather than the reflection of differing oral traditions. There are several signs that the phenomenon is a product of *Thomas's* redaction. One of them is the creation of continuity errors in the examples above. Such continuity errors in parallel narrative material are often indicators of the secondary nature of the work in which they appear. The phenomenon has similarities with examples of fatigue in the Synoptics,[11] whereby the inconcinnities[12] found in certain triple tradition and double tradition pericopae appear to have been generated by Matthew's and Luke's editorial fatigue. They make distinctive redactional changes at the beginning of pericopae but lapse into the wording of their source as they go through.[13] *Thomas* is a little different in that the inconcinnity is generated by the loss of material from the middle of the pericope, but the phenomenon is analogous, as narrative coherence is lost in secondary editing of a more coherent prior version.

But a further sign that this is due to the author's own editorial activity is that the feature is found across different types of material, not only in parables (Wheat and Tares; Rich Fool, above) and narrative (Tribute to Caesar, above), but also in discourse and sayings material. The phenomenon appears to be related not to specific forms but rather to a repeated pattern of editing material. In other words, the missing middle makes better sense on redaction-critical grounds, where the focus is on the author's redaction of his sources, than on form-critical grounds, where the focus is on the character of the tradition.

---

11. Goodacre, "Fatigue."

12. The term "inconcinnity" in this context is from W. D. Davies and Dale Allison, *A Critical and Exegetical Commentary on the Gospel According to Saint Matthew* (3 vols.; ICC; Edinburgh: T. & T. Clark, 1988-97), 1:107.

13. I argue that the phenomenon points to Markan priority in the triple tradition material and Luke's use of Matthew in double tradition material.

Log and Speck (Matt. 7:3-5 // Luke 6:41-42 // *Thom.* 26)

The next example of the feature is found in a pericope we have already discussed as showing the kind of verbatim agreement between *Thomas* and the Synoptics that points to a direct link between the texts, Matt. 7:3-5 // Luke 6:41-42 // *Thom.* 26,[14] in which all of Matt. 7:4 // Luke 6:42a is missing:

Matt. 7:3-5	Luke 6:41-42	*Thom.* 26
3 Why do you see the speck that is in your brother's eye, but do not notice the log that is in your own eye? 4 Or how can you say to your brother, "Let me take the speck out of your eye," when there is the log in your own eye? 5 You hypocrite, first take the log out of your own eye, and then you will see clearly to take the speck out of your brother's eye.	41 Why do you see the speck that is in your brother's eye, but do not notice the log that is in your own eye? 42 Or how can you say to your brother, "Brother, let me take out the speck that is in your eye," when you yourself do not see the log that is in your own eye? You hypocrite, first take the log out of your own eye, and then you will see clearly to take out the speck that is in your brother's eye.	Jesus said, "You see the speck in your brother's eye, but you do not see the log in your own eye. First take the log out of your own eye, and then you will see clearly to take out the speck that is in your brother's eye."*

* The translation here works with the Greek of P.Oxy. 1.1-4, where καὶ τότε assumes the presence of a first clause like the one found in Matthew and Luke here. See further above, 31.

As usual, *Thomas* relates the saying using many fewer words, but the abbreviation is done not by means of simple summary but rather by means of omitting a chunk of text from the middle of the passage. Although the omission here does not generate a glaring inconcinnity, the *Thomas* version lacks the narrative logic of the Synoptic version. In all three accounts, there is a statement first of all about seeing, but only Matthew and Luke then introduce the attempts at the removal of the speck, the necessary comic

14. Chapter 2, above.

prelude to the exhortation to remove the log from one's own eye. *Thomas* retains the removal of the log at the end, but in losing the prior attempt at the removal of the speck, he loses the joyful absurdity of the Synoptic passage. *Thomas's* inability to make the comedy work as well as it does in the Synoptic version is a reminder that *Thomas's* alleged oral qualities are often more rumored than real. The memorable version is the one that is found in Matthew and Luke, which lends itself so well to dramatic performance or recitation.[15]

Once again, *Thomas's* redactional pattern is clear. Funk and Hoover suggest that the Thomasine version is "simpler" and therefore more primitive than the version found in Matthew and Luke,[16] but this illustrates not only the form-critical fallacy of equating greater simplicity with greater primitivity,[17] but also the importance of paying attention to patterns of redaction in *Thomas*. In a pericope in which close verbatim agreement suggests a direct link between the texts, *Thomas* shows signs of having abbreviated his source text, producing a less coherent, secondary version.[18]

The Outside of the Cup (Matt. 23:25-26 // Luke 11:39-41 // *Thom.* 89)

There are still further examples of the missing middle, even in quite short sayings:

---

15. The comic potential of the Synoptic version is illustrated in the animated Jesus film *The Miracle Maker* (dir. Derek W. Hayes and Stanislav Sokolov, 1999).

16. "Thomas' version of this humorous comparison is simpler than the form found in Q, which suggests that the latter has been expanded. . . . Thomas does not use the word 'phony' — someone who pretends to be someone he or she isn't — so this element may be secondary. The Q version is also redundant (lines 4-5 in the Q version repeat lines 1-2)" (Funk and Hoover, *Five Gospels*, 488). But Matt. 7:4 // Luke 6:42a is not "redundant." The attempt at the removal of the speck is the comic presupposition for the conclusion of the passage.

17. See further on this below, 145-50.

18. Given the fragmentary nature of P.Oxy. 1, it is possible that the missing middle was not present in the Greek textual tradition but was made instead by the Coptic translator. However, arguments from textual silence often cut both ways, and it is an equal theoretical possibility that the Coptic translator eliminated examples of the missing middle by further abbreviating material in his *Vorlage*. See further below, 121.

Matt. 23:25-26	Luke 11:39-41	*Thom.* 89
25 Οὐαὶ ὑμῖν, γραμματεῖς καὶ Φαρισαῖοι ὑποκριταί, ὅτι καθαρίζετε τὸ ἔξωθεν τοῦ ποτηρίου καὶ τῆς παροψίδος, ἔσωθεν δὲ γέμουσιν ἐξ ἁρπαγῆς καὶ ἀκρασίας. 26 Φαρισαῖε τυφλέ, καθάρισον πρῶτον τὸ ἐντὸς τοῦ ποτηρίου, ἵνα γένηται καὶ τὸ ἐκτὸς αὐτοῦ καθαρόν.	39 εἶπεν δὲ ὁ κύριος πρὸς αὐτόν, Νῦν ὑμεῖς οἱ Φαρισαῖοι τὸ ἔξωθεν τοῦ ποτηρίου καὶ τοῦ πίνακος καθαρίζετε, τὸ δὲ ἔσωθεν ὑμῶν γέμει ἁρπαγῆς καὶ πονηρίας. 40 ἄφρονες, οὐχ ὁ ποιήσας τὸ ἔξωθεν καὶ τὸ ἔσωθεν ἐποίησεν; 41 πλὴν τὰ ἐνόντα δότε ἐλεημοσύνην, καὶ ἰδοὺ πάντα καθαρὰ ὑμῖν ἐστιν.	ΠЄΧЄ ΙC ΧЄ ЄΤΒЄ ΟΥ ΤЄΤΝЄΙШЄ ΜΠСΑ ΝΒΟΛ' ΜΠΠΟΤΗΡΙΟΝ ΤЄΤΝΡΝΟЄΙ ΑΝ ΧЄ ΠЄΝΤΑϨΤΑΜΙΟ ΜΠСΑ ΝϨΟΥΝ ΝΤΟϤ ΟΝ' ΠЄΝΤΑϤΤΑΜΙΟ ΜΠСΑ ΝΒΟΛ'
25 Woe to you, scribes and Pharisees, hypocrites! For you cleanse the outside of the cup and the plate, but inside they are full of greed and self-indulgence. Blind Pharisees! Cleanse first the inside of the cup and plate, so that the outside also will be clean.	And the Lord said to him, "Now you Pharisees cleanse the outside of the cup and the plate; but your inside is full of greed and evil. You fools! Did not the one who made the outside make the inside too? But give alms for the things that are within and, behold, all things are clean to you."	Jesus says, "Why do you wash the outside of the cup? Do you not understand that the one who made the inside is the one who made the outside too?"

In both Matthew and Luke, Jesus rebukes the (scribes and) Pharisees for cleansing the outside of the cup and plate. In parallel, *Thomas*, with no specific audience delineated, asks, "Why do you wash the outside of the cup?"[19] But whereas in Matthew and Luke Jesus then explains the point by

19. Typically, *Thomas*'s dehistoricizing creates an isolated saying with no clear referent for those who wash the outside of the cup. The saying works better in Matthew's and Luke's polemical context. The debate about the cleansing of the outside of the cup is an intra-Pharisaic one (see E. P. Sanders, *Jewish Law from Jesus to the Mishnah* [Philadelphia: Trinity Press International, 1990], 203-4), not at all appropriate for an imagined audience of Jesus' disciples, who in *Thomas* and the Synoptics are hardly depicted as scrupulous about particular Pharisaic oral traditions.

adding that they have greed and evil within, this middle section of the saying is missing in *Thomas*. The Synoptic conclusion, which speaks of both the outside and the inside, is then paralleled again in *Thomas*, following the Lukan wording.[20] It is another case of a missing middle generating an inconcinnity. In *Thom.* 89.2 there is no context for the mention of "the inside." Its comment that "the one that made the inside is the one who made the outside too" does not make sense without that missing element.[21] As Plisch notes, "It seems that there is a link missing that would bring the statement to the level of the metaphoric application."[22]

"What you will wear" (Matt. 6:25-30 // Luke 12:22-28 // *Thom.* 36 (P.Oxy. 655)

It might perhaps be objected that the missing middle is a feature of the Coptic scribe's inability to transcribe his text effectively, a kind of text-critical accident that has nothing to do with the author of *Thomas*. However, this does not appear to be the case since there is a strong example of the missing middle in one of the Greek witnesses, *Thomas* 36 in P.Oxy. 655.[23]

---

20. Plisch, *Gospel of Thomas*, 200, notes: "The second sentence has an almost verbatim parallel in Luke 11.40. . . . If we had proof that Luke 11.40 were a Lukan redaction, then *Gos. Thom.* 89 would literarily be dependent on Luke 11.40." If Goulder is right (*Luke*, 518-19, 525-26), then Luke is redacting Matthew here and so he is responsible for the wording. Plisch goes on to note that *Thomas* "lacks the undoubtedly Lukan addition, 'You fools!'" However, this rebuke would have been inappropriate in *Thomas*, where the audience is unnamed. Note that several textual and patristic witnesses have the reverse order of inside/outside in Luke, which increases the extent of the verbatim agreement between Luke and *Thomas*; cf. Schrage, *Verhältnis*, 170-71; but contrast Patterson, *Gospel of Thomas*, 62.

21. I am grateful to Simon Gathercole for pointing out this example of a missing middle to me.

22. Plisch, *Gospel of Thomas*, 201. Contrast Funk and Hoover, *Five Gospels*, 520, who report the Jesus Seminar's rating of the *Thomas* version as pink and the Synoptic version as gray.

23. For the synopsis in Greek and Coptic, see above, 62.

Matt. 6:25-30	Luke 12:22-28	*Thom.* 36 (P.Oxy. 655)
25 Therefore I tell you, do not worry about your life,	22 He said to his disciples, "Therefore I tell you, do not worry about your life,	Jesus says, "Do not be anxious] from morning [until evening and] from evening [until] morning, neither [about] your [food] and
what you will eat or what you will drink, or about your body,	what you will eat, or about your body,	what [you will] eat, [nor] about [your clothing] and
what you will wear. Is not life more than food, and the body more than clothing? . . . 27 And can any of you by worrying add a single hour to your span of life? 28 And why do you worry about clothing?	what you will wear. 23 For life is more than food, and the body more than clothing. . . . 25 And can any of you by worrying add a single hour to your span of life? 26 If then you are not able to do so small a thing as that, why do you worry about the rest?	what you [will] wear.
Consider the lilies of the field, how they grow: they neither toil nor spin, 29 yet I tell you, even Solomon in all his glory was not clothed like one of these. 30 But if God so clothes the grass of the field, which is alive today and tomorrow is thrown into the oven, will he not much more clothe you — you of little faith?	27 Consider the lilies, how they grow: they neither toil nor spin; yet I tell you, even Solomon in all his glory was not clothed like one of these. 28 But if God so clothes the grass of the field, which is alive today and tomorrow is thrown into the oven, how much more will he clothe you — you of little faith!"	[You are far] better than the [lilies] which [neither] card nor [spin]. As for you, when you have no garment, what [will you put on]? Who might add to your stature? He will give you your garment."

Thomas 36 has parallels to Matt. 6:25 // Luke 12:22 and Matt. 6:28b-30 // Luke 12:27-28, but it is missing Matt. 6:26b-28a // Luke 12:23-26. In other words, there is a large white space in the middle of the passage in *Thomas,* which can be seen clearly once it is laid out in synopsis alongside Matthew and Luke. The missing middle generates a minor inconcinnity.

Like the later Synoptics, *Thomas* begins with the exhortation not to be worried about food or clothing. In the section missing from *Thomas*, though, Matthew and Luke deal with the first of these issues, food. Where *Thomas* rejoins the Synoptics, they are talking about the second of these, clothing. *Thomas* therefore has the exhortation not to be worried about food and clothing, but only the poetic justification for avoiding worry about clothing. The missing middle does not here generate a glaring inconcinnity, but the fuller Synoptic version provides a logical progression from exhortation to poetic justification that, as usual, is better crafted and more rhetorically powerful than the *Thomas* version. It is another reminder to be wary of the notion that *Thomas* is somehow more characteristically "oral" than are the Synoptic Gospels. Its text is significantly less memorable than its Synoptic counterpart.[24]

The presence of this example in one of the Greek witnesses suggests that the missing middle is a feature of *Thomas*'s redaction, not of scribal error. Indeed, the Coptic text in this example actually eliminates the phenomenon by retaining only the first part of the saying.[25] It is possible that other examples have also been lost in the Coptic text.[26]

As far as I am aware, this feature of *Thomas*'s (lack of) storytelling ability has not been discussed in the scholarship before. It may be an example of canonical bias, whereby the Synoptics exercise a kind of normative influence on our reading of *Thomas*. Because of our familiarity with the Synoptic stories, we unconsciously find ourselves filling in the blanks in the story so that we do not notice that key antecedent elements have been dropped.

Our failure to notice the feature may also result from the lack of good *Thomas*-Synoptic synopses. Setting the Synoptic accounts alongside *Thomas* enables us to see the missing middle. Constructing synopses in our minds is not easy, and it is not surprising that we find ourselves searching for explana-

---

24. One further example of a missing middle in *Thomas* is in the Tenants in the Vineyard (Matt. 21:33-46 // Mark 12:1-12 // Luke 20:9-19 // *Thom.* 65-66). Gathercole, "Luke in the *Gospel of Thomas*," 128, notes that *Thomas*'s explanation for the killing of the son is strange: "The Synoptics' explanation may not make psychological or legal sense, but it at least makes narrative sense. The *Thomas* version is less clear, and looks like it might be an abbreviation which has made the narrative no longer make good sense: there is a missing presupposition here."

25. See the discussion above, 60-63.

26. Unfortunately, the only other example in this chapter to be witnessed in the Oxyrhynchus fragments is *Thom.* 26 in P.Oxy. 1.1-4, but only the end of the saying is present in the Greek.

tions along the lines of conciseness and primitivity rather than abbreviation and redaction.

One might ask what further evidence could help to explain the phenomenon in *Thomas*. Are we right to be seeking a redaction-critical explanation, whereby *Thomas* abbreviates his Synoptic source material, leaving out key middle sections, or would a form-critical explanation, whereby *Thomas* witnesses to independent oral forms of these stories, be preferable? One means of exploring the question would be to ask if contemporary analogies could shed light on the data. There is a striking example of the "missing middle" phenomenon in F. C. Bartlett's experiments with memory in the early 1930s.[27] He gave his subjects a text called "The War of the Ghosts" and asked them to read the text a couple of times, and then he tested them for recall of the piece after selected periods of time, with interesting results, including a good example of an individual retelling the story without its middle section (in his first retelling, twenty hours after his reading of the text).[28] This kind of memory of a written text might appear to provide a good parallel for *Thomas*'s familiarity with the Synoptics, but we should be cautious. Bartlett's experiments do not re-create anything like the conditions that may be in view in antiquity, with communal texts read aloud by the literate to the community over a period of time, not a single unfamiliar text read by a modern individual and then recalled. So while analysis of the way that moderns attempt to recall texts can stimulate our reflections on antiquity, we should be clear that this is a question of analogy, not experimental verification.

When in another context April DeConick[29] discusses Bartlett's work, she suggests taking it forward by developing experiments of our own. Spending time on field experiments, she proposes, could help us to get a handle on the working of memory in antiquity. Unfortunately, in the absence of a TARDIS, we do not have access to the workings of the ancient mind except in so far as those workings are crystallized in texts. But while the kind of fieldwork that is available to contemporary practitioners of oral history is not available to those doing ancient history, we should not be discouraged. Our "field" is ancient texts, and the good news is that *Thomas*

27. F. C. Bartlett, *Remembering: A Study in Experimental and Social Psychology* (1932; repr. Cambridge: Cambridge University Press, 1995).

28. Ibid., 72-73.

29. April DeConick, "Human Memory and the Sayings of Jesus," in Tom Thatcher, ed., *Jesus, the Voice, and the Text: Beyond the Oral and Written Gospel* (Waco: Baylor University Press, 2008), 135-80.

is not the only text in antiquity that features extensive parallels with the Synoptic Gospels.

The most striking early Christian parallel to this feature in *Thomas* is found in the writings of Justin Martyr.[30] The parallel is particularly illuminating not only because Justin may well be a close contemporary of *Thomas*[31] but also because he quotes and alludes to a lot of the sayings material from the Synoptics.[32] In *1 Apology*, in his discussion of swearing, for example, Justin omits a chunk of material from the passage in Matthew he is quoting:

Matt. 5:34-37	1 Apol. 16.5
34 ἐγὼ δὲ λέγω ὑμῖν μὴ ὀμόσαι ὅλως· μήτε ἐν τῷ οὐρανῷ, ὅτι θρόνος ἐστὶν τοῦ θεοῦ· 35 μήτε ἐν τῇ γῇ, ὅτι ὑποπόδιόν ἐστιν τῶν ποδῶν αὐτοῦ· μήτε εἰς Ἱεροσόλυμα, ὅτι πόλις ἐστὶν τοῦ μεγάλου βασιλέως· 36 μήτε ἐν τῇ κεφαλῇ σου ὀμόσῃς, ὅτι οὐ δύνασαι μίαν τρίχα λευκὴν ποιῆσαι ἢ μέλαιναν. 37 ἔστω δὲ ὁ λόγος ὑμῶν ναὶ ναί, οὒ οὔ· τὸ δὲ περισσὸν τούτων ἐκ τοῦ πονηροῦ ἐστιν.	Περὶ δὲ τοῦ μὴ ὀμνύναι ὅλως τἀληθῆ δὲ λέγειν ἀεί, οὕτως παρεκελεύσατο· Μὴ ὀμόσητε ὅλως. Ἔστω δὲ ὑμῶν τὸ ναὶ ναί, καὶ τὸ οὒ οὔ· τὸ δὲ περισσὸν τούτων ἐκ τοῦ πονηροῦ.

---

30. John Halsey Wood Jr. suggests that the use of Gospel material in second-century Christian writers could shed light on *Thomas*, "The New Testament Gospels and the *Gospel of Thomas*: A New Direction," *NTS* 51 (2005): 579-95. He discusses Justin Martyr on 590-91.

31. See chapter 9 below.

32. Some caution is, of course, required in seeking parallels in material where Synoptic dependence is itself disputed. For contrasting views, see Edouard Massaux, *The Influence of the Gospel of Saint Matthew on Christian Literature Before Saint Irenaeus*, vol. 3: *The Apologists and the Didache* (ET; New Gospel Studies 5/3; Macon, GA: Mercer University Press, 1993); and Koester, *Synoptische Überlieferung*; and the discussion by F. Neirynck in Massaux, xiii-xxiv. In order to avoid begging the question, the verbatim agreement between Justin and the Synoptics in the examples chosen here is so close as to make a direct link between them highly likely. For the methodological issues involved in discussing the use of the Gospels in the Apostolic Fathers, see Gregory, *Reception of Luke-Acts*, 7-15; and Gregory and Tuckett, "Reflections on Method."

Matt. 5:34-37	1 Apol. 16.5
34 But I say to you, Do not swear at all, either by heaven, for it is the throne of God, 35 or by the earth, for it is his footstool, or by Jerusalem, for it is the city of the great King. 36 And do not swear by your head, for you cannot make one hair white or black. 37 But let your word be "Yes, Yes" or "No, No"; anything more than this comes from the evil one.	And with regard to our not swearing at all, and always speaking the truth, he commanded as follows: "Do not swear at all; but let your Yes be Yes and your No, No; anything more than this comes from the evil one."

As in several examples of *Thomas*-Synoptic comparisons, the middle section of the Synoptic passage is missing. Justin has verbatim agreement with the opening of Matt. 5:34 (μὴ ὁμόσαι ὅλως, "Do not swear at all"), almost verbatim agreement with Matt. 5:37,[33] but all of Matt. 5:34b-36 is missing.[34]

Justin's parallel to Matt. 7:15-20 in *1 Apol.* 16.13 shows a similar pattern in its use of Matthew:

Matt. 7:15-20	1 Apol. 16.13
15 Προσέχετε ἀπὸ τῶν ψευδοπροφητῶν, οἵτινες ἔρχονται πρὸς ὑμᾶς ἐν ἐνδύμασιν προβάτων, ἔσωθεν δέ εἰσιν λύκοι ἅρπαγες. 16 ἀπὸ τῶν καρπῶν αὐτῶν ἐπιγνώσεσθε αὐτούς. μήτι συλλέγουσιν ἀπὸ ἀκανθῶν σταφυλὰς ἢ ἀπὸ τριβόλων σῦκα;	πολλοὶ γὰρ ἥξουσιν ἐπὶ τῷ ὀνόματί μου, ἔξωθεν μὲν ἐνδεδυμένοι δέρματα προβάτων, ἔσωθεν δὲ ὄντες λύκοι ἅρπαγες· ἐκ τῶν ἔργων αὐτῶν ἐπιγνώσεσθε αὐτούς.

---

33. The verbatim agreement enables us to identify the source as Matt. 5:34-37 rather than the parallel Jas. 5:12 (so also Koester, *Ancient Christian Gospels*, 363, though he sees Justin as quoting a catechism influenced by both). Cf. Massaux, *Influence*, 3:26-27, "A literary contact with Mt. is evident" (27).

34. Koester, *Ancient Christian Gospels*, 363, rightly notes: "The absence of Matt. 5.34b-36 is probably due to omission on the part of Justin."

Matt. 7:15-20	1 Apol. 16.13
17 οὕτως πᾶν δένδρον ἀγαθὸν καρποὺς καλοὺς ποιεῖ, τὸ δὲ σαπρὸν δένδρον καρποὺς πονηροὺς ποιεῖ. 18 οὐ δύναται δένδρον ἀγαθὸν καρποὺς πονηροὺς ποιεῖν, οὐδὲ δένδρον σαπρὸν καρποὺς καλοὺς ποιεῖν. 19 πᾶν δένδρον μὴ ποιοῦν καρπὸν καλὸν ἐκκόπτεται καὶ εἰς πῦρ βάλλεται. 20 ἄρα γε ἀπὸ τῶν καρπῶν αὐτῶν ἐπιγνώσεσθε αὐτούς.	πᾶν δὲ δένδρον, μὴ ποιοῦν καρπὸν καλόν, ἐκκόπτεται καὶ εἰς πῦρ βάλλεται.
15 Beware of false prophets, who come to you in sheep's clothing but inwardly are ravenous wolves. 16 By their fruits you will know them. Are grapes gathered from thorns, or figs from thistles? 17 In the same way, every good tree bears good fruit, but the bad tree bears bad fruit. 18 A good tree cannot bear bad fruit, nor can a bad tree bear good fruit.	For many will come in my name, dressed outwardly in sheep's clothing, but who inwardly are ravenous wolves. By their works you shall know them.
19 Every tree that does not bear good fruit is cut down and cast into the fire. 20 Therefore from their fruits you will know them.	Every tree that does not bear good fruit is cut down and cast into the fire.

The abbreviation of the saying by Justin is achieved not by means of summarizing but by means of omitting the middle section, here Matt. 7:17-18. The missing middle creates a less poetic, less coherent flow of thought in Justin than in Matthew. In Justin the tree and fruit imagery emerges suddenly with the image of judgment, rather than with Matthew's explication of good tree/good fruit, bad tree/bad fruit.

Justin does the same thing with respect to Luke:

Luke 12:48	1 Apol. 17.4
Παντὶ δὲ ᾧ ἐδόθη πολύ, πολὺ ζητηθήσεται παρ᾿ αὐτοῦ· καὶ ᾧ παρέθεντο πολύ, περισσότερον αἰτήσουσιν αὐτόν.	ᾧ πλέον ἔδωκεν ὁ θεός , πλέον ἀπαιτηθήσεται παρ᾿ αὐτοῦ.

Luke 12:48	*1 Apol.* 17.4
From everyone who has been given much, much will be demanded; and from the one who has been entrusted with much, much more will be asked.	To whom God has given more, of them shall more be required.

Justin quotes this saying of Jesus using nine words against Luke's sixteen, and the missing words are in the middle. It is interesting here that Justin indicates that he is quoting Jesus.[35] It may be that Justin is working from his memory of the text in which the middle section has disappeared.[36]

Conclusion

On several occasions the *Gospel of Thomas* features parallels to the Synoptics in which the middle section of the Synoptic passage is absent. That the missing middle is a product of *Thomas*'s familiarity with the Synoptics is made likely by the fact that it appears in a range of types of material: parable (*Thom.* 57, Wheat and Tares; *Thom.* 63, Rich Fool), brief narrative (*Thom.* 100, Caesar's Coin), extended poetic metaphor (*Thom.* 26, Log and Speck), brief sayings (*Thom.* 89, inside of the cup), and exhortation with poetic rationale (*Thom.* 36, Do not be anxious). The likelihood that the phenomenon is a feature of the *Gospel of Thomas* itself and not simply the Coptic witness is enhanced by the occurrence of the feature in one of the Oxyrhynchus papyri (P.Oxy. 655; *Thom.* 36).

The inconcinnities generated by the phenomenon suggest that *Thomas* has abbreviated the more coherent Synoptic accounts, probably in working from memory of their texts. It is a casualty of the author's inclination to abbreviate material, and he is an author who lacks the greater artistic and storytelling ability of the sources from which he is working.

35. "But if you pay no regard to our prayers and frank explanations, we shall suffer no loss, since we believe (or rather, indeed, are persuaded) that every man will suffer punishment in eternal fire according to the merit of his deed, and will render account according to the power he has received from God, as Christ intimated when he said, 'To whom God has given more, of him shall more be required.'"

36. As Koester notes (*Ancient Christian Gospels*, 364-65, but four times erroneously given as Luke 17:48), Luke 12:48 D is a little closer to Justin than the critical text: παντὶ δὲ ᾧ ἔδωκαν πολύ, ζητήσουσιν ἀπ' αὐτοῦ περισσότερον, καὶ ᾧ παρέθεντο πολύ, πλέον ἀπαιτήσουσιν αὐτον; but Justin is missing the middle whichever version he saw.

The examples of missing middles in Justin's quotations from the Synoptics[37] may illustrate that the phenomenon in *Thomas* has a comfortable parallel in a literary context in the mid-second century. They incline us against the view that *Thomas*'s frequent brevity with respect to the Synoptics is related in any way to primitivity. Such a view runs directly counter to a lot of the received wisdom on the origins of the *Gospel of Thomas*, as well as to a certain reconstruction of trajectories in early Christianity, and it will require further exploration. In the next chapter, we will look at the question of orality, literacy, and *Thomas*, exploring the grounds for the claim that *Thomas* is primitive in genre and form, and close to the oral traditions that characterized early Christianity.

---

37. There are other possible examples of the same thing, e.g., *1 Apol.* 16.7 // Matt. 19:16-17 // Mark 10:17-18 // Luke 18:18-19, where Justin omits the linking dialogue, "Why do you call me good?" (Mark and Luke) or "Why do you ask me about what is good?" (Matthew).

CHAPTER 8

Orality, Literacy, and *Thomas*

Introduction

There is an emerging consensus in recent studies of *Thomas* that *orality*[1] provides the key to studying the Gospel. The mode of *Thomas*'s origin, development, and composition is an oral one.[2] It is difficult to underestimate the importance of this perspective, but it is an issue that requires a little unraveling. Although often treated together, two elements in this discussion require separate attention. The first is a proposition that relates to Christian origins scholarship in general. The second relates more specifically to *Thomas*. The general claim is that in order to understand the full range of early Christian documents, one needs to take seriously the burgeoning literature on orality and to engage with a properly informed understanding of oral tradition.[3] The more specific claim is that the *Gospel of Thomas* can only be properly understood as the product of an "oral mind," the result of an "oral disposition" that contrasts with the scribal mentality that characterizes certain other early Christian documents.

---

1. The term "orality" has been developed in contradistinction to "literacy" and is most closely associated with the important and influential work of Walter Ong, *Orality and Literacy: The Technologizing of the Word* (London: Methuen, 1982). However, Ong's contrast between oral cultures and literate cultures often falls out of view in discussions of orality in scholarship on Christian origins, where clearly literate authors are said to be moving in an oral culture. Perrin, *Thomas and Tatian*, is an exception here.

2. Perrin, *Thomas and Tatian*, is an exception here.

3. For useful overviews see Kelly R. Iverson, "Orality and the Gospels: A Survey of Recent Research," *Currents in Biblical Research* 8 (2009): 71-106; and Holly E. Hearon, "The Implications of 'Orality' for Studies of the Biblical Text," *Oral Tradition* 19/1 (2004): 96-107.

These different claims are sometimes confused and they are sometimes discussed as if they are the same thing. Unfortunately, this pattern characterizes much of the discussion of orality and literacy in early Christianity, an area that is frequently marked by a lack of clarity. The two different claims are partly in contrast with one another, and since it is quite possible to have differing views on each, I will begin by addressing some of the aspects in the general discussion about orality and Christian origins, and I will then move to the elements in the discussion of *Thomas* as a product of an oral culture.[4]

The basic point that I hope to underline is that the world of early Christian texts and tradents is best understood as a world in which there was a vibrant interaction between orality and literacy, the ear and the eye, text and tradition. It is a very different world from the one we live in, but caricatures of our literate world can be damaging to a proper appreciation of how orality and literacy interacted in antiquity and how the *Gospel of Thomas* found its place in that world.[5]

Understanding these issues is important in the context of the argument of this book for several reasons. I have argued that *Thomas* is directly linked with the Synoptic Gospels, that its author is familiar with them. This kind of thesis inevitably risks being characterized as belonging to an outmoded "literary paradigm" that has been superseded by a new paradigm that stresses orality at every turn.[6] It is easy to caricature a theory in which there are direct links between texts as a matter of "scissors and paste,"[7] and to accuse those who hold such theories as belonging to another generation. It is only by careful consideration of the complex issues surrounding orality and

4. For a helpful discussion of some of the key issues in relation to *Thomas*, see especially Uro, "*Thomas* and the Oral Gospel Tradition."

5. See Rafael Rodriguez, "Reading and Hearing in Ancient Contexts," *JSNT* 32 (2009): 151-78, for a helpful critique of the recent discussion of orality and literacy in early Christianity.

6. DeConick, "Gospel of Thomas," 474, writes, "Did someone not sit down with a pen in hand and write it, perhaps relying on written sources like the New Testament Gospels? This type of answer [*sic*] reveals the enormous distance between ourselves and ancient people, between our world of information technology and their world of memory and story. Their culture was one dominated by memory and orality, punctuated only by occasions of reading and writing."

7. DeConick, for example, describes what she calls "the literate model" as a matter of "scissors and paste" (*Recovering*, 43, citing McL. Wilson, *Studies*, 48). She also criticizes Perrin's *Thomas and Tatian* as a "cut-and-paste model" (*Recovering*, 48). The now antiquated metaphor of "scissors and paste" is, of course, only ever used in scholarship to characterize and so criticize the views of opponents.

literacy in early Christianity that we will be able to navigate our way to a clear understanding of the relationship between *Thomas* and the Synoptics.

Moreover, many of the standard arguments in favor of *Thomas's* independence of the Synoptics are apparently enhanced when they are restated as part of a model that conceptualizes the world of *Thomas* as a world of rampant orality. Arguments about the brevity of *Thomas's* sayings, or about the lack of allegory in its parables, take an older form-critical view of the development of the tradition and update them by recasting them as examples of oral traditions appropriated by an author (or authors) with an oral mentality. Misperceptions about orality and literacy in antiquity can obscure the case for *Thomas's* familiarity with the Synoptics, and they need to be taken seriously.

In this chapter, we will begin by exploring the claim that a proper understanding of orality transforms the task of examining the literary deposit from early Christianity. I will argue that the corrective offered by scholars like James Dunn actually underestimates the importance of literacy among early Christian authors and tradents, whose world we should reconstruct as one characterized by a lively interaction between text and tradition. I will suggest further that *Thomas* is best understood as a representative of that same world of text and tradition, and that attempts to locate it as a special representative of a kind of oral mind are misguided.

Orality, Literacy, and Christian Origins

In an important article, James Dunn[8] offers a major challenge to students of Christian origins, arguing that we are so influenced by the "literary paradigm" within which we do our work that we are ill equipped to understand the "oral culture" within which the early Christian authors moved.[9] The literary paradigm is a kind of "default setting," and we need training to free

---

8. James D. G. Dunn, "Altering the Default Setting: Re-envisaging the Early Transmission of the Jesus Tradition," *NTS* 49/2 (2003): 139-75. See also Dunn, *Jesus Remembered.* Because Dunn does not have a lot to say about *Thomas* in his analysis of early Christian orality, his study marks a useful starting point for investigation of the general claims about orality. For Dunn's views on *Thomas*, see *Jesus Remembered*, 161-65.

9. Cf. Werner Kelber, *The Oral and the Written Gospel: The Hermeneutics of Speaking and Writing in the Synoptic Tradition, Mark, Paul, and Q* (Philadelphia: Fortress, 1983), 32: "Literacy is so deeply implanted in every twentieth-century biblical scholar that it is difficult to avoid thinking of it as the normal means of communication and the sole measure of lan-

ourselves from this way of thinking because it is seriously distorting our scholarship. Dunn summarizes his approach:

> In a word, we naturally, habitually and instinctively work within a *literary paradigm*. We are, therefore, in no fit state to appreciate how a *non-literary culture*, an *oral* culture, functions. And if we are to enter empathetically into such a culture it is essential that we become conscious of our literary paradigm and make deliberate efforts to step outside it and to free ourselves from its inherited predispositions. It becomes necessary to alter the default settings given by the literary shaped software of our mental computers.[10]

Appealing to the pioneering work of Albert Lord and Milman Parry, and quoting Walter Ong,[11] Dunn is particularly impressed with Kenneth Bailey's model of "informal controlled oral tradition," which is based on anecdotal evidence.[12] Dunn builds a case for understanding the origins,

---

guage." As with Dunn, the overstatement whereby literacy is configured as the "sole measure" of language among moderns is striking.

10. Dunn, "Altering," 142.

11. Albert Bates Lord, *The Singer of Tales* (Cambridge: Harvard University Press, 1960); Ong, *Orality and Literacy*. It is common for New Testament scholars to appeal to Lord and Parry without bearing in mind Lord's own disastrous attempt to apply his insights to the New Testament in Albert B. Lord, "The Gospels as Oral Traditional Literature," in William O. Walker Jr., ed., *The Relationships among the Gospels: An Interdisciplinary Dialogue* (San Antonio: Trinity University Press, 1978), 33-91. Lord's article illustrates the problem with attempting to transfer the insights from *The Singer of Tales* to the study of Christian origins without first understanding the nature of the Synoptic Problem and related issues.

12. Kenneth Bailey, "Informal Controlled Oral Tradition and the Synoptic Gospels," *AJT* 5 (1991): 34-54 = *Themelios* 20/2 (1995): 4-11; idem, "Middle Eastern Oral Tradition and the Synoptic Gospels," *ExpT* 106 (1995): 363-67. Dunn appeals repeatedly to the Bailey model, also in *Jesus Remembered* and in "Jesus in Oral Memory: The Initial Stages of the Jesus Tradition," in D. Donnelly, ed., *Jesus: A Colloquium in the Holy Land* (London: Continuum, 2001), 84-145. This aspect of Dunn's case has been weakened by Theodore J. Weeden's exposing of serious problems in Bailey's work, "Kenneth Bailey's Theory of Oral Tradition: A Theory Contested by Its Evidence," *JSHJ* 7 (2009): 3-43. Dunn's reply, "Kenneth Bailey's Theory of Oral Tradition: Critiquing Theodore Weeden's Critique," *JSHJ* 7 (2009): 44-62, defends Bailey's anecdotal evidence, asking, "Are personal experiences stretching over several decades to be dismissed simply because they are recorded with an anecdotal casualness that the scientific mind abhors?" (48), the answer to which is yes, if we are serious about academic study. At best, Bailey's materials can provide useful analogies for modeling early Christian tradition. Others who have appealed to Bailey include DeConick, *Recovering*, 29; idem, "Gospel of Thomas," 475; N. T. Wright, *Jesus and the Victory of God* (Christian Origins and the Question of God 2; London: SPCK, 1996), 133-36. See too Terence Mournet, *Oral Tradition and*

development, and even the writing down of the Jesus tradition under the heading of orality. He does not deny the role played by texts and by relationships between texts, but for Dunn orality is always at the forefront.[13]

Dunn's thesis, which coheres with a broader movement in New Testament studies,[14] provides a welcome corrective to our text-obsessed minds, our library- and study-based contemporary academic perspective on the world. Sometimes it takes a shock to jolt scholars out of the kind of complacent, unexamined assumptions that form the backdrop to their everyday activities, and Dunn is clearly attempting to turn on the electricity to achieve a massive paradigm shift. But shock treatment can be counterproductive; and while the stimulus to think is successful, the attempt to shift paradigms is less so.[15]

One of the difficulties with Dunn's perspective is its starting point. He overstates the case for the extent of our immersion in a literary culture. He describes us as "children of Gutenberg and Caxton." "We belong," he says, "to cultures shaped by the book. Our everyday currency is the learned article and monograph. Libraries are our natural habitat."[16] There is, of course, some truth in this; no one would deny the importance of the book in our culture. But what Dunn is talking about here is not so much our culture in general, but the academic subculture of research and writing. Even within that subculture, our literary research interacts with oral and aural elements.

Literary Dependency: Variability and Stability in the Synoptic Tradition and Q (WUNT 2/195; Tübingen: Mohr Siebeck, 2005), 90-91, 185-90, *et passim*, for a sympathetic critique of Bailey.

13. For discussion of Dunn, see also Samuel Byrskog, "A New Perspective on the Jesus Tradition: Reflections on James D. G. Dunn's *Jesus Remembered*," *JSNT* 26 (2004): 459-71; and Birger Gerhardsson, "The Secret of the Transmission of the Unwritten Jesus Tradition," *NTS* 51 (2005): 1-18.

14. It is a movement that owes a great deal to Kelber, *Oral and Written*. For a recent discussion of Kelber, see Tom Thatcher, "Beyond Texts and Traditions: Werner Kelber's Media History of Christian Origins," in Tom Thatcher, ed., *Jesus, the Voice, and the Text: Beyond the Oral and the Written Gospel* (Waco: Baylor University Press), 1-26.

15. Iverson, "Orality and the Gospels," 77, suggests that a "paradigm shift" influenced by the work of Parry, Lord, Havelock, and Ong is "still being played out today."

16. "Default," 142. While scholars of our generation may still be children of Caxton and Gutenberg, scholars of this generation are children of Bill Gates and Tim Berners-Lee. It is easy to underestimate the radical change in learning brought about by a generation of digital natives, who are usually taught by digital immigrants like us. See Marc Prensky, "Digital Natives, Digital Immigrants," On the Horizon 9/5 (2001); idem, "Digital Natives, Digital Immigrants, Part 2: Do they really think differently?" On the Horizon 9/6 (2001), reproduced at Marc Prensky, http://www.marcprensky.com/, accessed 23 August 2011. See further on this below.

Our primary means of communicating our scholarship is the classroom, which is all about speaking and hearing in interaction with the primary texts being studied and the secondary texts that help. The oral interaction in the classroom is a major contributor to the development of the scholar's thoughts.

In the preparation of our scholarship, the oral plays a key role. Dunn's own article began life as a Society for New Testament Studies presidential address in 2002. The interaction between written draft, oral presentation, revised drafts in the light of live questioning — these are the staples of the development of academic work. Thus where Dunn conceptualizes the scholar as living in the library, one might just as readily characterize the enterprise as one of interaction in which solitary library time is only one feature, and not necessarily the most important feature.

Outside that academic subculture, our world is still permeated by orality. Many more people receive their news through television and radio — oral media — than through newspapers. And many who do use newspapers are now no longer simply reading them, but they are combining the reading experience with watching online videos, listening to podcasts, and so on. We are living in a culture in which the very term "reader" is once again changing. The avid "reader" of *The Guardian* or *The New York Times* now incorporates activities that involve no reading at all, listening to podcasts and audio streaming and watching embedded video.

This is not to say, of course, that our world is a nonliterary one but to point out that it is easy for academics to underestimate the extent to which orality and literacy interact in our own culture. Dunn suggests, "In an overwhelmingly literary culture our experience of orality is usually restricted to casual gossip and the serendipitous reminiscences of college reunions,"[17] a surprising statement given the many other manifestations of orality in our culture.[18] The spoken word is everywhere. For many, the written word is secondary. To be literate does not mean that the written word is always and inevitably primary, or that we always think along literary lines. The case of knowledge of the Bible is itself instructive. As those who have taught the New Testament know, the student's knowledge of the texts is often received through oral tradition, not through direct familiarity with the text. Few

17. "Default," 149.

18. If "literacy" is broadly defined as the ability to read (and sometimes to write), orality should be defined as the ability to communicate by the spoken voice, without prejudice to the specific questions of primary orality, secondary orality, and the oral cultures, oral societies, or oral minds who are engaging in the communication.

people who think they know the Christmas story get their knowledge directly from reading Matthew 1–2 and Luke 1–2, let alone the *Protevangelium of James* or the *Gospel of Pseudo-Matthew*. Their knowledge is conveyed through our culture's oral tradition and its harmonized and legendary versions of the story so frequently retold and reenacted.[19]

The point is not to attempt to narrow the gap between the ancient world and the contemporary world. The key task of the ancient historian is to convey some sense of the great differences between the worlds we study and our own, and to avoid anachronistic readings influenced by our own way of looking at things.[20] The point rather is that in our attempts to conceptualize the ancient world, we should be careful not to lapse into caricature of the contemporary world, and so to warp our perception of Christian origins. If we were to imagine the person who in a millennium is reading Dunn's scholarship, looking for information about how we communicate with one another in the early-twenty-first century, that researcher would have little idea of how we actually live our lives. We live in libraries ("our natural habitat") and we trade in monographs and learned articles ("our everyday currency"). Where Dunn is exploring the analogy of a computer's "default setting," he conceives of the computer solely in word-processing terms and not as a communications device that incorporates oral and aural features. For many contemporary academics, the computer has two basic functions, word processing and email, literate activities in continuity with the typewriter and the letter writing that they replaced.[21]

---

19. Knowledge of film versions like *Jesus of Nazareth* (dir. Franco Zeffirelli, 1977) and *The Nativity Story* (dir. Catherine Hardwicke, 2006) further informs the contemporary mind, and the aural/visual encounter remains primary. There is rich potential for research into this kind of encounter, all the more interesting in that such film versions are themselves informed by interaction with traditions of harmonized retellings of the biblical versions.

20. On the cultural difference see Philip Esler, *New Testament Theology: Communion and Community* (Minneapolis: Fortress, 2005), 171-72.

21. Of course, some academics understand and use technology effectively in their research and teaching, but there remains a gap between scholars and students. Scholars' perceptions of their abilities with technology are different from students' perceptions of their abilities. See, for example, Scott Jaschik, "Technology Gap," Inside Higher Ed, November 5 2009, http://www.insidehighered.com/news/2009/11/05/survey.

Secondary Orality

Indeed, the computer analogy may be appropriate in a way not anticipated by Dunn. His analogy conceptualizes the computer as a writing machine, a kind of glorified electronic typewriter, but it is much more than that: a communications device, a telephone, a radio, a television set, a games console, and so on. Just before the dawn of the computer revolution, the radical change in communications culture was already encouraging Ong to conceptualize our culture as something other than a purely literate one. "The electronic age," he said, "is also an age of 'secondary orality,' the orality of telephones, radio, and television, which depends on writing and print for its existence."[22]

Ong was prescient in his realization of the emerging importance of secondary orality, something he was already discussing in 1971,[23] but the generation that separates us from Ong's important studies has demonstrated an explosion in secondary orality of the kind that he could hardly have imagined. Biblical scholars who repeatedly appeal to Ong as if his work will lend theirs a trendy legitimacy would do well to reflect on our own cultural distance from Ong. When he conceptualizes secondary orality, his list of electronic devices now looks dated. He speaks, for example, of "the 'secondary orality' of present-day high-technology culture, in which a new orality is sustained by telephone, radio, television and other electronic devices that depend for their existence and functioning on writing and print."[24]

Ong's reference to "telephone, radio, television and other electronic devices" illustrates that the computer revolution has hardly dawned. When, twelve years later, Robert Fowler is exploring "How the secondary orality of the electronic age can awaken us to the primary orality of antiquity," his list of what is involved in the discussion of secondary orality includes the following: "However, by means of our computers, telephones, televisions, VCRs, CD players, and tape recorders, hypertext breaks into our cozy study, grabs us by the scruff of the next [*sic*], and plunges us full-bore into the advent(ure) of secondary orality."[25]

22. Ong, *Orality and Literacy*, 3.

23. Walter Ong, *Rhetoric, Romance and Technology: Studies in the Interaction of Expression and Culture* (Ithaca: Cornell University Press, 1971), chapter 12, especially 299.

24. *Orality and Literacy*, 11.

25. Robert Fowler, "How the Secondary Orality of the Electronic Age Can Awaken Us to the Primary Orality of Antiquity, or What Hypertext Can Teach Us About the Bible, with Reflections on the Ethical and Political Issues of the Electronic Frontier," paper presented to

Fowler provides a snapshot of a moment in the development of the culture of secondary orality, and there are items in this list that were absent from Ong's list. And now Fowler's 1994 list looks dated. VCRs and tape recorders have gone the way of vinyl before them. Tape is no more. We would now talk about DVDs, blu-ray, DVRs, downloads, blackberries, iTunes, podcasts, P2P, streaming — and this list too will soon begin to look dated to those now reading this book written in 2012. It is easy to see that one is living in a revolution when the items in the list are changing so rapidly.

Reflection on this revolution in secondary orality illustrates the extent to which academics can underestimate how orality works in our culture, a fact that influences the way that the discussion of antiquity is framed. On one level, there is nothing surprising here; we speak of what we know. Ong himself is a case in point. When he discusses television and radio, he instinctively thinks in terms of political figures and their oratory.[26] On the only occasion that he specifies a particular radio program, it is "a recently published series of radio lectures" by Claude Lévi-Strauss.[27] Perhaps it is unsurprising, therefore, that Ong thinks in terms of television, radio, and electronic devices "that depend for their existence and functioning on writing and print." There is, of course, a lot of truth in this. The existence of radio and television is inconceivable without writing, and a great deal of television and radio depends on the carefully planned script, especially drama and documentary. Nevertheless, television and radio, to say nothing of the Internet, podcasting, and more, have gone beyond "print," even if the interaction between orality and literacy remains essential.[28] A lot of the content of television, radio, the Internet, and podcasts is spontaneous and not formally dependent on writing or print. Sports coverage and some reality TV programs are obvious examples, but it is a discussion that could provide many more.

The difficulty for academics who reflect on these issues is that they are inclined to play down orality in contemporary culture, a situation that leads to exaggerated, even romanticized notions of the primary orality of the past. While it is indeed essential for the ancient historian to grasp the

---

the Semiotics and Exegesis Section, Society of Biblical Literature Annual Meeting, Chicago, November 19, 1994, reproduced at http://homepages.bw.edu/~rfowler/pubs/secondoral/index.html.

26. *Orality and Literacy*, 136-37.

27. Ibid., 174.

28. Podcasting, for example, is an oral medium that is often unscripted, but the process of editing, tagging, and uploading is inconceivable without literacy.

utter difference of the ancient world from ours, and to attempt to understand how orality and literacy interacted in antiquity, misconceptualizing the contemporary world can make the problem worse, not least by encouraging a kind of binary opposites approach according to which the ancient world is characterized by orality and our world is characterized by literacy. However useful it might be, in teaching and summary communication, to emphasize this kind of complete contrast, the reality is more complex. It is a matter of understanding the different ways in which orality and literacy interact then and now.

In so far as contemporary orality and literacy can be reduced to simple descriptors, terms like "print-determined" or "print-dominated"[29] are not particularly helpful. Instead, we should engage seriously with the secondary orality of our culture without overemphasizing elements in the rarefied atmosphere of the academic subculture.

"Secondary Orality" in New Testament Scholarship

The meaning of the term "secondary orality" in Ong's work is clear, and it has been developed to embrace the ways in which the orality of the electronic media impacts on contemporary literacy.[30] In recent years, however, a new and completely different usage has become common in New Testament scholarship. The new meaning of "secondary orality" relates it to the ancient world rather than the contemporary world, and uses it to refer to indirect familiarity with texts through oral tradition. It has become especially prevalent in discussions of *Thomas* to describe a familiarity with the Synoptic Gospels that is mediated through oral tradition.

The new use of the term derives from Werner Kelber, who uses it in this way in his influential 1983 book, *The Oral and the Written Gospel*: "Obviously, orality derived from texts is not the same as primary orality, which operates without the aid of texts. The passion narrative is largely built on texts and texts recycled into the oral medium, that is, secondary orality."[31]

Later, Kelber explains the properties of this "secondary orality." Texts

---

29. Dunn, "Default," 150, speaks of "our print-determined default setting" and the "blinkers of a mindset formed by our print-dominated heritage"; cf. Kelber, *Oral and Written*, xv, "I have written this book out of a concern for what seemed to be a disproportionately print-oriented hermeneutic in our study of the Bible."

30. Cf. Ruth Spielmann, "Secondary Orality," *TIC Talk* 53 (2002): 1-4.

31. Kelber, *Oral and the Written Gospel*, 197.

were "fixed and in a sense dead, permanently open to visual inspection and the object of unceasing efforts at interpretation," but at the same time they were "meant to be read aloud and heard"; and so, "If this text enters the world of hearers by being read aloud, it functions as secondary orality." The contrast with "primary orality" is striking in that "the story narrated is one that was never heard in primary orality, for it comprises textually filtered and contrived language."[32]

The difficulty with Kelber's usage of the term is not only that it is confusing to co-opt a term that is already used to refer to something completely different, but also that it works with a static and unidirectional model, whereby fixed text is appropriated orally. It plays down the interaction between text and tradition, underestimating the role played by texts in the earliest period, and overestimating the fixed nature of texts from Mark onward.[33] The term "secondary" orality here functions to emphasize that it is an orality that is derivative of the fixed text, with no link to the oral tradition from which the text was derived.

For Kelber, "secondary orality" does not yet have the nuance it has developed more recently. Kelber is speaking about texts being read aloud, not about knowledge of texts mediated through oral tradition. There is no discussion of interaction between text and tradition, and there is not yet a specific reference to *Thomas*. The term is used with reference to *Thomas* for the first time in Klyne Snodgrass's article on *Thomas*,[34] where he attempts to make clear that he is not suggesting that *Thomas* copied from the Synoptics but rather that *Thomas* is "witness of a 'secondary orality.'" This is the usage that has subsequently become popular in discussions of *Thomas*, and which is associated especially with Risto Uro.[35] Like Kelber, Uro uses it in self-

32. Ibid., 217-18. Kelber's departure from Ong's use of the term "secondary orality" is self-conscious: "In communications theory secondary orality usually refers to electronically mediated sound. We would suggest a differentiation of three types of orality: primary orality, textually mediated or secondary orality, and electronically mediated or tertiary orality" (*The Oral and the Written Gospel*, 226 n. 118). This categorization has not caught on.

33. In recent work, Kelber has shown some modification of his earlier views on fixed texts, largely under the influence of Parker, Living Text; e.g., Werner Kelber, "Orality and Biblical Studies: A Review Essay," RBL 12 (2007): 22-25, http://www.bookreviews.org/pdf/2120_6744.pdf.

34. Snodgrass, "Gospel of Thomas," 28. Snodgrass footnotes Kelber for "the expression," apparently realizing that he is using it differently.

35. Uro's key article on the topic is "'Secondary Orality' in the Gospel of Thomas? Logion 14 as a Test Case," *Forum* 9/3-4 (1993): 305-29; repr. as "*Thomas* and the Oral Gospel Tradition," in Risto Uro, ed., *Thomas at the Crossroads*, 8-32. For the concept Uro also cites

conscious differentiation from the standard usage in orality studies,[36] but his usage aligns with that of Snodgrass, to refer to the indirect dependence on the Synoptic Gospels mediated orally.[37] DeConick uses the term in the same sense,[38] as a convenient shorthand for the possibility of oral mediation of Synoptic texts to *Thomas*.

The use of the term in the study of early Christianity is problematic not just because of the confusion with its use in Ong but also because it leads to an unrealistic appreciation of the dynamics of early Christian discourse. What is required is something a little more nuanced. The use of "secondary orality" with reference to Christian origins effectively elevates a kind of primary orality to an importance it never had, and it detracts attention from the fact that texts were often composed and almost always mediated orally. In other words, we should be thinking about a kind of dynamic interaction between orality and literacy, between text and tradition, throughout the early period.

Wherever we look in early Christianity, we see this interaction between text and tradition. Traditions crystallize in texts, and texts stimulate the tradition. When Luke sets out to write an account of the things that have been fulfilled among the early Christians (Luke 1:1-4), he self-consciously claims to have knowledge of both texts and traditions, of other narratives and of the things that have been passed on by eyewitnesses. And the analysis of the Gospel itself makes sense as the product of that interaction, between written texts and oral traditions.[39]

Moreover, it is well known that Papias also witnesses to the desire to access material about Jesus not only through texts but also by word of mouth.[40] Once again, it is a matter of both eye and ear, text and tradition. So

---

Ernst Haenchen, "Literatur zum Thomasevangelium," *Theologische Rundschau* 27 (1961): 147-78 (178).

36. Uro, *Thomas at the Crossroads*, 10 n. 11.

37. For a further comment, see also Risto Uro, *Thomas: Seeking the Historical Context of the Gospel of Thomas* (London: Continuum, 2003), chapter 5, especially 109.

38. As far as I can tell, it does not appear in the first of her two sister volumes, *Recovering* , but it occurs frequently in the second, *Original Gospel*, at 18, 21, 22, 24, 53, 89, 94, 111, 134, 140, 167, 169, 188, 194, 200, 201, 208, 215, 235, 261, and 269.

39. I have argued elsewhere that one should pay serious attention to the role played by oral tradition in the composition of Luke (*Goulder and the Gospels*, part 2, especially 284-86; *Case Against Q*, 64-66).

40. The famous statement about the "living, abiding voice" is in Eusebius, *HE* 3.39.4, but it is worth adding that Eusebius's quotations of Papias (3.39.1-16) feature multiple references to hearing and memory alongside the references to the literary works like Mark and Matthew,

too Justin Martyr. The means by which the Christians he knew were accessing the gospel materials was by the reading aloud, in church, of what they conceptualized as "the memoirs of the apostles," and this reading aloud was subsequently interpreted and expounded.[41]

This is not simply a matter of what was happening at the end of the first century and in the first half of the second. The same interaction characterizes the evidence as far back as we can go. Indeed, the difficulty with "secondary orality" is the implication that there was a primary orality, which conjures up a world of illiterate tradents and detracts from an understanding of the roles played by orality and literacy in early Christianity. To see the point, it is worth reflecting on the question of the literacy of those who passed on the tradition from the first.

Literate Tradents

A facetious comment attributed to the pseudonymous blogger N. T. Wrong underlines the literacy of the biblical authors: "Of those who wrote biblical books, the literacy rate was 100%."[42] Everyone, of course, knows this, but not everyone reflects on the roles played by the literate elite in a largely illiterate culture.[43] In order to understand a text, we begin by exploring the world of the author, a world that presupposes literacy even where that author is surrounded by illiteracy. It is true that the majority of the hearers of early Christian texts were illiterate, from the slave at the dinner table to the stall holder at the marketplace; but those composing texts, copying texts, and reading texts aloud were by definition literate. In other words, it is essential to take seriously the role played by the literate in a culture where there was widespread illiteracy, and to come to terms with the role played

---

1 John and 1 Peter. Papias's knowledge of the Synoptic Gospels alongside his claims to knowledge of tradition combined with "strange parables and teachings of the Savior" and "other more mythical things" sounds like a good analogue for the *Gospel of Thomas*.

41. Justin Martyr, *1 Apol.* 67, "the memoirs of the apostles or the writings of the prophets are read, as long as time permits; then, when the reader has ceased, the president verbally instructs, and exhorts to the imitation of these good things."

42. N. T. Wrong, "The Relative Unimportance of Oral Culture for Interpreting Biblical Books," The N. T. Wrong Blog, 14 November 2008, http://ntwrong.wordpress.com/2008/11/15/the-relative-unimportance-of-oral-culture-for-interpreting-biblical-books/.

43. Studies of the question invariably stress illiteracy in the majority of the population as if this establishes the oral mind-set of the authors of the texts.

by this elite. As Harry Gamble says, "In a community in which texts had a constitutive importance and only a few people were literate, it was inevitable that those who were able to explicate texts would acquire authority for that reason alone."[44]

In early Christianity, there were many poor illiterates, but the literate elite were those who had command over the traditional material.[45] Therefore descriptions of the world in which early Christians moved as an "oral culture" or of their mind-set as an "oral mentality" are unhelpful.[46] Their world is one more accurately characterized as involving a rich interaction between orality and literacy, what Vernon Robbins calls a "rhetorical culture."[47] Nor is this world one that only emerges with the writing of the

---

44. Harry Gamble, *Books and Readers in the Early Church: A History of Early Christian Texts* (New Haven: Yale University Press, 1995), 9-10. For the issue of the power wielded by the literate elite, see Joanna Dewey, "From Storytelling to Written Text: The Loss of Early Christian Women's Voices," *BTB* 26 (1996): 71-78; idem, "Textuality in an Oral Culture: A Survey of Pauline Traditions," in Joanna Dewey, ed., *Orality and Textuality in Early Christian Literature* (Semeia 65; Atlanta: Scholars Press), 37-65; for a recent critique see Rodriguez, "Reading and Hearing," 168-70.

45. One of the values of the model proposed by Birger Gerhardsson, *Memory and Manuscript: Oral Tradition and Written Transmission in Rabbinic Judaism and Early Christianity;* with *Tradition and Transmission in Early Christianity* (combined ed.; Biblical Resource Series; Grand Rapids: Eerdmans, 1998), is that it takes seriously the roles played by literate teachers in the earliest Christian movement, in contrast to the model proposed by Bailey and followed by Dunn (see above, 131-32), which provides a poor analogy for the circumstances of the earliest Christian tradents. Bailey is dealing with groups of illiterates who share material with one another, without influence from a literate elite group.

46. Cf. Rodriguez, "Reading and Hearing," 157, "Nevertheless, we find compelling reasons to demur at the concept of an 'oral mentality,' and especially at the hopelessly vague 'oral culture,' both of which continue to be influential within NT research. Analyses of oral tradition and its functions in wider cultural patterns, including the use of written texts, have pointed out for well over a decade how remarkably imprecise and vacuous is the concept *oral mentality.*" On the pervasiveness of literacy in antiquity, see also Kim Haines-Eitzen, *Guardians of Letters: Literacy, Power, and the Transmitters of Early Christian Literature* (Oxford: Oxford University Press, 2009), especially chapter 1.

47. Vernon Robbins, "Oral, Rhetorical, and Literary Cultures: A Response," in J. Dewey, ed., *Orality and Textuality,* 75-92; and "Interfaces of Orality and Literature in the Gospel of Mark," in R. Horsley, J. Draper and J. Foley (eds.), *Performing the Gospel: Orality, Memory, and Mark: Essays Dedicated to Werner Kelber* (Minneapolis: Fortress, 2006), 125-46. In relation to *Thomas,* however, Robbins overestimates the extent of its "oral intertexture"; see below, 143-45. On rhetorical culture, and the interaction between oral and written composition, see also DeConick, *Rediscovering,* 26-37. For the interplay between oral and written traditions, see Uro, "*Thomas* and Oral Gospel Tradition," 15-19.

Gospels. From the early decades of the Jesus movement, it seems that the oral tradition presupposes literacy and literate tradents.

Almost all of the early Christian tradents we know appear to have been literate.[48] The best known, Paul, was of course literate, and his sharing of Jesus tradition in places like 1 Cor. 7:10-11, 9:14, and 11:23-26 is a case of a literate tradent sharing Jesus tradition with another literate tradent (the reader of the letter), who will then share that tradition with his or her hearers. Here there is a clear example of the kind of interaction between orality and literacy that characterizes the development of Christian origins, or, more specifically, between literate tradents and illiterate (and literate) hearers of the tradition. Presumably Apollos too was literate (e.g., Acts 18:24), and so were Silas, Timothy, and, it seems, Phoebe, Barnabas, Prisca, Aquila, and many others. If we can trust Luke, it is broadly implied that James too is literate (Acts 15:20), and his importance in the emerging Christian movement (cf. Josephus, *Ant.* 20) may also suggest literacy.

It is reasonable to assume that such people were participating as literate tradents in a culture in which there was interaction between orality and literacy, but it is possible also to go further than this. The tradition itself presupposes literate tradents. In 1 Cor. 15:3-5 Paul presents what he has received as of first importance and which he also passed on to the Corinthians (παρέδωκα γὰρ ὑμῖν ἐν πρώτοις ὃ καὶ παρέλαβον), "that Christ died for our sins *according to the Scriptures*, and that he was buried, and that he was raised on the third day *according to the Scriptures*." In other words, the content of the tradition invokes what is written. It is difficult to imagine illiterate tradents having success with the sharing of material that itself presupposes literacy in this way.[49]

---

48. The exceptions are Peter and John, who are represented by Luke as ἀγράμματοι (Acts 4:13), sometimes translated as "illiterate." It may be that Luke here implies "uneducated" or "unschooled" rather than illiterate given that he also depicts Peter as quoting extensively, verbatim, from the Hebrew Bible (or perhaps more accurately here in Acts, the LXX). Nevertheless, it is a useful reminder of the possible existence of illiterate tradents in the early period.

49. Cf. Gerhardsson, "Secret," 13, for a critique of Dunn along related lines: "The gospel tradition, both the sayings of Jesus and the narratives about him, differs from non-Jewish oral tradition also by being strongly impregnated with OT words, themes and motifs, allusions, and sometimes also quotations. This fact shows, moreover, that Jesus and his disciples did not move within an oral society. Sacred writings played an important role in Jewish life, and had for many centuries influenced thinking and speaking, and listening to lessons, in services, at studies, in discussions and on other occasions within the spiritual life of the community."

Is Thomas an Oral Gospel?

The pertinent question for our purposes, however, is whether *Thomas* too participates in that world in which text interacts with tradition or whether it proceeds from a different mind-set and a different social location, a gospel with a fundamentally oral state of mind to be contrasted with the Synoptics and their scribal dimensions. It is a key question in any study of *Thomas*'s use of sources to find out if *Thomas*'s relationship to the tradition is different from the scribal relationship that characterizes intra-Synoptic relationships. For Vernon Robbins, the key to studying *Thomas*'s relationship to the tradition is to understand its "oral intertexture." He draws attention to "orality as a social location in the Gospel of Thomas" by making the following important observation:

> An amazing fact about the *Gos. Thom.* is its complete lack of appeal to written text. In contrast to the canonical gospels, the narrator never says, "As it is written in Isaiah the prophet" (Mark 1:1), "For so it is written by the prophet" (Matt 2:5), "As it is written in the book of the words of Isaiah the prophet" (Luke 3:4), or "For these things took place that the writing might be fulfilled" (John 19:36). In addition, the narrator of the *Gos. Thom.* never attributes to Jesus a statement like "Have you never read what David did . . ." (Mark 2:25), "It is written, 'One does not live by bread alone'" (Luke 4:4//Matt 4:4), "This is he of whom it is written . . ." (Matt 11:10), "What is written in the law? How do you read?" (Luke 10:26), or "It is written in the prophets, 'And they shall all be taught by God'" (John 6:45). All the canonical gospels contain an orientation toward "what is written" both at the level of the narration of the story and in speech attributed to Jesus. [50]

The observation is brilliant, but the conclusion that Robbins derives from this observation is problematic. He sees this lack of interest in written text as a symptom of *Thomas*'s social location, so that *Thomas*'s relationship to the Synoptic Gospels is that of "oral intertexture" rather than "scribal intertexture." But some reflection on the "scribal" features isolated by Robbins confirms that these come less from social location than from generic

50. Vernon K. Robbins, "Rhetorical Composition and Sources in the Gospel of Thomas," in Society of Biblical Literature 1997 Seminar Papers (Atlanta: Scholars Press, 1997), 86-114 (88), reproduced at http://www.religion.emory.edu/faculty/robbins/Pdfs/RhetCompThomas .pdf. "Mark 1:1" is an error for Mark 1:2.

preference. In so far as we can discover anything about *Thomas*'s location, it is a scribal one. The document is prefaced with the claim that it is "the secret words of the living Jesus *which Didymos Judas Thomas wrote down*."[51] The appearance of orality is a necessity of the genre chosen, the book of sayings. At the risk of stating the obvious, sayings are by their nature oral and any book of sayings will inevitably have the characteristics of speech, of orality, at least if its author has done his or her job properly.[52]

So in *Thomas* we should not expect to see repeated comments from the narrator of the kind that we find in narratives like Matthew, Mark, and Luke. Nor would we expect to find narrative reflection on Jesus' deeds of the kind we find there. *Thomas* does not report any deeds of Jesus, so its author hardly has the context to say, "These things happened in order to fulfill. . . ." The book does not have a prominent narrator, and the author's fundamental conceit is that this is a collection of secret sayings. The interpretation of the sayings is not revealed in the text; they are to be sought and found as a means to eternal life (Incipit; *Thom.* 1).

It is worth adding that *Thomas*'s lack of reference to reading and writing (after the Incipit) probably says as much about its attitude to the Old Testament as it does about its attitude to scribal culture in general. *Thomas* takes a negative stance toward the Hebrew Scriptures. The disciples, who appeal to the twenty-four prophets who spoke about Jesus, are told that they are speaking about the dead (*Thom.* 52). These dead prophets are never mentioned in *Thomas*. Indeed, the only relevant Old Testament character is Adam and the only relevant story is Genesis 1–2.[53]

---

51. Robbins does not refer to the Incipit in this article.

52. Cf. Kelber, "Sayings Collection," 222-23, for useful reflections on the interface between writing and orality in *Thomas*, including the claim that "the sayings gospel is perhaps best described as an interface between orality and writing, seeking a rapprochement with both worlds" (223). However, the idea of two gospel genres in the early period, the narrative gospel and the sayings gospel, each with "different compositional and transmissional processes," requires an early *Gospel of Thomas* to be aligned with the Q hypothesis so that there are two representatives of the sayings gospel genre in the first century rather than none.

53. On *Thomas* and the Old Testament, see further below, 187-91. Robbins, "Rhetorical Composition," 88-89, contrasts the allusion to Ps. 118:22 in Matt. 21:42 // Mark 12:10-11 // Luke 20:17 with *Thom.* 66. While Mark's Jesus shows "extended scribal relation to that written text," *Thomas*'s Jesus "does not refer to his speech as written text, and the recitation embeds a brief word string of the biblical text in the manner of proverbial memory and performance. . . . The *Gos. Thom.* version is free from 'scribal' influence." But this is a function not only of *Thomas*'s attitude to the Old Testament, which it never explicitly quotes, but also of its genre. Mark's Jesus is engaging in controversy dialogues with opponents over shared

The point is confirmed when we remember that a similar situation obtains in many other texts found in the Nag Hammadi library. Like the *Gospel of Thomas*, the *Book of Thomas the Contender* has an introductory saying about what is written down (here by Mathias, 138.1-4), but afterward there are no references to books, scribes, writing, or reading. *The Gospel of Philip*, the *Acts of Peter and the Twelve Apostles*, the *Dialogue of the Savior*, and the *Second Apocalypse of James* are all likewise lacking in any references to reading or writing. *Allogenes* refers only to writing what is revealed, once, at the end of the book (68.16-21). So too the *Apocalypse of Adam* has one reference to writing, at the end of the book, when the revelations are written "upon a rock of truth," not having been committed to a book (85.3-11). In each case, it is a function of genre and theological preference, the absence of self-conscious engagement with the Hebrew Bible, and the pretense of enigmatic pronouncement or revelatory discourse.

In other words, what we have in *Thomas* is not a matter of "orality as social location" but rather sayings gospel as generic preference. It is in this generic decision, to write a book of sayings rather than, say, another narrative gospel, that we gain insight into how *Thomas* used the Synoptics. It is too easy to confuse genre (sayings book) with origins and tradition history. Indeed, it is a mark of the success of *Thomas's* project that we go digging for oral traditions behind the book, ultimately looking for a location in the historical Jesus' own ministry, rather than reflecting on how it is that one puts a book like this together, and what its author's choice of genre tells us about his theological preferences.

The Legacy of Form Criticism

The difficulty, however, is that several of *Thomas's* sayings resemble the imagined appearance of those sayings in the primitive Jesus tradition. This appearance of primitivity is not easily unimagined and requires a little extra thought. The idea that *Thomas* features primitive sayings emerges from the legacy of classical form criticism of the Gospels, and it is an approach that is particularly well illustrated by the work of the Jesus Seminar. Robert Funk's "Rules of Oral Evidence,"[54] which guided their work, are anything

---

foundations (the Hebrew Scriptures), whereas *Thomas's* Jesus proclaims enigmas to his inner circle of confidants.

54. Robert W. Funk, "Rules of Oral Evidence: Determining the Authentic Sayings of Jesus," *The Fourth R* 4/2 (1991): 8-10; repr. in Bernard Brandon Scott, ed., *Finding the Histori-*

but "rules."[55] They are form-critical assertions that do not stand up to scrutiny. The most serious problem is related to the bogus "rule" about simplicity. According to Funk, "At the earliest stage of the tradition we should expect to find single aphorisms and parables and not extended clusters or discourses."[56] He spells it out in the following way:

The simpler, the earlier
A. The simpler forms of sayings and parables are more likely to be original with Jesus
B. More complicated forms may mask earlier and simple forms.[57]

Funk illustrates the phenomenon by drawing attention to Luke's version of the first beatitude, "Blessed are the poor" (Luke 6:20), suggesting that Luke has retained the Q version whereas Matthew has "spiritualized" it.[58] The simple illustration masks a sleight of hand. As soon as one is discussing the first beatitude, one has left the realm of form criticism and entered the world of source and redaction criticism. Funk does not believe that Matthew and Luke have independently derived this beatitude from a freely circulating oral version, retained by one and "spiritualized" by the other. He thinks that both have a copy of a Q text that each modifies in his own way. And in source criticism, there is no such rule as "the simpler, the earlier." The evangelists may well expand material they inherit; they may distill or summarize it. Earlier sources may feature more elaborate material; they may feature less elaborate material. Even if this were a genuine example of a form independently derived from one or more oral originals, though, there is still no such rule as "the simpler, the earlier." It only appears in the guise of a "rule" because frequent repeti-

---

cal Jesus: Rules of Evidence (Jesus Seminar Guides; Sonoma: Polebridge, 2008), 25-29. Page references are to the reprinted version.

55. For critiques of the "rules of evidence" of others in the Jesus Seminar, see William Herzog, *Jesus, Justice and the Reign of God: A Ministry of Liberation* (Louisville: Westminster John Knox, 2000), 36-41. For a general comment, see Rafael Rodriguez, *Structuring Early Christian Memory: Jesus in Tradition, Performance, and Text* (LNTS 407; London: T & T Clark, 2009), 19-21.

56. Funk, "Rules," 27.

57. Ibid.

58. Although my point here is to draw attention to the way in which alleged oral evidence is illustrated from literary parallels, the point is also weak on the level of the literary parallels — the first beatitude in Luke makes good narrative, theological, and contextual sense as Luke's redaction of Matt. 5:3; see my *Case Against Q*, chapter 7.

tion and use in New Testament studies lend it that appearance.[59] The Jesus Seminar uses it repeatedly, as when, for example, they write with respect to *Thom.* 26: "Thomas' version of this humorous comparison is simpler than the form found in Q, which suggests that the latter has been expanded."[60] Or on *Thom.* 31 they write: "The earliest form of the saying is probably the aphorism consisting of a single line found in Thom 31:1; Luke 4:24; and John 4:44 (the simpler form is usually the earlier). This adage is characteristic of the short, easily remembered, and, in this case, ironical remark that lent itself to oral transmission, and was typical of Jesus as a sage and prophet."[61]

This kind of perspective is not limited to the Jesus Seminar. It is often found elsewhere. Koester, for example, sees the "Mothers and Brothers" pericope in *Thom.* 99 as "a brief chria, lacking any of Mark's elaborate introductory setting of the stage and discourse."[62] Or Gerd Lüdemann, in commenting on the parable of the Sower (Mark 4:2-9 // *Thom.* 9), says, "On the whole we must regard the version of Thomas as older than that of Mark, because it is simpler."[63]

But "simplicity" is in the eye of the beholder. In discussions of *Thomas's* parallels with the Synoptics, the "simpler" form often turns out simply to be the shorter one, the one that takes up less space on the page. *Thomas's* brevity is more clearly a function of the author's redaction than of his source material. *Thomas* is often more brief than Matthew, Mark, and Luke in Synoptic parallels. The table below illustrates the number of words taken by each of the Synoptics and *Thomas* to tell the parallel parables:[64]

59. With respect to the *Gospel of Thomas*, McArthur already warned in 1960 that "the shorter is not necessarily the more primitive" ("Gospel According to Thomas," 67).

60. Funk and Hoover, *Five Gospels*, 488.

61. Ibid., 491. For the *Thomas* version as showing familiarity with Luke's redaction of Mark, see above, 84-86.

62. Koester, *Ancient Christian Gospels*, 110. Koester erroneously gives the reference in Mark as 3:31-34 rather than 3:31-35. See further n. 65 below. Koester's treatment of *Thomas* 100 (*Ancient Christian Gospels*, 112) is similar — it is another "brief chria" lacking the extra Markan material.

63. Gerd Lüdemann, *Jesus after Two Thousand Years: What He Really Said and Did*, with contributions by Frank Schleritt and Martina Janssen (London: SCM, 2000), 28. Fred Lapham, *Introduction to the New Testament Apocrypha* (London: T & T Clark, 2003), 115, notes that some see *Thomas's* Sower as more primitive because it is shorter, but he rightly notes that dependent texts are often shorter, including Luke's triple tradition material.

64. For purposes of comparison, I have used English translations for each (Lambdin for *Thomas* and the RSV for the Synoptics) in order that the word lengths are not artificially skewed given the differences between the Coptic and Greek; I have also limited the counts to Jesus' words so that the lengthier Synoptic narrative introductions do not inflate their figures.

Parable	Matthew	Mark	Luke	Thomas
Sower	101	106	75	78
Tenants	150	183	166	127
Banquet	252	—	200	243
Tares	151	—	—	82
Rich Fool	—	—	117	55
Mustard Seed	56	73	49	32
Leaven	23	—	29	32
Lost Sheep	113	—	175	52

Although Luke is usually taken to be later than Mark, he is shorter than Mark in the Sower, Mustard Seed, and Tenants.[65] Similarly, *Thomas*'s pericopae are often shorter than their Synoptic parallels (Sower, Mustard Seed, Tenants, Tares, Rich Fool, Lost Sheep). And where *Thomas* takes fewer words to narrate parables than do the Synoptic parallels, the abbreviation is sometimes at the cost of the coherence of the piece. The abbreviations are sometimes made in unhelpful places, especially in the middle of the piece (see chapter 7 above). Here *Thomas*'s brevity has little to do with form-critical primitivity[66] and much more to do with editorial tendency.[67]

The problem with oversimplified pictures about brevity and simplicity in the early tradition is that they often forge ahead without engaging with E. P.

65. Luke's greater brevity in these places is telling and it is reflected in his redaction of Mark outside the parable tradition too. The Mother and Brothers pericope (Matt. 12:46-50 // Mark 3:31-35 // Luke 8:19-21 // *Thom.* 99) is greatly abbreviated in Luke as it is also in *Thomas*. Patterson, *Gospel of Thomas*, 67-68, sees the Lukan and Thomasine versions as "less embellished" and derived from a "less developed, parallel tradition," but it is much more straightforward to see Luke abbreviating Mark, as often, and to see *Thomas* here doing the same.

66. Cf. Baarda, "Gospel of Thomas," 60, "The form-critical argument that a short form is always more authentic than the longer form seems strong, but is in my view questionable," commenting on *Thom.* 100.

67. The same point could be extended to other second-century authors like Justin Martyr, whose version of the parable of the Sower is much shorter than any of the Synoptic versions (*Dialogue with Trypho* 125.1-2); cf. *1 Clem.* 25.5. Massaux, *Influence of the Gospel*, 14, comments on Justin's parallel with Matt. 19:11-12 in *1 Apol.* 15.4, "This method [of copying and inverting] seems to show that the sayings of Christ, brief and short, as reported by Justin, sometimes owe their brevity to the apologist himself."

Sanders's *Tendencies of the Synoptic Tradition.*[68] The book appears to have bypassed a generation of scholars of a particular persuasion.[69] Since some still remain unfamiliar with the book,[70] it is worth quoting Sanders's own conclusion from the study in the later textbook coauthored with Margaret Davies:

> When we study in detail the form critical "laws" of the development and change of the material, we discover that none of them holds good. A comparison of the quotations of Jesus' sayings in second- and third-century literature with the synoptic versions does not reveal that the sayings tended to become longer and more detailed, or shorter and less detailed. Individual tellers might expand or abbreviate, might elaborate or epitomize. There are no general laws about length and detail.[71]

But the tendencies model is not easily shifted. It is easy to understand and easy to apply. It is one of those tools that proves its usefulness to the biblical scholar in applications that explain the development of the Gospel tradition and promise to shed light on the historical Jesus. And it is pedagogically powerful. In classroom sessions where lecturers have an hour to

68. E. P. Sanders, *The Tendencies of the Synoptic Tradition* (Cambridge: Cambridge University Press, 1969).

69. The difficulty caused by ignoring Sanders is pointed out by Snodgrass, "Gospel of Thomas," 21. For a recent helpful summary and comment, see Christopher Tuckett, "Form Criticism," in Werner Kelber and Samuel Byrskog, eds., *Jesus in Memory: Traditions in Oral and Scribal Perspectives* (Waco: Baylor University Press, 2009), 20-38 (33); for a recent critique see Mournet, *Oral Tradition*, 25-36.

70. But see the comment in Kelber, *The Oral and the Written Gospel,* 7, which commends Sanders for his critique of the form critics while criticizing him for presuming that the developments of oral tradition and written tradition are comparable: "In taking this course he acted out of the conviction he shared with Bultmann — and a majority of New Testament scholars, one suspects — concerning the irrelevance of a distinction between oral and written tradition: '. . . the tendencies of one are presumably the tendencies of the other'" (quoting Sanders, *Tendencies,* 8). The criticism results from a failure to appreciate the purpose of Sanders's study, which is to supply what was lacking in the form critics' approach to the literature: "The form critics did not derive the laws from or apply the laws to the Gospels systematically, nor did they carry out a systematic investigation of changes in the post-canonical literature. It is the purpose of this study to meet this last defect" (*Tendencies,* 26). Moreover, the focus of Sanders's study includes the Synoptic Problem, in which Kelber has no interest (see further below, n. 80).

71. E. P. Sanders and Margaret Davies, *Studying the Synoptic Gospels* (Philadelphia: Trinity Press International, 1989), 127-28, commenting in context on Bultmann, *History*; Dibelius, *From Tradition to Gospel*; and Vincent Taylor, *The Formation of the Gospel Tradition* (London: Macmillan, 1933).

explain form criticism to new students, the tendencies approach offers the chance of illustrating an observable evolutionary model of early Christian tradition. But the model is wrong, and however great the apparent utility, it needs to be abandoned.

The Mode of *Thomas's* Access to the Synoptics

Before leaving the topic of this chapter, it is worth asking about the manner of *Thomas's* use of the Synoptic Gospels. If the idea of "scissors-and-paste" access is a caricature of the theory of literary dependence,[72] is there a more nuanced way that the interpreter can imagine *Thomas's* mode of accessing the Synoptic Gospels? Since the author does not inform us how he used his source material, it is a matter of informed speculation, based on clues drawn from the internal evidence and from the way that others proceeded.

One major clue is the presence of several sequences of words in verbatim agreement between *Thomas* and the Synoptics (chapter 2 above), which means that the author is highly likely, on occasions, to have consulted the Synoptic Gospels directly. These will be occasions where the author has obtained a copy of Matthew or Luke,[73] either his own or copies belonging to his church or community, and has looked up a passage in order to check the wording. It is a reasonable guess that the author would be dictating his work, like many authors in antiquity,[74] so it is unnecessary to imagine the writing taking place simultaneously with source consultation.[75] It is quite possible too that the author used wax tablets in order to make notes for his composition.[76]

The other major clue that the *Gospel of Thomas* provides is the order of its sayings. The relative lack of parallels in order between *Thomas* and

---

72. See above, 129.

73. The relative scarcity of Johannine material makes it less likely that the author has a copy of a Four Gospels codex, though it is possible that he has access to a copy of a Gospels codex and focuses primarily on Matthew and Luke.

74. Including, of course, our best-known witness, Paul (Rom. 16:22; cf. 1 Cor. 16:21; Gal. 6:11).

75. For a study of the issues involved with writing in antiquity, and how this impacts the Synoptic Problem, see R. A. Derrenbacker Jr., *Ancient Compositional Practices and the Synoptic Problem* (BETL 186; Leuven: Peeters, 2005).

76. See John C. Poirier, "The Roll, the Codex, the Wax Tablet, and the Synoptic Problem," *JSNT* 35 (2012): 3-30.

the Synoptics suggests that the author was regularly accessing the Synoptic materials from his memory of the texts he was using. While it is not impossible that the author was physically finding his key texts, the logistical efforts involved in that enterprise are far greater than those involved with recalling texts from memory. Moreover, memory is associative, and many of *Thomas's* links look as if they could be the result of simple associations in memory. It is commonly said that *Thomas* works by "catchword" (*Stichwort*) connection, and it is undoubtedly the case that many of the links between sayings make sense on this basis. These links may often be the result of memory associations,[77] and it is worth adding that the links between sayings are not limited to the word level. Sometimes there are links between sayings in thought and imagery, which may also be signals of memory association. The case of *Thom.* 79 (chapter 6 above) makes the point clearly. In material that shows a marked dependence on Luke, the author associates material from disparate parts of the Gospel (Luke 11:27-28 and 23:28-29) that share the same imagery and vocabulary. It is the kind of association that may show that the author has a good mental recall of the text of Luke.[78]

Nevertheless, if *Thomas* is often accessing the Synoptic Gospels through memory of the texts, this may mean that some of the variations from the Synoptics are due to memory distortion as well as intentional redaction. The phenomenon of the missing middle (chapter 7 above) may itself be an illustration of this. The author is recalling texts in an incomplete way, and leaving out key sections from the middle of the passages in question. Once again, though, the possibility of consultation of the texts, alongside access from memory, should not be ruled out. Sequences of sayings like 63 (Rich Fool), 64 (Great Banquet), 65 (Tenants in the Vineyard), and 66 (Rejected Stone) may point to the author working in sequence through the Gospel of Luke (12:15-21; 14:15-24; 20:9-16, 17).

77. See Patterson, *Gospel of Thomas*, 100-102, for a list of catchwords and the suggestion that "one could well imagine an editor assembling these sayings simply as he or she remembered them, catchwords triggering the recollection of each new saying. In this case the catchwords will not have been part of any conscious design on the part of the editor, but simply the result of his or her own process of remembering" (102). Patterson imagines the process as taking place with respect to "an oral stage in the tradition," but catchwords are just as likely to work with respect to memory of texts too.

78. If this explanation of the catchword connections is on the right lines, it makes it less likely that the catchwords in *Thomas* relate to "a long history of oral composition" (DeConick, *Recovering*, 48). The catchwords may be the result of memory associations in the author's recall rather than evolving as mnemonic triggers for the person performing the text.

Conclusion

A chapter like this runs the risk of being misheard. Many scholars are currently rediscovering the importance of oral tradition; others are seeing their approach to Christian origins transformed by consideration of orality. When one is in the midst of a changing perception in the scholarship, whether or not it ends up being a genuine "paradigm shift," it can be difficult to retain the right balance. Consideration of orality in the wider academic guild has undoubtedly played a major and often successful part in encouraging the reassessment of orality and literacy in early Christianity.[79] The danger, however, is that enthusiasm for the new perspective can distort as well as enlighten, and the eagerness to embrace the study of orality can lead to ignorance of areas like the study of the relationship between the texts. It is a case in point that a great deal of the study of orality takes place to the neglect of any serious understanding of issues in the Synoptic Problem.[80] Moreover, our desire to understand orality in the ancient world should not be confused with our ability to gain access to the oral traditions and oral performances that are, in their very nature, lost, except in so far as they are crystallized in the texts that we have been studying all along.[81]

I have suggested in this chapter that while it is helpful to reflect on the

79. Note also the emerging study of memory in much recent New Testament scholarship. See especially Anthony Le Donne, *The Historiographical Jesus: Memory, Typology, and the Son of David* (Waco: Baylor University Press, 2009); and Alan Kirk, "Memory," in Kelber and Byrskog, eds., *Jesus in Memory*, 155-72, and the literature cited there.

80. The common confusion of the Two-Source Theory with the literary relationship between the Synoptic Gospels illustrates the difficulty; see, e.g., Werner Kelber, "The Two-Source Hypothesis, the classic explanatory model accounting for the interrelationship of the three synoptic gospels, has been traditionally formulated as a literary problem that is to be examined in literary terms and subject to a literary resolution, leaving no room for oral interfacing, the poetics of gospel narrativity, and memorial activities" ("Oral Tradition in Bible and New Testament Studies," *Oral Tradition* 18/1 [2003]: 40-42 [41]). The Two-Source Theory is a solution to "the literary problem"; it is not the problem itself. See similarly Dunn, "Altering the Default Setting," 158; idem, *Jesus, Paul, and the Gospels* (Grand Rapids: Eerdmans, 2011), 27-28, where "the force of the standard two-source theory" is found in the degree of agreement between the Synoptic Gospels. That Dunn thinks that the degree of agreement between the Synoptics establishes the plausibility of the Two-Source Theory may illustrate the presence of a "default setting" in his scholarship.

81. There is a massive contrast here between the study of recent oral tradition and the study of oral tradition in antiquity. Oral history projects now allow us to access the stories and memories of individuals who have never committed them to writing. The study of orality in antiquity remains a matter of the study of texts.

role played by orality in antiquity, there are the potentials for the distortion both of the contemporary world and the ancient world. There is sometimes an inclination to caricature our own literate world in the light of the academic subculture in which we move and, at the same time, to exaggerate the role played by orality in antiquity by making claims that do not take seriously the importance of the literacy of the elite who carried the traditions and composed the texts. Understanding the world in which the early Christians moved is about understanding the role played by both texts and traditions. In the light of the interaction between orality and literacy, the emergence of the term "secondary orality" within New Testament studies should probably be avoided, and it should be retained only to describe contemporary electronic communications.

The *Gospel of Thomas* has played a special role in the discussion of orality, but the claim that it has a fundamentally oral disposition or that it is the product of an oral state of mind requires some caution. The appearance of orality is a product of *Thomas's* genre, the sayings gospel, itself no doubt influenced by its theological preference, its inclination to play down the Old Testament, and its characterization of Jesus as the enigmatic "Living One," the interpretation of whose sayings has the potential to impart eternal life. If this reading is right, the sayings that have parallels with the Synoptics do not emerge from a primitive oral tradition but from *Thomas's* self-conscious extraction of congenial material. This, of course, raises the question about how and why *Thomas* would engage in this kind of use of the Synoptics, and this is the topic of Chapter 10.

CHAPTER 9

Dating *Thomas* and the Gospels

Preliminaries

When one reflects on the case for *Thomas*'s familiarity with the Synoptics, there are broader, related questions that require exploration, questions about how, when, and why *Thomas* read the Synoptics. At first sight, the most straightforward of these questions relates to dating, the subject of the current chapter. Its apparent straightforwardness might, however, be misleading. The subject requires some care, beginning with discussion of the dating of other early Christian works, especially those to which *Thomas* is related.

One of the aspects of studying the dating of early Christian documents is the temptation to shoot too quickly for absolute dates, without first attempting to establish relationships between documents. I have waited until chapter 9 to discuss the issue for this reason, to avoid attempting to pinpoint *Thomas* to a particular date without first assessing its relationship to the Synoptic Gospels. One of the virtues of B. H. Streeter's classic *Four Gospels*[1] is that it takes seriously the necessity to work on Gospel relationships before attempting to establish the dates of the Gospels. However much we might find matters like the Synoptic Problem not to our taste, it is essential to get on top of such things if we are to get some feeling for the most plausible relationship of the Gospels to one another. It is a necessary prior step before attempting to fix the Gospels to a specific date or range of dates.

Another aspect of the problem is the pedagogical advantage of keep-

---

1. Burnett Hillman Streeter, *The Four Gospels: A Study of Origins Treating of the Manuscript Tradition, Sources, Authorship and Dates* (London: Macmillan, 1924).

ing the dating simple. Like other issues in the study of Christian origins, our research is affected by the need to teach the topic in a comprehensible way, to find a compelling narrative, and to make the points memorable. The standard picture used in introductory courses on the New Testament and Christian origins is remarkably easy to grasp, and it is pedagogically useful. Every decade in the first century from the 40s on is covered. Paul writes in the 40s and 50s, Mark in the 60s, Matthew in the 70s, Luke in the 80s, and John in the 90s. Other assorted items that are of lesser interest punctuate this pattern, and the noncanonicals are safely dated in the second century and beyond. This broad dating leads to a developmental model with easy-to-define markers and phases. The oral period lasts for a generation, during which Paul witnesses to the expansion of Christianity; Mark is the first to write a life of Jesus, utilizing those oral traditions but under Paul's influence; then, firmly in the post-70 period, Matthew builds on Mark but re-Judaizes it, while Luke does the same thing either at the same time or a little later. The picture is completed with John, writing his spiritual Gospel in the 90s or the turn of the century. The neatness of the picture, though, should act as a warning to reexamine the basis for these judgments. How secure is the general picture, what are the complications, and how does it impact on *Thomas*?

Before we take a closer look at these issues, it will be worth asking some preliminary questions in order to make sure that the discussion is placed on as sound a footing as possible. Several of these issues recapitulate themes that we have visited already, but it is nevertheless important to underline that the process of discussing ancient literary works, and relationships between ancient literary works, involves a necessary element of simplifying. The process of attempting to articulate the key issues in a coherent fashion inevitably means that the model might be mistaken for the reality.

What Is a Literary Work?

It is easy to engage in this kind of discussion without thinking through the broader issues of what it means to talk about "texts" and "literary works" in antiquity. It is somewhat hackneyed to point out the obvious facts that none of the autographs have survived and that there were no printing presses, but textual critics rightly remind us to behave as if we actually know that that is the case.[2] Too often, we lapse into treating the scholarly constructs as if they are the actual artifacts that they can only aspire to be. At the very least,

---

2. See especially Parker, *Living Text*.

we need to keep reminding ourselves in discussions like this that we are not dealing with fixed points and known entities but with reconstructions and approximations.

A Work's Evolution

There is a related issue here, that the more we become text-critically sensitive, the more we are inclined to reflect on the evolution of the literary works we think we know. When we try to date Mark's Gospel, what are we dating? Something that approximates to our scholarly reconstructions of Mark 1:1–16:8 or something akin to what the vast majority of witnesses have, a Mark that goes on beyond 16:8? When we try to date John, are we imagining a version with or without the *Pericope Adulterae*, with or without chapter 21? When we date *Thomas*, are we dating textual antecedents to the Oxyrhynchus fragments, where Coptic *Thomas*'s saying 77 is found with saying 30, or constructs more akin to the Coptic? This kind of question is sometimes framed as if it is exclusive to antiquity, but even in the print culture of the twentieth century, a literary work's history is often about a date range rather than a fixed point in time. When we refer to John Knox's *Chapters in a Life of Paul*, are we dating it to its original influential edition in 1954 or the revised version of 1989, in which he reacts to critics of his earlier work?[3] Sometimes our attempts to date literary works too precisely ignore what we know to be the case: documents are not static entities even today, let alone in antiquity.[4]

Text and Tradition

There is a further related issue that can lead to confusion. We sometimes speak as if a literary work is as early as the traditions it contains. Or, to put it in another way, we confuse tradition history with a document's dating. Thus a document first penned in the year 80 CE might contain good traditions from the early 30s. One first penned in the 60s might be full of historically dubious legends. We should be careful to make sure that in attempting to date a document we are not simply dating the traditions contained in that literary work.

It is not my intention, though, to talk only about the difficulties in-

---

3. John Knox, *Chapters in a Life of Paul* (1954; rev. ed., London: SCM, 1989). To make it still more complicated, we could insist too that even the 1954 edition featured revised versions of articles written in the 1930s.

4. Cf. Patterson, *Gospel of Thomas*, 115, for similar caution. But see further below, 161-62.

volved in the task at hand, but rather to make sure that certain warnings are in place before embarking on the journey ahead. It is important to be clear that this discussion of the dating of literary works takes place in a context that admits that there are complexities but that aims for the greatest degree of clarity possible.

Arguments for an Early Date

Establishing the latest possible date for the *Gospel of Thomas* is relatively straightforward. A work can be no later than its earliest textual witness, and in the case of *Thomas*, this is P.Oxy. 1, dated by Grenfell and Hunt to c. 200 CE, a date that has continued to command consensus.[5] Where *Thomas* falls in the period that dates from the earliest years of the Christian movement, though, is more difficult to establish. Here one's verdict will be determined in large part by the answers given to questions about *Thomas*'s familiarity with the Synoptics.[6] Although an independent or autonomous *Thomas* does not require an early date,[7] clearly it becomes increasingly difficult to imagine a late *Thomas* remaining uninfluenced by the Synoptic Gospels, especially Matthew.

For Stephen Patterson, there are three major indications of *Thomas*'s early date. The first argument is its appeal to authority.[8] Like Matt. 16:13-20 or the deutero-Pauline epistles, *Thomas* sits comfortably in the "last decades of the first century," as a text that appeals to the authority of particular individuals, not as "apostles" or as members of "the twelve." The Incipit and

5. See above, 28-29 n. 12. The scholar who presses closest to this *terminus ad quem* is Perrin, *Thomas and Tatian*, for whom the *terminus a quo* is set by Tatian's *Diatessaron*, setting up a fairly narrow window for the composition of *Thomas*, at the end of the second century. For his defense of this dating, see Perrin, *Thomas, the Other Gospel*, 97-99.

6. Cf. Ron Cameron, "Thomas, Gospel of," *ABD* 6:535-40 (536), "If *Gos. Thom.* is a sayings collection based on an autonomous tradition, and not a gospel harmony conflated from the NT, then a date of composition in, say, the last decades of the 1st century would be more likely than a mid-to-late-2d-century date."

7. As recognized by Patterson, *Gospel of Thomas*, 113.

8. The argument is developed from Koester, "Introduction," 39, "the type of appeal to apostolic authority," and 40-41. Although Koester states the case for an early date as if it is self-evident, these arguments are controversial. In 1977 Bruce Lincoln spoke of the Gospel's dating in "the first half of the second century A.D." as "now generally accepted" ("Thomas-Gospel and Thomas-Community: A New Approach to a Familiar Text," *NovT* 19 [1977]: 65-76 [65 n. 1]).

Thom. 13 (Peter, Matthew, and Thomas) and *Thom.* 12 (James) illustrate this phenomenon, and Patterson says:

> The text thus dates to a period in which authority was still *personal*, or dependent upon a leader's personal charisma and powers of persuasion, and not yet *apostolic* properly speaking. The latter depends upon a nostalgia, in which "the apostles" have become venerated figures in the community's foundational stories, a view not shared by Thomas (cf. esp. Thom 43, 51, and 52). All of this would suggest a date close to Paul, who feels no compunction about maligning the reputation of an apostolic leader when he feels so compelled (cf. Gal 2:11-12), or to Mark, who often portrays the "disciples" as simple dunderheads. By contrast, at the end of the first century Luke can smooth over all of these difficulties to portray a single, harmonious, apostolic church guided and unified by the Holy Spirit.[9]

The sketch is intriguing, but the argument becomes unconvincing as soon as we begin reflecting on the literature. The earliest works do, in fact, refer to "the apostles" and "the twelve" as authoritative groups. Indeed, 1 Cor. 15:1-11 lists appearances to Peter and "the twelve," and to James and "all the apostles," in the context of an authoritative teaching that Paul has received and passed on "as of first importance." This is hardly Paul speaking with a kind of nostalgic distance. Individual authority in these undoubtedly first-century Christian texts can quite easily be flanked by appeal to apostolic status (cf. 1 Cor. 9:1), and the deutero-Paulines likewise appeal to "the foundation of apostles and prophets" (Eph. 2:20).[10]

Unlike these first-century texts, *Thomas* does not appeal to "apostolic" authority as apostolic authority. James (*Thom.* 12), for whom heaven and earth came into being, comes closest to playing this role. He is, of course, a major figure in early Christianity (1 Cor. 15:7; Gal. 1:19; 2:9, 12; Acts 15:13; 21:18), but this James is not so much the brother of Jesus as James "the Just" (ΔΙΚΔΙΟΣ) of later Christian reflection. The designation of "the Just" is not found in the Gospels, Acts, or Paul but is characteristic of later Christian

---

9. Patterson, *Gospel of Thomas*, 116. *Thomas* is getting a little earlier here as one progresses through the argument, beginning — along with the deutero-Paulines and Matthew — in the latter decades of the first century, and ending up — along with Paul and Mark — nearer to the mid-first century.

10. For some nuanced reflections on "authority and autonomy" in *Thomas*, see Uro, *Thomas*, 80-105.

sources like Hegesippus and Clement of Alexandria.[11] The presence of James, then, is certainly consonant with a later date,[12] all the more as others of *Thomas's* favorite characters similarly straddle both centuries (Salome, Mary, and Thomas).[13]

Patterson's second argument reverts to the issue of *Thomas's* alleged generic similarity to Q, and the position they share as examples of sayings collections within early Christianity: "The sayings collection as a literary form belongs to the earliest period of Christian literary activity, as evidenced by Q."[14] Like the source behind Mark 4, Q was absorbed into narrative gospels and so obliterated. The loss of *Thomas* then ensures the triumph of the narrative gospel and the death of this primitive form. For Q skeptics, arguments like this will have little appeal, and for them *Thomas* does not have the analogical mooring in the first century. Others too might perceive problems with the argument. Although a key ingredient of Koester and Robinson's *Trajectories* model, *Thomas* fits just as easily into a scheme where it provides a bridging text to the revelation discourses of the second century and beyond. It is not an example of a lost literary form from the first century but rather an emerging literary form in the second. *Thomas* does not yet feature that explicit post-resurrection setting that characterizes texts like *Dialogue of the Savior*, but it marks a clear step in that direction, with its "living Jesus" and its lack of historicizing tendency.[15]

Patterson's third argument is based on the lack of Christological titles in *Thomas*. Following Koester, he notes that *Thomas* does not use the titles "Messiah," "Lord," or "Son of Man."[16] "Koester invites comparison," Patter-

---

11. Eusebius, *HE* 2.1.3; 2.23.4. On James in *Thomas* see John Painter, *Just James: The Brother of Jesus in History and Tradition* (Edinburgh: T & T Clark, 1999), 160-63; and Uro, *Thomas*, 84-88 and 93-97.

12. See also the apparent prominence of James to the Naassenes (Hippolytus, *Refutation of All Heresies* 5.7.1; cf. 10.9.3), noted by William R. Schoedel, "Naassene Themes in the Coptic Gospel of Thomas," *VC* 14 (1960): 225-34 (232-33).

13. Salome: *Thom.* 61; Mark 15:40; 16:1; *First Apocalypse of James* 40.25-26; Mary: *Thom.* 114; Mark 15:40–16:8 and parallels. As in many second- and third-century works, including the *Gospel of Mary, Pistis Sophia,* and *Dialogue of the Savior,* Mary in *Thomas* is not specifically "Magdalene," in contrast with all four canonical Gospels. Indeed, it is often impossible to work out which Mary is being referenced in the second- and third-century texts. See further the essays collected in F. Stanley Jones, *Which Mary? The Marys of Early Christian Tradition* (SBLSymS 19; Atlanta: Society of Biblical Literature, 2002).

14. Patterson, *Gospel of Thomas,* 117.

15. On the sayings gospel argument, see also above, 9-14.

16. Patterson, *Gospel of Thomas,* 118, citing Koester, "Introduction," 40. See also Koester,

son notes, "with other early sayings collections such as Q, which he has long argued originally did not include sayings identifying Jesus with an apocalyptic Son of Man."[17] Unfortunately, there are no "other early sayings collection such as Q," and even within Q the absence of Christological titles is something that one can only establish by means of a literary stratigraphy[18] that is by no means accepted by all Q scholars. The support for this argument, therefore, is a matter of accepting a particular means of stratifying a hypothetical document. Yet even granting those arguments does not establish an early date for *Thomas*. It only tells us about *Thomas's* Christology, or lack of it.[19] After all, the earliest extant Christian works, like 1 Thessalonians, are rich in Christological titles, especially "Christ" and "Lord."

Patterson's arguments for *Thomas's* early date do not settle the issue. The key difficulty, though, remains the evidence for *Thomas's* familiarity with the Synoptic Gospels. In order to gain a sense of *Thomas's* date, it is necessary to reflect on the dating of the Synoptic Gospels themselves.

Dating the Synoptic Gospels

If, as I have argued in the previous chapters, *Thomas* is familiar with the Synoptic Gospels, the book of course postdates them. If *Thomas* knew and used the Synoptic Gospels, then the *terminus a quo* for the composition of *Thomas* can be determined in the attempt to find the dates at which the Synoptic Gospels were written.[20] This is no easy task, and is itself a matter of debate. Nevertheless, there are reasons not to be daunted. First, the case for Markan priority remains strong, and it is the broad consensus in New

---

Ancient Christian Gospels, 86. The occurrence of "Son of Man" in *Thom.* 86 is regarded as "not titular."

17. Patterson, *Gospel of Thomas*, 118. See also Patterson et al., *Fifth Gospel*, 43.

18. Patterson, and later Koester, endorse Kloppenborg's stratigraphical analysis of Q in support of the view that "the early, formative layer of Q" is the one with which *Thomas* should be compared (Patterson, *Gospel of Thomas*, 118; Koester, *Ancient Christian Gospels*, 87).

19. Note too that *Thom.* 13 features discussion of Christology, and implies a rejection of the conceptions of Jesus represented by the mainstream Christian figures Peter and Matthew, in favor of a Christology of enigma and revelation associated with the hero Thomas.

20. Contrast Patterson, *Gospel of Thomas*, 113, "The fact that Thomas is not dependent upon the synoptic gospels is informative insofar as it means that these texts, the latest (Luke) having been written perhaps near the end of the first century, do not offer a *terminus a quo* for Thomas." He speaks of this "fact" again in 113 n. 1, though rightly noting that an independent *Thomas* is not necessarily an early *Thomas*, contrasting Stevan Davies, *Gospel of Thomas*, 145.

Testament scholarship for good reason.[21] My advocacy of Markan priority combined with Luke's use of Matthew[22] is more controversial, but it only impacts the current discussion marginally. On the Farrer theory, Luke is writing later than Matthew, and so *Thomas* becomes the fourth document in a trajectory from Mark to Matthew to Luke to *Thomas*, but this is not greatly different from the Two-Source Theory, where *Thomas* would still be a fourth document, but without the direct line of genealogical descent passing through Matthew to Luke to *Thomas*. For Two-Source theorists who hold that *Thomas* knows the Synoptics, it does not make a great deal of difference, for dating discussions, whether Matthew and Luke are independent. Indeed, for some Two-Source theorists, Luke is writing later than Matthew, notwithstanding his independence of him.[23]

Second, the case for a post-70 dating for Mark is strong, and gaining in momentum in recent scholarship. Although it might be overstating the case to speak about a post-70 Mark as an emerging consensus, several recent works place the onus on those wishing to argue the opposite. The importance of this is obvious. Since Mark is the first in the sequence of literary works, dating Mark is a very helpful way of moving forward. If Mark postdates 70, so do Matthew, Luke, and *Thomas*.

Before tackling that question, however, it is important to underline a key point about the dating game. The discussion is inevitably clouded by the complications of textual tradition (observable) and textual tradition (hypothesized). We discussed above some of the difficulties involved with a literary work's evolution, its range of dates, and the inevitable difficulties that this can cause the historian. Nevertheless, it is possible to speak reasonably about the dating of the literary works as long as one bears these kinds of difficulties in mind. History, especially ancient history, often needs to deal in approximations. It is a heuristic and not a descriptive discipline, and reasoned discussion of the date of given works is achievable provided one proceeds with care. Too often, appeal to uncertainty is given as an excuse for failure to think through literary relationships and dates in a disciplined way.

---

21. Nevertheless, scholars should avoid the complacency of simply appealing to consensus on issues like this lest like other consensus views, it turns out to be weaker than we had imagined. My defense of the case for Markan priority is found in *Case Against Q*, chapter 2; *Synoptic Problem*, chapters 3–4; and "Fatigue in the Synoptics."

22. Defended in my *Case Against Q*.

23. Most radically this is the case for scholars like Burton L. Mack, for whom Matthew is dated in the late 80s and Luke in 120; see his *Who Wrote the New Testament? The Making of the Christian Myth* (San Francisco: HarperSanFrancisco, 1995), 161 and 167.

It is important, for example, to distinguish clearly between the date of a given work and the date of the traditions it contains and to avoid allowing document dating to get bound up with tradition history. How, then, should we conceive the question of dating a literary work? It should refer, one might argue, to the date of the given literary work as an observable, substantive entity with recognizable parameters such that it distinguishes itself from other works.[24] Matthew, for example, is recognizably Matthew and not Mark, even though it contains a lot of Mark. Luke is recognizably Luke; it is not Matthew and it is not Mark, even though it contains a lot of the shape and the substance of those works. In this kind of discussion, then, we need to be clear about what it is we are trying to date. We are dating the literary works to which our texts bear witness, and not prior oral traditions, written traditions, or hypothetical earlier versions of the work in question. In this context, we are not investigating the dating of elements within the larger, later literary work; we are attempting to date the work itself.

A work can be no earlier than its most recent datable tradition. This is why, when we come to Mark, the question of its knowledge of the destruction of the temple is so important. If Mark is familiar with the events of 70, the presence of traditions earlier than 70 is irrelevant. Thus when Gerd Theissen argues that Mark's Little Apocalypse (Mark 13) and Passion Narrative (Mark 14–15) can be dated to the late 30s or early 40s, he is nevertheless still able to locate the production of Mark's Gospel in the early 70s, so distinguishing clearly between the date of the literary work and the history of its constituent elements.[25]

James Crossley's *Date of Mark's Gospel*[26] provides a case in point. Crossley argues against the consensus that Mark should be dated somewhere in the region 65–75 CE, suggesting instead that Mark's knowledge of Jewish law, and the assumptions he makes about it, make best sense at a very early point, as early as the mid- to late 30s or early 40s. One of the book's virtues is that it effectively strengthens the case for a law-observant historical Jesus,

---

24. The most important word here is "substantive." It is right to stress the fluidity of the boundaries to a given literary work, but it is easy also to use this as an excuse to refrain from serious discussion about the dating of that literary work as a substantive entity. It is worth asking, for example, whether DeConick's hypothetical "Kernel Gospel" is any more the *Gospel of Thomas* than Matthew's Gospel is Mark's Gospel.

25. Gerd Theissen, *The Gospels in Context: Social and Political History in the Synoptic Tradition* (Minneapolis: Fortress, 1991), 125-65 and 166-200.

26. James G. Crossley, *The Date of Mark's Gospel: Insight from the Law in Earliest Christianity* (JSNTSup 266; London: T & T Clark International, 2004).

and Crossley's arguments to that end are effective. The book is less persuasive, though, in closing the gap that is usually theorized between Jesus in the early 30s and Mark in the late 60s or early 70s.[27] The notion that the originating circumstances of the tradition correlate directly with the perspective of the evangelist is problematic. It may be that Mark is sometimes a faithful retailer of traditional material.[28] It is always going to be a tall order to demonstrate that assumptions apparently made in given traditions are identical with assumptions made by the author of the work in which they appear.

Moreover, where there are clear signs of Markan redaction, they point away from Crossley's thesis. In the key passage about hand washing in Mark 7, the narrator's framing of the material explains that hand washing before eating food is something practiced by "the Pharisees *and all the Jews*" (καὶ πάντες οἱ Ἰουδαῖοι). This does not set up the debate as an intra-Jewish one of the kind that Crossley's thesis requires. The practice of hand washing is established as something that "all the Jews" do, and which Jesus' disciples do not do (7:2, 5), setting up a contrast that Jesus' words then speak into, a contrast that makes good sense on the standard grounds that Mark is addressing later Christian concerns. For Crossley, the reference here to "all the Jews" is a Markan exaggeration,[29] but this concedes the ground about the accuracy and precision of Mark's knowledge of Judaism that is a major and necessary element in his case.[30]

27. Cf. David Gowler's review of Crossley's subsequent *Why Christianity Happened* in *CBQ* 69 (2007): 815-16 (816), "Jesus' Torah observance could still have been adequately represented by Mark in the 60s."

28. Cf. Charles Talbert's review in *Perspectives in Religious Studies* 33/4 (2006): 524-27 (527), "This is a provocative thesis. Its arguments, however, are a house of cards, exegetically and logically. If Jesus is portrayed as a Torah-observant Jew in the Synoptics, it is debatable that Matthew and Luke reflect early church controversies in their support of such a view. It may be simpler to say that Jesus is so portrayed because that was the church's memory of him. Such a portrayal, in discontinuity with early church controversies, argues for the historicity of the depiction." See David Instone Brewer's review in *JTS* 57/2 (2006): 647-50, for a similar critique, though Instone Brewer is attracted by Crossley's "startling exegesis" of Mark 7:19.

29. Crossley, *Date*, 184-85. Crossley refers to a similar exaggeration in *Letter of Aristeas* 305-6, but this does not help his case given that the author of *Aristeas* is assuming the persona of a Gentile, affecting an outsider perspective to make his point.

30. There is a further difficulty with Crossley's attempts to date the Gospel early — his assumption that Gentile Christians in the early period were observing biblical laws (*Date*, chapter 5). Paula Fredriksen, in an article not discussed by Crossley, argues persuasively that in the early period it was assumed that Gentiles were included in the people of God without the necessity for conversion to Judaism. The idea of circumcising Gentiles was an innovation

If Crossley's effort to rethink the dating of Mark is unsuccessful, it is nevertheless worth asking how secure the standard dating is. Since 2003 four studies have reinforced the grounds for locating Mark in the aftermath of 70.[31] Although these four disagree with one another on the details (e.g., the precise referent of Mark 13:14),[32] all agree on the significance of Mark 13:1-2, "Do you see these great buildings? Not one stone will be left upon another which will not be torn down." For many, so blatant a prediction of the destruction of the temple in Jerusalem settles the question of Mark's date — it is written in full knowledge of the disastrous events of 70. For Kloppenborg, "The fact that this seems to correspond so precisely to what occurred invites the conclusion that it was formulated (or reformulated) *ex eventu*."[33] For Roskam, "the evangelist could not have presented the prediction of the destruction of the temple as an utterance of Jesus with such firmness unless he was very certain about its fulfilment."[34] Objections to this view are ably discussed by Incigneri,[35] who stresses Mark's "over-arching concentration on the Temple,"[36] the destruction of which is so important in his narrative that it is implausible to imagine that it was still standing when Mark wrote.[37]

One of the standard arguments against the idea that Mark shows knowledge of the destruction of Jerusalem is the reassertion of the text's

---

in some parts of the emerging Christian movement, in Antioch, Jerusalem, and Galatia. See "Judaism, the Circumcision of Gentiles and Apocalyptic Hope: Another Look at Galatians 1 and 2," *JTS* 42 (1991): 532-64. Crossley's assumption that avoidance of biblical law was introduced later, and that it involved a change of policy for Paul, is unnecessary.

31. Brian J. Incigneri, *The Gospel to the Romans: The Setting and Rhetoric of Mark's Gospel* (Biblical Interpretation Series 65; Leiden: Brill, 2003); H. N. Roskam, *The Purpose of the Gospel of Mark in Its Historical and Social Context* (NovTSup 114; Leiden: Brill, 2004); Adam Winn, *The Purpose of Mark's Gospel: An Early Response to Roman Imperial Propaganda* (WUNT 245; Tübingen: Mohr Siebeck, 2008); and John S. Kloppenborg, "Evocatio Deorum and the Date of Mark," *JBL* 124/3 (2005): 419-50. Incigneri, Roskam, and Kloppenborg are written independently of one another, and independently of Crossley.

32. Roskam follows Lührmann in seeing a reference to the Roman general or his army (*Purpose*, 90-91); Incigneri is certain that Titus is in view (*Gospel*, 130-33).

33. Kloppenborg, "Evocatio deorum," 431. The key text is Josephus, *J.W.* 7, especially 7.1-4.

34. Roskam, *Purpose*, 86.

35. Incigneri, *Gospel*, chapter 3, "No Stone upon Another," is a detailed and persuasive argument in favor of a post-70 date for Mark.

36. Ibid., 154.

37. For the centrality of the temple theme in Mark, see further Thomas R. Hatina, "The Focus of Mark 13:24-27 — The Parousia, or the Destruction of the Temple?" *BBR* 6 (1996): 43-66.

own character here as prediction. In his *Introduction to the New Testament*, for example, David A. DeSilva suggests, "The primary reason many scholars tend to date Mark's Gospel after 70 CE is the presupposition that Jesus could not foresee the destruction of Jerusalem — an ideological conviction clearly not shared by all."[38] But this kind of appeal, while popular, tends not to take seriously the literary function of predictions in narrative texts like Mark.[39] Successful predictions play a major role in the narrative, reinforcing the authority of the one making the prediction and confirming the accuracy of the text's theological view.[40] It is like reading Jeremiah. It works because the reader knows that the prophecies of doom turned out to be correct. It is about *when prophecy succeeds.*

The text makes sense as Mark's attempt to signal, in a post-70 context, that the event familiar to his readers was anticipated by Jesus, in word (13:2, 14) and deed (11:12-21) and in the symbolism of his death, when the veil of the temple was torn in two (15:38). The framing of the narrative requires knowledge of the destruction of the temple for its literary impact to be felt. It is a perspective that is underlined by the first of the taunts leveled when Jesus is crucified, "So! You who are going to destroy the temple and build it in three days, come down from the cross and save yourself!" (15:29-30).[41] For the irony to work, the reader has to understand that the temple has been destroyed;[42] the mockers look foolish from the privileged perspective of the post-70 reader, who now sees that Jesus' death is the moment when the temple was proleptically destroyed, the Deity departing as the curtain

38. David A. DeSilva, *An Introduction to the New Testament* (Downers Grove, IL: InterVarsity Press, 2004), 196. Similarly Donald Guthrie, *New Testament Introduction* (Downers Grove, IL: InterVarsity Press, 1971), 54, and often elsewhere.

39. Cf. Kloppenborg, *"Evocatio deorum,"* who stresses the role played by the literary motif of *evocation deorum* echoed here in Mark, e.g., 446, "This raises a crucial distinction between omens and rituals that (allegedly) occurred before the events, and their literary and historiographic use in narrative."

40. Cf. Winn, *Purpose of Mark's Gospel*, 57-58.

41. I am grateful to Ken Olson for alerting me to the importance of this text in a paper, "You who would destroy this temple," presented at the British New Testament Conference Synoptics Seminar in September 2005. Olson points out that the other taunts on the cross are presumed true: Jesus saved others (15:31), he is the Christ, the king of Israel (15:32), the Son of God (15:39).

42. Cf. Incigneri, *Gospel*, 152-53, "Ironically, it is true: he *is* in the process of destroying it and building a new one, commencing with his willingness to die so that all will hear the gospel. As the readers know that the new temple, the Church, had already been built, for the irony of 15.29 to work fully, the Temple, too, must already have been destroyed." Cf. Donald H. Juel, *A Master of Surprise: Mark Interpreted* (Minneapolis: Fortress, 1994), 82.

is torn, the event of destruction interpreted through Gospel narrative and prophecy.

Dating of Subsequent Gospels

If Mark is written after 70, and if Matthew, Luke, and *Thomas* all postdate Mark, it is worth asking whether indications in Matthew, Luke, and *Thomas* correlate with this picture. For J. A. T. Robinson, it was the lack of reference to 70 anywhere in the New Testament that proved decisive in his attempts at redating:

> the single most datable . . . event of the period — the fall of Jerusalem in AD 70, and with it the collapse of institutional Judaism based on the temple — is never once mentioned as a past fact. It is, of course, predicted; and these predictions are, in some cases at least, assumed to be written (or written up) after the event. But the silence is nevertheless as significant as the silence for Sherlock Holmes of the dog that did not bark.[43]

The claim is unimpressive, though, given that most of the literary works in question are either written in the pre-70 period (Paul's Letters) or set in the pre-70 period (Gospels and Acts). What is remarkable is that literary works set a generation before 70 appear to speak so clearly about the destruction of the temple. For Robinson, "That Jesus could have predicted the doom of Jerusalem and its sanctuary is no more inherently improbable than that another Jesus, the son of Ananias, should have done so in the autumn of 62."[44] The problem for this perspective is that Jesus ben Ananias's prophecy occurs in a literary work that postdates 70, Josephus's *Jewish War*. As with Mark, it is important to ask the question about the literary function of the prediction in the narrative, here in a work that climaxes with the story of Jerusalem's destruction.[45]

Indeed, a comparison between Jesus ben Ananias in Josephus and Je-

---

43. John A. T. Robinson, *Redating the New Testament* (London: SCM, 1976), 13.

44. Ibid., 15.

45. Cf. C. A. Evans, "Predictions of the Destruction of the Herodian Temple in the Pseudepigrapha, Qumran Scrolls and Related Texts," *JSP* 10 (1992): 89-147, which attempts "to determine as precisely as possible the significance of Jesus' prophecy and the way it would have been understood by his contemporaries" (91) rather than to look at the literary function of predictions of the destruction of the temple in narratives like Mark.

sus of Nazareth in Matthew and Luke provides further striking parallels. The oracle Matt. 23:37-39 // Luke 13:34-35 has marked similarities with the oracle in *Jewish War* 6.300-301, the same threefold focus on the people, the city, the temple. Jesus ben Ananias cries "a voice against Jerusalem," and Jesus laments "Jerusalem, Jerusalem." Jesus ben Ananias singles out "the holy house," and Jesus says, "Behold, your house is forsaken." Jesus ben Ananias raises "a voice against this whole people," just as Jesus exclaims, "how often would I have gathered your children." Moreover, the same context in Josephus features a portent of voices being heard in the temple saying, "we are departing from hence" (μεταβαίνομεν ἐντεῦθεν, *J.W.* 6.299), similar to the implication here in Matthew and Luke that God has left the temple — "Behold your house is forsaken and desolate" (Matt. 23:38).[46] Such prophecies and portents function similarly in each of the texts and they point to a post-70 dating.

Finding references to the destruction of the temple in *Thomas* might be thought less likely. Given its genre (sayings gospel in which narratives about the temple are absent) and theological proclivity (the relative lack of so-called apocalyptic eschatology), one might not expect to see references in *Thomas* to the destruction of the temple. However, *Thom.* 71, "I shall destroy this house and no one will be able to rebuild it," does appear to be a reference to this event, in a saying that is reminiscent of Jesus' reported words in Matthew and Mark:[47]

Matt. 26:61	Mark 14:58	*Thom.* 71
Οὗτος ἔφη· Δύναμαι καταλῦσαι τὸν ναὸν τοῦ θεοῦ καὶ διὰ τριῶν ἡμερῶν οἰκοδομῆσαι.	Ἡμεῖς ἠκούσαμεν αὐτοῦ λέγοντος ὅτι Ἐγὼ καταλύσω τὸν ναὸν τοῦτον τὸν χειροποίητον καὶ διὰ τριῶν ἡμερῶν ἄλλον ἀχειροποίητον οἰκοδομήσω·	ΠΕΧΕ ΙⳠ ΧΕ ϯΝΑϢΟΡ[ϢῬ ΜΠΕΕ]ΙΗΕΙ ⲀΥⲰ ΜΝ̄ ⲖⲀⲀΥ ΝⲀϢΚΟΤϤ Ν̄[ⲤⲀΒ̄ⲖⲖⲀⲒ̈] . . .*

---

46. See further my *Case Against Q*, 23-28, in which I argue for the post-70 dating of Matthew and Luke. At that point, I had not seen how strong the case was for a post-70 Mark.

47. Cf. also John 2:19, which has the saying on Jesus' lips (as in *Thomas*).

Matt. 26:61	Mark 14:58	*Thom.* 71
"This man said, 'I am <u>able to</u> <u>destroy</u> the temple of God <u>and</u> to <u>build it</u> after three days.'"	"We heard him say, '<u>I will destroy this</u> temple made with hands <u>and</u> after three days, I will <u>build</u> another not made with hands.'"	Jesus says, "<u>I will destroy this</u> house, <u>and</u> no one will be <u>able</u> <u>to</u> <u>build</u> it [except me].ᵃ"

ᵃThe saying falls at the bottom of a damaged page. This reconstruction, ⲚⲤⲀⲂⲖⲖⲀⲒ ("except me") is due to Hans-Martin Schenke, "Bemerkungen zu #71 des Thomas-Evangeliums," *Enchoria: Zeitschrift für Demostistik und Koptologie* 27 (2001): 120-26; also followed by Plisch, *Gospel of Thomas*, 171. DeConick, *Original Gospel*, 226, mentions the damage also at the top left of the next page of the manuscript and notes, "This makes the reconstruction of the last portion of saying 71 and the last portion of 72 very difficult," but this should read ". . . the first portion of 72."

There are hints of the Synoptic saying in *Thomas*'s formulation, Mark's bold "I will destroy this temple" resembling *Thomas*'s "I will destroy this house," and Matthew's redactional reformulation with "I am able . . ." (δύναμαι . . .) perhaps leading to *Thomas*'s "no one will be able to build it" (ⲘⲚ ⲖⲀⲀⲨ ⲚⲀϢⲔⲞⲦϤ).[48] The matter of special interest in *Thomas*'s formulation is this latter clause, which hints at a date after Bar Kokhba's rebellion, placing *Thomas* after 135 CE. Now no one will be able to rebuild the temple.

This raises the question whether anything else might corroborate the hint. Is there anything else in *Thomas* that points to the post-135 period? *Thomas* 68 provides a strong clue that *Thomas* indeed postdates 135, in material that appears in a redactional addition to material paralleled in Matthew and Luke:

48. Bethge's Greek retroversion here is λέγει Ἰησοῦς· καταλύσω [τοῦτον τὸν] οἶκον καὶ οὐδεὶς δυνήσεται οἰκοδομῆσαι αὐτόν [πλὴν ἐμοῦ].

Matt. 5:10-11	Luke 6:22	*Thom.* 68
10 μακάριοι οἱ δεδιωγμένοι ἕνεκεν δικαιοσύνης, ὅτι αὐτῶν ἐστιν ἡ βασιλεία τῶν οὐρανῶν. 11 μακάριοί ἐστε ὅταν ὀνειδίσωσιν ὑμᾶς καὶ διώξωσιν καὶ εἴπωσιν πᾶν πονηρὸν καθ᾽ ὑμῶν ψευδόμενοι ἕνεκεν ἐμοῦ.	Μακάριοί ἐστε ὅταν μισήσωσιν ὑμᾶς οἱ ἄνθρωποι, καὶ ὅταν ἀφορίσωσιν ὑμᾶς καὶ ὀνειδίσωσιν καὶ ἐκβάλωσιν τὸ ὄνομα ὑμῶν ὡς πονηρὸν ἕνεκα τοῦ υἱοῦ τοῦ ἀνθρώπου.	ΠΕΧΕ ΙC ΧΕ ΝΤⲰΤΝ ϨΜΜΑΚΑΡΙΟC ϨΟΤΑΝ ΕⲨⲰΑΝΜΕCΤΕ ΤΗΥΤΝ ΝCΕΡΔΙⲰΚΕ ΜΜⲰΤΝ ΑΥⲰ CΕΝΑϨΕ ΑΝ ΕΤΟΠΟC ϨΜ ΠΜΑ ΕΝΤΑΥΔΙⲰΚΕ ΜΜⲰΤΝ ϨΡΑΪ ΝϨΗΤϤ᾽
10 Blessed are those who are persecuted for the sake of righteousness because theirs is the kingdom of the heavens. 11 Blessed are you when they insult and persecute you and speak falsely every evil against you for my sake.	Blessed are you when people hate you and ostracize you and cast out your name as evil for the sake of the Son of Man.	Jesus says, "Blessed are you when they hate you and persecute you. But they (themselves) will find no place at the place where they have persecuted you."

The first half of the saying closely parallels Matt. 5:10-11 and Luke 6:22, the eighth and fourth beatitudes in their respective lists.[49] *Thomas*'s formu-

---

49. Matt. 5:11 is sometimes called the ninth beatitude, but it is more clearly an explication and application of the eighth beatitude in 5:10, applying it directly ("Blessed are you . . .") to the audience, just as 6:14-15 ("For if you forgive others . . .") expounds and applies a key part of the Lord's Prayer (6:9-13). Luke 6:22 picks up Matt. 5:11 since it is congenial to his second person plural approach throughout his beatitudes and woes. For the beatitudes as deriving

lation has elements in common with both Matthew and Luke, from which it may derive.[50] The new, interpretive clause added in *Thomas* appears to reflect a post-135 date, as Hans-Martin Schenke suggests:

> This saying reads — according to the only possible understanding of the text as it is transmitted — "And they (i.e. your persecutors themselves) will not (any longer) find a (dwelling-)place there where they persecuted you." The reference here can only be to Palestine, or more especially, to Jerusalem. This threat of retaliation, as a *vaticinium ex eventu*, shares in principle the same perspectival voice as Thomas 71, except that it no longer points to the destruction of the temple that took place in the year 70 C.E., but indeed to the banishment of the Jews from Jerusalem after the year 135 C.E., at the end of the Bar Kochba rebellion.[51]

The dating of this saying to the post–Bar Kochba period is, of course, a strong indicator of the date of the *Gospel of Thomas*. Plisch sees the force of Schenke's case and agrees that the saying points to a date after 135. He suggests, however, that the second clause "found its way into the *Gospel of Thomas* as a commenting gloss."[52] It is true that the clause has the character of a "commenting gloss" or "an interpretative clause,"[53] but given the coherence of *Thom.* 68 with *Thom.* 71, the "commenting gloss" is more likely the author's comment on the (known) Synoptic parallels than a later scribe's comment on a (hypothetical) earlier version of the text. Where our textual base is thin, as it is with the *Gospel of Thomas*, it is always worth considering conjectures about scribal additions and textual accretions; but in the case of *Thom.* 68, the basis for the conjecture is weak, and the evidence it provides for a date in the post–135 period should be taken seriously.

---

from Q, see C. M. Tuckett, "The *Beatitudes*: A Source-Critical Study," with a reply by M. D. Goulder, *NovT* 25 (1983): 193-216.

50. Bethge's and Greeven's retroversions are identical: λέγει Ἰησοῦς· μακάριοί ἐστε ὅταν μισήσωσιν ὑμᾶς καὶ διώξωσιν ὑμᾶς, and they are especially close to Luke, with a five-word verbatim agreement. DeConick, *Original Gospel*, 220, is not persuaded that *Thomas* is here familiar with the Synoptics (though her "Luke 5.22" should read "Luke 6.22"). Patterson, *Gospel of Thomas*, 51-53, treats *Thom.* 68-69 together and argues for independence from the Synoptics.

51. Schenke, "On the Compositional History," 28.

52. Plisch, *Gospel of Thomas*, 166.

53. DeConick, *Original Gospel*, 222. For her, the first clause is a "kernel" saying (219-20), like almost all the Synoptic parallels, and the second sentence is an "accretion" (221-22), like almost all of the non-Synoptic material. DeConick is not, however, persuaded of the post–135 date (222).

Conclusion

It is important, at the end of the chapter as at the beginning, to remember that the dating of literary works is precarious, and that the issue is complicated by questions about texts, traditions, and successive editions. Even in the case of a once-lost work like *Thomas*, we are dealing with a living literary work that changed. But the fact that *Thomas*, like other works from antiquity, was not a rigidly fixed text should not tempt us into sidestepping the telltale signs of when the work was written. The dating of the *Gospel of Thomas* to the 140s makes good sense of a book that witnesses to the destruction of the temple (*Thom.* 71) and apparently presupposes the Bar Kokhba revolt (*Thom.* 68), indications that cohere with the work's familiarity with the Synoptic Gospels, all of which themselves appear to postdate 70. But if *Thomas* is a product of the mid-second century, written by an author who was familiar with the Synoptic Gospels, this raises a fascinating question: Why did *Thomas* use the Synoptics?

CHAPTER 10

Secrecy, Authority, and Legitimation: How and Why *Thomas* Used the Synoptics

I have argued in this book that the author of the *Gospel of Thomas* was familiar with the Synoptic Gospels and that he shows his knowledge of them in his composition. If a date in the 140s makes best sense of the evidence, it is worth asking how and why *Thomas* used the Synoptics. After all, it is by no means a given that early Christian sayings collections should feature extensive parallels to the Synoptic Gospels. *Thomas's* multiple cases of Synoptic sayings contrasts with works like the *Gospel of Mary* and the *Dialogue of the Savior*, which are relatively poor in such material. In this final chapter, I suggest that *Thomas's* use of the Synoptics is an authenticating device, a means by which the author can charge his newer, stranger material with an authenticity it derives by association with older, more familiar material. It is no accident, in other words, that *Thomas* interlaces Synoptic and non-Synoptic material, two or three sayings at a time, always keeping the sound of the Synoptic Jesus close at hand while interweaving sayings from *Thomas's* enigmatic, secret Jesus.

One of the difficulties, though, with some scholarship on the *Gospel of Thomas* is the extent of the influence from form criticism.[1] Redaction criticism has still not made the kind of impact on *Thomas* that it has in studies of the Synoptic Gospels. The treatment of *Thomas* as a mine rather than as a literary artifact can discourage us from spending time trying to appreciate the book as a whole, and attempting to hear its distinctive voice. It is easy to understand the temptation. The desire to find more material on the his-

---

1. See above, 145-50 and elsewhere.

torical Jesus and the first generations of the Christian movement has led us into the temptation to treat the writer of *Thomas* as an archivist rather than an author, and to see our task as one that involves sifting, categorizing, and dating the materials we find, discovering kernels, cores, and other kinds of traditional material. A redaction-critical approach would spend less time mining and more time looking for the voice of the redactor, attempting to understand the key moments in the work, the repeated emphases, and the molding of the source material.

The warnings were already seen by some of the early investigators of *Thomas*, but they have not always been heeded.[2] Grant and Freedman here had some insight into the new discovery at a time when redaction criticism was just beginning to break onto the scene.[3] They saw that the interpreter should begin by taking seriously the Incipit of the book:

> In form, the sayings contained in the Gospel of Thomas fulfill the expectations which a reader would derive from the Preface to the book. Since they are words spoken by "Jesus the Living," the reader would expect to find that they resembled what is to be found in the Church's gospels. Since they are secret words, he would expect most of them to be at least slightly different from what was known publicly. And, since a blessing is given to him "who will find the interpretation of these words," the reader would expect to find many of them mysterious, or at least set in a new context which makes understanding difficult. All these features are to be found in the sayings and in their arrangement.[4]

Although the quotation appears a little dated because of the gender-exclusive language and the references to "the Church's gospels," it is nevertheless a prescient overview of *Thomas*. Like a lot of early scholarship on *Thomas*, it is more forgotten than refuted. Certain viewpoints that now appear a little naïve, alongside a now unfashionable emphasis on *Thomas*'s Gnostic character, all too easily provide excuses for scholars to ignore those like Grant and Freedman. In several respects, however, they show an appreciation of what *Thomas* is about, how it understands itself and how it

---

2. Cf. Grant and Freedman, *Secret Sayings*, 103: "To analyze the Gospel of Thomas on the basis of the literary forms it employs, however, does not do us much good."

3. Grant and Freedman's *Secret Sayings* was published in 1960, the same year that Hans Conzelmann's seminal redaction-critical work, *The Theology of St Luke* (London: Faber & Faber, 1960), was translated into English.

4. Grant and Freedman, *Secret Sayings*, 102.

was formed, not least because they knew the importance of beginning in the right place, for it is a good idea to begin, as the King advised the White Rabbit, at the beginning.

Thomas's Literary Conceit

These are the secret sayings that the living Jesus spoke and that Didymos Judas Thomas wrote down. And he said, "Whoever finds the interpretation of these sayings will not taste death."

(Incipit; Saying 1)

It might sound trite to suggest that the best way to understand the nature of *Thomas* is to take its opening seriously, and yet some have ignored certain signals in the Incipit and first saying. One of these, the importance of the author as scribe, who establishes the genre and outlook of the book as a collection of "secret sayings," is routinely overlooked in favor of a romanticized notion of an oral mind and an oral culture. If *Thomas's* oral nature is a consequence of his generic preference rather than his social location (chapter 8, above), the book requires a conceit like the one chosen by *Thomas*: Jesus speaks and Didymos Judas Thomas writes.

For the literary conceit to work effectively, the *Gospel of Thomas* uses the technique of authorial self-representation, itself a clear indication of the lateness of *Thomas* in comparison with the Synoptic Gospels.[5] The Synoptic Gospels are anonymous and avoid attempting to project an authorial presence to lend authority to their work.[6] Only Luke among the Synoptics has a

---

5. Ismo Dunderberg, "*Thomas* and the Beloved Disciple," in Uro, ed., *Thomas at the Crossroads*, 65-88, especially 80-88, uses the term "authorial fiction," itself derived from John Kloppenborg, *The Formation of Q: Trajectories in Ancient Wisdom Collections* (Studies in Antiquity and Christianity; Philadelphia: Fortress, 1987), 263-316. I prefer the term "authorial self-representation" because it characterizes the process more precisely and less prejudicially, and uses terminology familiar in literary criticism.

6. Baum, "Anonymity," argues that the anonymity of the Gospels follows in the tradition of the anonymity of the history books of the Hebrew Bible, in contrast with the tendency for authors to be named in Greco-Roman texts contemporary with the Gospels. Baum's observations may shed some light on the discussion here, but he sees too sharp a division between the canonical Gospels and "the author of the Coptic Gospel of Thomas" (122). It is true that John is anonymous while *Thomas* is not, but both have similar degrees of authorial self-representation. Further, anonymity is not necessarily used because of the "priority of the subject matter" or the desire of the authors to remain invisible behind authoritative traditions, as

narrator who uses the first person (Luke 1:1-4; cf. the "we passages" in Acts), and even here the author himself remains anonymous. By contrast, *Thomas* has a bold declaration of authorship right at the beginning. There is some comparison here with John's Gospel, which in this respect is on the road to the kind of authorial self-representation that is explicit in *Thomas*. The author of the Fourth Gospel makes claims to have been present at the events he is narrating, at the cross in 19:35, and then as the author approaches the end of the book:

John 21:24: Οὗτός ἐστιν ὁ μαθητὴς ὁ μαρτυρῶν περὶ τούτων καὶ <u>ὁ γράψας ταῦτα</u>, καὶ οἴδαμεν ὅτι ἀληθὴς αὐτοῦ ἡ μαρτυρία ἐστίν.

This is the disciple who testifies to these things and <u>the one who wrote these things down</u>, and we know that his testimony is true.

This is similar in style and literary function to the Incipit of *Thomas*:

<u>οὗτοι</u> οἱ λόγοι οἱ ἀπόκρυφοι οὓς ἐλάλησεν Ἰησοῦς ὁ ζῶν καὶ <u>ἔγραψεν</u> Ἰούδας ὁ καὶ θωμᾶς

<u>These</u> are the secret sayings which the living Jesus spoke and which Judas who is also Thomas <u>wrote down</u>.

Both texts speak about "these things" or "these words" in a way that draws attention to the contents of the Gospel alongside a declaration of authorial witness to those words or deeds. In both, the authorial self-representation legitimizes the message of the book in a way absent from the earlier Gospels but found explicitly in later Christian works like the *Protevangelium of James* and the *Gospel of Peter*.[7] John's claim enables the author to establish his Gospel's authority — he knows that the things he reports are true because he was

---

Baum claims. Anonymity may have a marked rhetorical function, for example, the attempt to present a narrative as having an inevitable course with an inevitable goal, the unalterable result of divine activity in history.

7. *Protevangelium* 25.1, again with γράφω (write) and οὗτος (this), ἐγὼ δὲ Ἰάκωβος ὁ γράψας τὴν ἱστορίαν ταύτην . . . ("And I, James, the one who wrote this account . . ."); *Gospel of Peter* 60, "But I, Simon Peter, and my brother Andrew, took our nets and went off to the sea. . . ." Cf. Dunderberg, "*Thomas* and the Beloved Disciple," 88, commenting on John and *Thomas*, "The way authenticating figures are presented in these gospels connects them with Christian writings that are later than the earliest gospels, in which such ascriptions are still lacking. However, in these gospels authorial fiction has assumed less concrete forms than in some other early Christian writings. This indicates that they still stand at the threshold of the

there. In *Thomas* the same is true, but there is also a further step: not only was the author present but he was privy to secret teachings, teachings that provide the way to salvation (Incipit; cf. *Thom.* 13).

The importance of secrecy in *Thomas* should not be played down. It is a casualty of the many discussions about whether *Thomas* is Gnostic, according to which we ask about the applicability of an external label,[8] that we pay too little attention to the work's self-description as a "secret" book. *Thomas* is an apocryphal gospel. It is proud to conceptualize itself in this way, as presenting "the secret words" or "the hidden words" (οἱ λόγοι οἱ ἀπόκρυφοι)[9] that the living Jesus spoke. This is not to use the term "apocryphal" in the disparaging and marginalized sense of orthodox Christians looking at works of which they disapprove. Rather, it is to underline the way that the work wishes to be characterized, as owning a label that provides the key for the proper understanding.

There is, in other words, a trajectory among these early Christian texts, from the absence of authorial self-representation in Mark and Matthew, to hints in Luke and Acts (with the first person found in Luke 1:1-4 as well as in the "we" passages in Acts), to the marked but nevertheless still unnamed authorial presence in John, to the explicit self-representation of Didymos Judas Thomas in *Thomas*'s Incipit, a naming that also leads the reader to pay special attention to *Thom.* 13.

A similar literary conceit is common in second- and third-century Christian works. It is fundamental to the attempt to claim apostolic authority for an unusual text, and to lend legitimacy to works that are properly called apocryphal. The pretense of the apostolic scribe being present in Jesus' lifetime, hearing his sayings and writing them down, proved a powerful way of claiming authority and legitimation. An elaborate version of this maneuver is found in the *Apocryphon of James* (1.8–2.19):

---

development which gradually led to increasingly concrete ways of authenticating pseudepigraphical writings in early Christianity."

8. Although see *Thom.* 3.5-6, "When you come to know (γνῷ) yourselves, then you will be known (γνώσεσθαι), and you will realize that you are children of the living Father. But if you do not come to know (γνώσεσθε) yourselves, then you exist in poverty and you are poverty." See also below, 181-82. The point about *Thomas* as apocryphal, however, is that ἀπόκρυφοι is a descriptor that characterizes the sayings as announced in the Incipit.

9. The word ἀπόκρυφοι has to be reconstructed here in P.Oxy. 654, but it is practically certain that this is what stood behind Coptic ⲈⲐⲎⲠ (erroneously transcribed as ⲈⲐⲎⲦ in DeConick, *Original Gospel*, 44) since it fits the space comfortably and coheres with the apparent purpose of the Gospel. ϨⲰⲠ, ϨⲎⲠ, ϨⲞⲠ- (to be hidden) is among *Thomas*'s favorite vocabulary: here, 5, 6, 32, 33, 39, 83, 96, 108, 109.

Since you asked that I send you a secret book which was revealed to me and Peter by the Lord, I could not turn you away or gainsay (?) you; but I have written it in the Hebrew alphabet and sent it to you and you alone. But since you are a minister of the salvation of the saints, endeavor earnestly and take care not to rehearse this text to many — this that the Savior did not wish to tell to all of us, his twelve disciples. But blessed will they be who will be saved through the faith of this discourse.

I also sent you, ten months ago, another secret book which the Savior had revealed to me. Under the circumstances, however, regard that one as revealed to me, James; but this one. . . .

. . . the twelve disciples [were] all sitting together and recalling what the Savior had said to each one of them, whether in secret or openly, and [putting it] in books. [But I] was writing that which was in [my book] — lo, the Savior appeared, [after] departing from [us while we] gazed after him.[10]

It is in some respects the fruition of a growing consciousness of predecessor works, from the πολλοί (many) of Luke's preface (Luke 1:1), to the many other books that could fill the world in the last verse of John (John 21:25), now to the explicit claim that there were multiple books about Jesus. The author acknowledges the existence of other gospels, written by apostles, some public and some not, but makes a claim to special, secret revelation, hidden even from other disciples, and it is a revelation that brings salvation. These are themes that are present also in *Thomas*, and they are given prominence, first here at the beginning of the book and then, with further reflection, in *Thom.* 13:[11]

Jesus said to his disciples, "Compare me to someone and tell me whom I am like." Simon Peter said to him, "You are like a righteous angel." Mat-

---

10. Translation by Francis E. Williams in James M. Robinson, ed., *The Nag Hammadi Library in English* (San Francisco: HarperCollins, 1990), 29-37 (30). For a discussion of the *Apocryphon of James*, see Ron Cameron, *Sayings Traditions in the Apocryphon of James* (HTS 34; Philadelphia: Fortress 1984). For a useful introduction, see Koester, *Ancient Christian Gospels*, 187-200.

11. See similarly *Book of Thomas the Contender* 138, "The hidden sayings that the Savior spoke to Judas Thomas, which I, Matthaias, in turn recorded. I was walking, listening to them speak with each other" (trans. Marvin Meyer, in Marvin Meyer, ed., *The Nag Hammadi Scriptures* [New York: HarperCollins, 2007], 239).

thew said to him, "You are like a wise philosopher." Thomas said to him, "Master, my mouth is wholly incapable of saying whom you are like." Jesus said, "I am not your master. Because you have drunk, you have become intoxicated by the bubbling spring that I have measured out." And he took him and withdrew and told him three things. When Thomas returned to his companions, they asked him, "What did Jesus say to you?" Thomas said to them, "If I tell you one of the things that he told me, you will pick up stones and throw them at me; a fire will come out of the stones and burn you up."

This revealing exchange should be taken seriously. Its importance is sometimes played down, not least because there is no chance that the exchange is authentic, and *Thomas* research can be so interested in the historical Jesus and early Christian tradition that it damages our ability to appreciate the book on its own terms. The Incipit, which announces this book as "the secret sayings of the living Jesus, which Didymos Judas Thomas wrote down," introduces Thomas and warns the reader to pay special attention to any future appearance of the character. So when Thomas reappears, in *Thom.* 13, the reader should be ready to read and the hearer ready to listen. This is how the *Gospel of Thomas* flags the importance of what is said here, and a redaction-critical approach to the book alerts us to its importance.

As well as legitimizing the role of *Thomas*'s alleged author, the exchange cleverly situates the book over against Christian Gospels that are already becoming authoritative by virtue of their popularity and greater antiquity.[12] The singling out of Peter may be because of his connection with Mark's Gospel, already witnessed in this period in Papias,[13] and the mention of

12. See Francis Watson, "The Fourfold Gospel," in Stephen C. Barton, ed., *The Cambridge Companion to the Gospels* (Cambridge: Cambridge University Press, 2000), 34-52 (37-39); and Perrin, *Thomas: The Other Gospel*, 107-24. Cf. Larry W. Hurtado, *Lord Jesus Christ: Devotion to Jesus in Earliest Christianity* (Grand Rapids: Eerdmans, 2003), 462, "Whereas the Synoptic scenes all reflect the familiar early Christian advocacy of Jesus' messianic status over against inadequate estimates from outside the circle of faith, *Gos. Thom.* 13 clearly represents an intramural effort to ridicule the christological beliefs of other Christian circles in favor of another religious outlook that is cryptically presented in *Gos. Thom.* This secret view of Jesus accounts for the absence of familiar christological titles in *Gos. Thom.*" Cf. Valantasis, *Gospel of Thomas*, 78, "The real subject of this narrative sequence does not revolve about Jesus' identity, but Thomas' authority as a spiritual guide and revealer."

13. Eusebius, *HE* 3.39.14-15. The point is only that Peter is already associated with Mark's Gospel in this period, the early to middle second century, when *Thomas* was written (above, chapter 9), with no prejudice to questions of the historical origin of Mark's Gospel.

Matthew may also be because of the Gospel now bearing his name, his main claim to fame in early Christianity.[14] It is not these disciples but Thomas who has it right, in an exchange that encourages the initiate to go beyond the public writings in those other Gospels, and to trump them with its own private revelation.[15]

It would be well nigh impossible for the author of *Thomas* to think of replacing the Synoptic Gospels at this point, and he does not try that. Instead, his best bet is to accept their existence but to attempt to transcend them by means of the fiction of special revelation and hidden sayings to a key figure, Judas Thomas the twin. The incident remains intriguing because of the forbidden "three words" spoken to Thomas, and while guessing at what is implied may be irresistible,[16] the point is, of course, that the reader of the Gospel cannot know what was said without extra revelation. It is here that the *Gospel of Thomas* points most clearly beyond itself to an interpreter who will unlock the secrets of the book. The book is constructed as a gateway text that invites the reader into a world that might sound like the world of early Christianity, but which has its own, private knowledge, to be revealed only to those here represented by the character of Thomas.[17]

---

14. Surprisingly, Patterson himself notes the possibility: "The rather pointed criticism of Matthew and Peter in *Thom.* 13 suggests that perhaps the author of this saying has in view the Gospel of Matthew and the particular form of Christianity associated with it"; see Patterson, et al., *Fifth Gospel*, 42. Compare Matthew's prominence in the *Dialogue of the Savior*.

15. That Luke and John are not represented in the exchange coheres with a dating for *Thomas* in the 140s (see above, chapter 9). At this point, these Gospels are a little newer on the scene in comparison with Mark and Matthew. Of course, it would be harder to find a way of plausibly representing Luke in this exchange, but featuring John would have been very straightforward.

16. The most intriguing suggestion remains that of Grant and Freedman, *Secret Sayings*, 134: "We conclude that the words are probably the secret words of the Naassenes: *Caulacau, Saulasau, Zeesar* (Isaiah 28:10; Hippolytus, *Ref.*, 5, 8, 5); according to the Basilidians, Jesus 'descended in the name Caulacau' (Irenaeus, *Adv. haer.*, 1, 24, 6). It is his secret Gnostic name which he is revealing to Thomas."

17. Lincoln, "Thomas-Gospel," 68-69, speaks of "a seeming paradox in the nature of *Thomas*," adding, "On the one hand, it proclaims itself to be secret, or to contain secrets, as in the Prologue . . . . But on the other hand, the text was widely circulated, and states that this is as it should be" (e.g., saying 33). Lincoln continues, "This contradiction, however, can be accounted for by recognizing that *Thomas*, like Ptolemaeus' *Letter to Flora* and numerous other religious documents, is a text that is addressed at the same time to initiates and non-initiates alike. Thus, the *fact* that the *Thomas*-community possessed secret knowledge was proclaimed loudly to outsiders, but the *nature* of that knowledge and its true meaning were disclosed only

The Authenticating Voice of the Synoptic Jesus

The use of Synoptic parallels in order to authenticate the sayings in the *Gospel of Thomas* provides a reason why *Thomas* uses the Synoptic Gospels so much (half of the book) and how it can have so much additional material too (half of the book). The Synoptic material legitimizes the strange new material, interweaving the familiar with the unique, so providing a new and quite different voice for Jesus that at the same time is plausible enough to sound authentic to *Thomas*'s earliest audiences.[18] The Synoptic sayings are, in other words, the necessary baggage that *Thomas* chooses to carry to make the voice of his newly constructed "living Jesus" sound sufficiently similar to the known voice of Jesus familiar to his audience.[19] They are there to evoke the authority of Jesus, with one foot in the tradition and one foot in the new Thomasine theology. It is a reinvention of the Synoptic Jesus, a redactional rewriting of his distinctive voice. The hearer thinks that this is Jesus because he talks like the Synoptic Jesus, at least half the time. It is just that this Jesus does not talk about the Son of Man or the future kingdom of God, and instead encourages followers to become solitary, to make the two one, and to cast off the things of bodily existence.

This theory has the further advantage of explaining why *Thomas* is apparently so reticent to employ Johannine sayings. If his reason for using Synoptic material is legitimation, extensive borrowing from John's Gospel may have been less effective. At a time when John is still battling for acceptance in some Christian circles, *Thomas*'s cause would not have been furthered by borrowing sayings that do not have the Synoptic ring. *Thomas* wants his Jesus to sound like the Jesus familiar to his audience, and the sayings from John are not going to help with that.

---

within the community itself in a program of detailed instruction which must have lasted over a period of several years."

18. The Fourth Gospel does something similar but uses a completely different technique. Rather than mixing his new sayings material with sayings taken over from the Synoptics, John inserts his new sayings material into a Synoptic-type narrative culminating in the passion and resurrection.

19. Cf. M. R. James, "The New Sayings of Christ," *Contemporary Review* 72 (July-December 1897): 153-60, already on the basis of P.Oxy. 1: "It is something in favour of the new sayings that they are found in company with the old. Something, not everything. The forger is well advised, it may be answered, who does not trust entirely to his own powers of invention, but uses some materials at least which he finds ready to his hand. On the other hand, if these *Logia* can be in any sense described as a forgery, they are a forgery of a class totally new to us" (157). On *Thomas* as an ancient forgery, see Ehrman, *Lost Christianities*, 47-66.

The way in which the Synoptic material is appropriated in order to generate authenticity is sometimes at the level of entire sayings or parables. The parables of the Sower (*Thom.* 9), the Mustard Seed (*Thom.* 20), and the Leaven (*Thom.* 96), for example, are taken over with only limited revisions. Similarly, the sayings about the Log and Speck (*Thom.* 26), the great harvest (*Thom.* 73), and foxes' holes (*Thom.* 86) are all repeated with only minor changes. In these cases, the Synoptic sayings function in the broader context as a means of allaying the impact of the striking new sayings, reorienting the reader who might otherwise suspect that *Thomas's* Jesus does not speak with the same authority as the more familiar Jesus of the Synoptic Gospels.

On other occasions, echoes of Synoptic sayings lend distinctive Thomasine sayings a veneer of authenticity, as in *Thom.* 106, where a drastically abbreviated version of the Synoptic Mountain saying (Matt. 17:20; Luke 17:6; Mark 11:23; Matt. 21:21; cf. 1 Cor. 13:2) is blended into typically Thomasine material about making the two one:

> Jesus says, "When you make the two one, you will become the sons of man, and when <u>you say, 'Mountain, move away,' it will move away.</u>"

Here the first half of the saying is typical Thomasine redaction, about the desirability of singularity and becoming one (*Thom.* 4, 11, 22, 23), but it is given an added, authenticating ring by being associated with the Synoptic saying about moving the mountain. In all of the Synoptic versions of the saying, "faith" (πίστις, πιστεύω) is the key;[20] but faith has no role to play in *Thomas's* theology, occurring only once (ΠΙϹΤΕΥΕ, *Thom.* 91), in one of the interlocutors' foils in need of correction by Jesus, in another passage that uses Synoptic imagery in the service of an adjusted theology:

> They said to him, "Tell us who you are so that we may believe (ΠΙϹΤΕΥΕ) in you." He said to them, "<u>You examine the face of the sky and the earth,</u> but the one who is before you, you have not known (ϹΟΥШΝ), and you do not know (ϹΟΟΥΝ) how to assess this opportunity."[21]

The metaphor is derived from the parallel in Matt. 16:2-3 // Luke 12:54-

---

20. *Thomas* 48 has a similar version of the same saying, again without the "faith" element found in the Synoptic parallels.

21. "Assess this opportunity" is Plisch's translation (*Gospel of Thomas*, 204).

56.[22] The interlocutors' language of faith in Jesus, so familiar from the New Testament and other early Christian works, is corrected by the preferred Thomasine language of "knowledge."[23] But the change is effected, as in *Thom.* 106, by borrowing memorable Synoptic imagery, there of the moving mountain and here of the examination of the sky and the earth. The imagery remains but the theology has changed.

There are other ways that the Synoptic material is used. Sometimes *Thomas* takes an entire Synoptic saying and simply adds a minor twist in order to make it reflect his distinctive theology, as with *Thom.* 16, for example, where the addition of the final clause turns a Synoptic saying about the devastation wrought by the eschaton into a comment on the ultimate aspiration of Thomasine solitary existence. It is one of the most lengthy and sustained parallels between *Thomas* and the Synoptics, yet the saying is transformed by the new clause:[24]

22. Plisch, *Gospel of Thomas*, 204, notes the similarity in literary structure between Luke and *Thomas*, though he contrasts Luke's δοκιμάζειν with the retroverted πειράζειν in *Thomas* and suggests "independent traditions." DeConick, *Original Gospel*, 260-61, suggests "an early multiform developed in the field of oral performance." She has δοκιμάξειν for δοκιμάζειν three times (260).

23. ⲤⲞⲞⲨⲚ ⲤⲞⲨⲰⲚ+ (know) occurs 25 times in *Thomas* in 20 sayings: *Thom.* 3 (3x), 5, 12, 16, 18, 19, 31, 46, 51, 56, 65 (2x), 67, 69, 78, 80, 91 (2x), 97, 103, 105, 109 (2x). The language here (in *Thom.* 91) picks up from γινώσκετε in Matt. 16:3 and οἴδατε in Luke 12:56, but the knowledge in *Thomas* is knowledge of Jesus and, typically, not of the eschaton, as in Matthew and Luke.

24. The saying is double tradition, Matt. 10:34-36 // Luke 12:51-53 but *Thomas*'s wording is closer to the Lukan version. If Goulder (*Luke*, 2:553-56) is right that Luke is here redacting Matthew, then *Thomas* is here showing familiarity with the Lukan redaction of Matthew. But Q theorists too incline toward reconstructing Q in line with Matthew here; see especially the IQP reconstruction (with Luke 12:52 not included in the critical text of Q) and note Tuckett's arguments for *Thomas*'s familiarity with Matthean and especially Lukan redaction of this saying, "Q and Thomas," 356-57; idem, "Thomas and the Synoptics," 146. Contrast Patterson, *Gospel of Thomas*, 25-26, who argues for *Thomas*'s independence; and DeConick, *Original Gospel*, 96, who appeals to "pre-synoptic oral variants."

Luke 12:51-53	*Thom.* 16
51 δοκεῖτε ὅτι εἰρήνην παρεγενόμην δοῦναι ἐν τῇ γῇ; οὐχί, λέγω ὑμῖν, ἀλλ' ἢ διαμερισμόν.	ΠΕΧΕ ΙC ΧΕ ΤΑΧΑ ΕΥΜΕΕΥΕ ΝϬΙ ῬῬϢΜΕ ΧΕ ΝΤΑΕΙΕΙ ΕΝΟΥΧΕ ΝΟΥΕΙΡΗΝΗ ΕΧΜ ΠΚΟCΜΟC ΑΥϢ CΕCΟΟΥΝ ΑΝ ΧΕ ΝΤΑΕΙΕΙ ΑΝΟΥΧΕ ΝϨΝΠϢΡΧ ΕΧΝ ΠΚΑϨ ΟΥΚϢϨΤ ΟΥCΗϤΕ ΟΥΠΟΛΕΜΟC.
52 ἔσονται γὰρ ἀπὸ τοῦ νῦν πέντε ἐν ἑνὶ οἴκῳ διαμεμερισμένοι, τρεῖς ἐπὶ δυσὶν καὶ δύο ἐπὶ τρισίν, 53 διαμερισθήσονται πατὴρ ἐπὶ υἱῷ καὶ υἱὸς ἐπὶ πατρί, μήτηρ ἐπὶ τὴν θυγατέρα καὶ θυγάτηρ ἐπὶ τὴν μητέρα, πενθερὰ ἐπὶ τὴν νύμφην αὐτῆς καὶ νύμφη ἐπὶ τὴν πενθεράν.	ΟΥΝ ϮΟΥ ΓΑΡ ΝΑϢϢ[ΠΕ] ϨΝ ΟΥΗΕΙ ΟΥΝ ϢΟΜΤ ΝΑϢϢΠΕ ΕΧΝ CΝΑΥ ΑΥϢ CΝΑΥ ΕΧΝ ϢΟΜΤ ΠΕΙϢΤ ΕΧΜ ΠϢΗΡΕ ΑΥϢ ΠϢΗΡΕ ΕΧΜ ΠΕΙϢΤ
	ΑΥϢ CΕΝΑϢϨΕ ΕΡΑΤΟΥ ΕΥΟ MΜΟΝΑΧΟC
51 Do you think that I have come to bring peace to the world? No, I tell you, but rather division!

52 From now on five in one household will be divided, three against two and two against three; 53 they will be divided: father against son and son against father, mother against daughter and daughter against mother, mother-in-law against her daughter-in-law and daughter-in-law against mother-in-law. | Jesus said, "People think, perhaps, that it is peace which I have come to cast upon the world. They do not know that it is division which I have come to cast upon the earth: fire, sword, and war. For there will be five in a house: three will be against two and two against three, the father against the son and the son against the father.

And they will stand as solitaries." |

Here the intrusion of the new, non-Synoptic Thomasine element at the end of the saying replaces the last part of the saying in Luke and renders it unintelligible. The math in Luke 12:52-53 is coherent.[25] There are five people in the house, a father and a mother, a married son and his wife, and a

25. Goulder, *Luke*, 1:104-5 and 2:554, notes Luke's preference for fives and tens; see my analysis in *Goulder and the Gospels*, 267-70.

daughter, so there can be "three against two and two against three." *Thomas* begins with five in the house, continues with "three against two and two against three," but then only gets as far as listing father and son, rendering all of the previous sentence pointless.[26] It is a typical act of Thomasine abbreviation of the kind that is now familiar,[27] but here the inconcinnity may result from the author's rush to get to a redactional addition that transforms the saying and gives it a new meaning.

Given *Thomas*'s disdain for "division,"[28] the saying might at first appear out of place,[29] but *Thomas* is attracted by the anti-familial potential of the saying, as elsewhere,[30] and to deliver the desired meaning he adds this clause, "And they will stand as solitaries," as typical a piece of Thomasine redaction as one could find, including the vocabulary ⲘⲞⲚⲀⲬⲞⲤ ("solitary"; cf. *Thom.* 49 and 75) and ⲰⲨⲈ ⲈⲢⲀⲦ⸗ ("stand," *Thom.* 18 [2x], 23 [2x], 28 [2x], 50 [2x], 75, and 99).[31]

Eschatology

One of the elements in these Thomasine transformations of Synoptic sayings is the adjustment of the eschatological viewpoint found there. Warnings of coming judgment and imminent apocalypse have little place in

26. Contrast Koester, *Ancient Christian Gospels*, 94, "Also missing in the *Gospel of Thomas* is the pedantic, and certainly secondary, enlargement of the family relationships at the end of Luke 12:53." It is not so much a matter of pedantry as coherence, but for Koester the term "secondary" is naturally found alongside "enlargement" because of the form-critical trajectory of simple to complex.

27. See above, especially Chapter 7.

28. Cf. Snodgrass, "Gospel of Thomas," 31, "*Thomas* has followed Luke in the redactional change from μάχαιραν (Matthew 10:34) to διαμερισμόν, which is a *hapax legomenon*." DeConick, *Original Gospel*, 94, misreads Snodgrass: "K. Snodgrass points out that διαμερισμός is a *hapax legomenon*, occurring in Luke six times and Acts twice." The word would not, of course, be a hapax if it occurred six times in Luke. Those figures are for the related verb διαμερίζειν (Snodgrass, "Gospel of Thomas," 31 n. 50).

29. Cf. *Thom.* 72, "I am not a divider, am I?"; and see above, 92.

30. See above (Chapter 6) on *Thom.* 79, for example.

31. DeConick, *Original Gospel*, 98-99, rightly notices the redactional nature of the new sentence, though she uses her standard language of "accretion." My suggestion, however, is that the Synoptic saying (her "kernel saying") was not a primary piece of tradition that naturally gained the new clause by "accrual" (99), but rather that the author selected the Synoptic saying in order to give his celebration of the one who stands solitary the sound of the authentic Synoptic Jesus.

Thomas, for whom salvation is found in interpreting the sayings of the living Jesus, knowing oneself and becoming a living spirit through singularity and the solitary existence that characterized Eden. The difficulty is, of course, that the Synoptic Gospels are so shot through with an apocalyptic eschatology that it is difficult fully to excise it even when engaging in drastic reappropriation of imagery and language.[32]

Thomas's distinctive take on eschatology is clear from *Thom.* 18:

> The disciples said to Jesus, "Tell us how our end will be." Jesus said, "Have you discovered, then, the beginning, that you look for the end? For where the beginning is, there will the end be. Blessed is he who will take his place in the beginning; he will know the end and will not taste death."

The saying provides the key to *Thomas*'s attitude to eschatology. As so often, the views of the disciples or other interlocutors represent views that require correction. The disciples are represented as focusing on the eschaton, just like the Synoptic Gospels and a lot of other early Christian literature, whereas *Thomas* wishes to stress instead "the beginning."[33] This is signature *Thomas* material, with the theme of not tasting death (ϥⲛⲁϫⲓ ϯⲡⲉ ⲁⲛ ⲙ̄ⲙⲟⲩ) returning after its introduction in *Thom.* 1.[34] The aspiration of the Thomasine Christian is to return to Eden, to the prefallen state, so that the corporeal existence and everything associated with it, like sex and clothing and eating corpses (*Thom.* 60), no longer obtains.

Thomas's clear redactional focus on protology rather than eschatology has a major effect on the author's selection of Synoptic material. There are, of course, no eschatological discourses here, like Mark 13, and the Synoptic parables have their apocalyptic edges shaved off. Where he repeats Synoptic references to the kingdom of God, he chooses those that are most conducive to his perspective and reconfigures them. Luke 17:20-21 is a particular favorite, and there are elements from the passage at both ends of the Gospel ("the kingdom of God is within you . . .," *Thom.* 3; "They will not say, 'Look, here!' or, 'Look there!' . . . ," *Thom.* 113).

---

32. See especially the residual apocalyptic of Matthew's Wheat and the Tares in *Thom.* 57 (above, 77-79).

33. See Stevan Davies, "The Christology and Protology of the Gospel of Thomas," *JBL* 111 (1992): 663-82; and Elaine Pagels, "Exegesis of Genesis 1 in the Gospels of Thomas and John," *JBL* 118 (1999): 477-96.

34. ϥⲛⲁϫⲓ ϯⲡⲉ ⲁⲛ ⲙ̄ⲙⲟⲩ. See also *Thom.* 19 and 85. The phrase is familiar from Matt. 16:28 // Mark 9:1 // Luke 9:27 and John 8:51-52, 58.

The shift in perspective between the Synoptics and *Thomas* is clear in relation to attitudes to death. Where Matthew and Mark speak about the future, natural death is scarcely ever in view. Instead, people are snatched away at the eschaton, or go to their judgment (e.g., Matt. 13:39-43, 49; 16:27; 19:27-30; 22:13; 24:29-31; 25:30, 31-46; Mark 13:26-27). The perspective begins to change, though, with Luke. Now natural deaths appear, notably on two occasions in the L parable material, the Rich Fool (Luke 12:13-21) and Dives and Lazarus (Luke 16:19-31), both of which feature rich men dying, and not at the end of the age. In the second of these example stories, the rest of the world continues on its ordinary way while Dives is in Hades and Lazarus is in Abraham's bosom. These other worlds coexist while Dives's brothers still have the chance to repent on earth.

Thomas, typically, is further along the same trajectory. Although there are references to violent death (e.g., *Thom.* 98), the references to natural death are more common than they are in the Synoptics:

> *Thomas* 59: Jesus said, "Take heed of the living one while you are alive, <u>lest you die</u> and seek to see him and be unable to do so."

Thomas 59 occurs in a cluster of material in which life and death is a key thread, from *Thom.* 58-61 and again in 63. Dying is the moment that prevents the hearer from taking heed of Jesus. Not surprisingly, the Rich Fool is one of the parables *Thomas* finds attractive — it nicely illustrates the perspective found in *Thom.* 59. Indeed, *Thomas*'s parallel to the Rich Fool (Luke 12:15-21 // *Thom.* 63) ends with the narration of the man's death ("that same night he died") rather than the death simply being implied in God's address, as in Luke.

Natural death is now a feature in the parable material, and *Thom.* 109 exhibits the same phenomenon:

> Jesus said, "The kingdom is like a man who had a hidden treasure in his field without knowing it. And <u>after he died</u>, he left it to his son. The son did not know (about the treasure). He inherited the field and sold it. And the one who bought it went ploughing and found the treasure. He began to lend money at interest to whomever he wished."

Perhaps the clearest example of the phenomenon occurs in *Thomas*'s version of the double tradition saying in Matt. 24:40-41 // Luke 17:34-35. *Thomas* is closest to Luke's version of the saying, but both Matthew and Luke speak of people being "taken" rather than dying:

Luke 17:34-35	*Thom.* 61
I tell you, in that night there will be two in one bed. One will be taken and the other left. There will be two women grinding together. One will be taken and the other left.	Jesus said, "Two will rest on a bed: <u>the one will die</u>, and the other will live."

Thomas comes from a time when natural deaths are finding their way into the representation of Jesus' teaching. It is a sign that *Thomas* belongs to a slightly later historical context, but it is also a sign of its author's need to rework the eschatological material that is so pervasive in the Synoptics.

For the author of the *Gospel of Thomas*, incorporating the Synoptic material into his very different work is not a straightforward task. It is not only the difference in genre but also the difference in perspective that will have made the task a challenging one. Where they speak about faith, *Thomas* wishes to speak about knowledge. Where they speak about the eschaton, *Thomas* wishes to speak about becoming solitary. It is not surprising that from time to time *Thomas* is tough to read. There is one area, however, where *Thomas's* incorporation of Synoptic material represents a particular challenge: the issue of the use of the Old Testament.

The Old Testament

Thomas's perspective on the Hebrew Scriptures differs radically from the perspective in the Synoptics. The distinctive, non-Synoptic elements in *Thomas* provide the clue to its perspective. As with eschatology, Jesus' response to one of the disciples' foil questions is instructive,[35] with the disciples again representing an expected viewpoint that requires refutation.

35. Cf. Milton Moreland, "The Twenty-Four Prophets of Israel Are Dead: Gospel of Thomas 52 as a Critique of Early Christian Hermeneutics," in Jon Ma. Asgeirsson, April D. DeConick, and Risto Uro, eds., *Thomasine Traditions in Antiquity: The Social and Cultural World of the Gospel of Thomas* (Leiden: Brill, 2006), 75-91 (77): "By framing the teachings of Jesus as cryptic retorts to the disciples' questions, Thomas stressed the imperatival teaching of Jesus, presenting Jesus as the true authority figure who clearly initiated and supported only the Thomasine community. For the true followers — the ones who could interpret the sayings (the Thomasine community) — the inquiring disciples' lack of understanding in the dialogues is directly proportionate to Jesus' knowledge (and thus the knowledge of those true followers who know 'what is in front of their face' [Gos. Thom. 5])."

Thomas 52 has the disciples expressing a view of the Old Testament that sounds like the view found in the canonical Gospels, Paul, Hebrews, and elsewhere, and Jesus' reply is unambiguously negative:

> His disciples said to him, "Twenty-four prophets spoke in Israel, and all of them spoke in you." He said to them, "You have omitted the one living in your presence and have spoken (only) of the dead."

This saying is signature *Thomas* material. The "Living One" (ⲡⲉⲧⲟⲛⲍ) is its favorite title for Jesus, signaled in the Incipit and again in sayings 59 and 111, where it occurs, as here, in contrast with "death" and "the dead." The disciples' foil statement is corrected by a single statement from Jesus in the distinctive Thomasine fashion (cf. *Thom.* 6, 12, 18, 20, 24, 37, 43, 51, 53, 99, 113). The "twenty-four prophets" must refer to the twenty-four books of the Hebrew Scriptures, a number first attested in *4 Ezra* 14.45.[36] There is a straightforward disdain here for the Scriptures. Jesus is the "Living One"; the prophets of the Old Testament are "the dead."

The saying is in striking contrast to the pervasive, unremitting patterns, allusions, and quotations of the Old Testament in the Synoptic Gospels. The contrast here between *Thomas* and the Synoptics should not be ignored or played down.[37] It is the only place where *Thomas* speaks of ⲓⲥⲣⲁⲏⲗ (Israel), and her prophets are not celebrated. Far from calling the heroes of Hebrew Scripture "the dead," the Synoptic Jesus corrects the Sadducees' mistaken view of the resurrection by reconfiguring "the God of Abraham, Isaac, and

---

36. *Thomas* 52 has further links with *4 Ezra* 14.44-47, the earliest extant witness to Old Testament books numbering "twenty four," in particular the self-conscious appeal to special, private revelation to be found outside the public books. I am grateful to Stephen Carlson, "Thomas and the Twenty-Four Prophets," Hypotyposeis blog, http://www.hypotyposeis.org/weblog/2007/05/thomas-and-twenty-four-prophets.html (30 May 2007), for this point. See Plisch, *Gospel of Thomas*, 133, for the oddity of the number twenty-four here with "prophets." For more on the number twenty-four here, see Baarda, "Thomas and the Old Testament," 11-12.

37. Funk and Hoover's remark (*Five Gospels*, 503), "The saying appears to reflect a time when Christianity was no longer a Judean sect, but had become largely gentile," drastically underestimates the character of a saying that severs the living Jesus from the Old Testament. DeConick, *Original Gospel*, 185, suggests: "The disciples are rebuked for thinking that the prophets bore witness to Jesus, when, in fact, Jesus, the Living God, is the one whose testimony must be heard and heeded," and she compares John 5:36-40, "this tradition . . . in a nascent form." But John affirms what *Thomas* does not affirm, that "the scriptures . . . bear witness to me" (John 5:39). Augustine, *Contra adversarium Legis et Prophetarum* 2.4.14, witnesses to the saying; but, in contrasting it with Luke 24:27, illustrates that he did not think it so innocuous.

Jacob" as "God of the living and not the dead" (Matt. 22:32 // Mark 12:27 // Luke 20:38). It is important here to listen to *Thomas's* distinctive voice and to avoid harmonizing his views with those of the Synoptic (and other early Christian) authors. The book's radical stance on the Old Testament is explicit in saying 52, and it is not contradicted by anything elsewhere in *Thomas*.[38]

Since the author of *Thomas* shows disdain for the Old Testament in the unique material, it is not surprising that his selection and redaction of Synoptic material appears to reflect the same attitude. Scripture fulfillment themes are entirely absent from *Thomas*.[39] There is not a single occasion when *Thomas* self-consciously draws attention to an explicit Old Testament quotation. Where Old Testament texts appear in *Thomas*, they are apparently mediated through the Synoptics and there is no independent access to them.[40] *Thomas* 21.10, "When the grain ripened, he came quickly with his sickle in his hand and reaped it," is reminiscent of Joel 3:13 (4:13 LXX), "Put in the sickle, for the harvest is ripe!" but it appears to have been mediated to *Thomas* through Mark 4:29, "Immediately he puts in the sickle because the harvest has come,"[41] which is closer to Joel than *Thomas* is.[42]

The same pattern recurs elsewhere in *Thomas*. His version of the Mus-

38. *Thomas's* only reference to an Old Testament character is Adam (sayings 46 and 85), which coheres with *Thomas's* interest in a restored Eden. *Thomas* 46, a version of Matt. 11:11 // Luke 7:28, is typical of *Thomas's* redaction of the Synoptics, eliminating all references found in those contexts to prophecy and prophets (Matt. 11:9-10, 13-14; Luke 7:26-27). In *Thomas*, "From Adam to John the Baptist" simply means all human beings from the first man to the most recent. See Gilles Quispel, "Das Thomasevangelium und das Alte Testament," in W. C. van Unnik, ed., *Neotestamentica et Patristica: Eine Freundesgabe, Herrn Professor Dr. Oscar Cullmann zu seinem 60. Geburtstag überreicht* (NovTSup 6; Leiden: Brill, 1962), 243-48, for the case that *Thomas* reverenced the Old Testament; and for a refutation see Tjitze Baarda, "The Gospel of Thomas and the Old Testament," *PIBA* 26 (2003): 1-28.

39. See further in the discussion of Vernon Robbins, above, 143-45.

40. The exception is *Thom.* 17, which (distantly) echoes Isa. 64:4 but does not appear in the Gospels. The closest early Christian parallel is 1 Cor. 2:9, but the saying is often found in early Christian agrapha, e.g., *Acts of Peter* 39 and *Acts of Thomas* 36. See McL. Wilson, *Studies*, 102-3; and Grant and Freedman, *Secret Sayings*, 137.

41. *Thomas's* ΟΥϭΕΠΗ (in a hurry) may reflect Mark's redactional εὐθύς (immediately). ϭΕΠΗ appears only here in *Thomas*. Greeven and Bethge both retrovert with ταχέως.

42. Patterson, *Gospel of Thomas*, 29, notes that Mark is closer to Joel but suggests that *Thomas* derives the saying from his own tradition-historical stream. Cf. Robbins, "Rhetorical Composition," 89, who notes that this saying and *Thom.* 66 come closest to verbal recitation of the Old Testament, but adds that *Thomas's* relationship to these Old Testament texts is not "scribal" as it is in the Synoptics.

tard Seed (*Thom.* 20) features the note that the branch (singular) "becomes a shelter for birds of the sky" (ⲛϥϣⲱⲡⲉ ⲛⲥⲕⲉⲡⲏ ⲛ︤ⲍ︦ⲁⲗⲁⲧⲉ ⲛⲧⲡⲉ), which is further removed from Dan. 4:12, Ezek. 17:23, and 31:6 than are the Synoptic versions (Matt. 13:31-32 // Mark 4:30-32 // Luke 13:18-19).[43] Similarly, the wording of *Thom.* 66, "Jesus says, 'Show me the stone that the builders rejected. It is the cornerstone,'" is further removed from Ps. 118.22 (LXX) than is the Synoptic quotation in the same context (Matt. 21:42 // Mark 12:10-11 // Luke 20:17), at the end of the parable of the Tenants in the Vineyard (Matt. 21:33-46 // Mark 12:1-12 // Luke 20:9-19).[44] Moreover, the absence of reference to Isaiah 5 in *Thomas*'s version of the Tenants in the Vineyard parable (*Thom.* 65) coheres with the same tendency.[45]

The point may go deeper still, to the very nature of *Thomas*'s choice of genre, the sayings gospel. The Synoptic evangelists' use of narrative is intimately connected with the view that the gospel is narrated in fulfillment of Scripture. Building on the earliest Christian conviction that *Christ died for our sins according to the Scriptures* (1 Cor. 15:3), the evangelists narrate Jesus' story as the story of his fulfillment of Scripture, the Messiah born in Bethlehem who evangelizes the poor and heals the lame, whose destiny is to die and rise as the prophets foretold. Their use of Scripture is not a secondary overlay to the evangelizing project but appears to be integral to the very

43. Already observed in Montefiore, "A Comparison of the Parables of the Gospel According to Thomas and of the Synoptic Gospels," in H. E. W. Turner and H. Montefiore, *Thomas and the Evangelists*, Studies in Biblical Theology 35 (London: SCM Press, 1962), 51. Montefiore also notes the absence of Old Testament allusions in *Thom.* 65, the Tenants in the Vineyard, and he comments that *Thom.* 16 is "further away from Micah 7:6 than the synoptic versions in Matt. 10:35 and Luke 12.52f," drawing attention to *Thom.* 52 (51 n. 4). However, Plisch, *Gospel of Thomas*, 79, regards it as self-evident that the Old Testament references in the Synoptics are secondary: "the end of the parable seems much simpler and more original than its synoptic parallels where the wording was clearly changed with allusions to the Old Testament in mind."

44. See Gathercole, "Luke in the *Gospel of Thomas*," 127-31, for the case that *Thomas* is here dependent on Luke. *Thomas* and Luke, unlike Mark and Matthew, lack a parallel to Ps. 118:23 (LXX).

45. Luke too (Luke 20:9) loses most of the Isa. 5:2 reference, and it is Luke's version of the parable that is closest to *Thomas*'s. For the links between *Thomas* and Luke here, see Gathercole, "Luke in the *Gospel of Thomas*," 127-31. Kloppenborg, *Tenants in the Vineyard*, 263, notes that "this is the *only* saying in the Gos. *Thom.* where the synoptic parallel has a biblical reference which Thomas entirely lacks," and adds, "It is logically fallacious to infer from a *single* instance to a general tendency in order to 'explain' that single instance." The point is true with respect to biblical references that *Thomas* "entirely lacks," but *Thomas* has a clear tendency to be further removed from the Old Testament where it shares parallels with the Synoptics.

idea of writing a gospel. Given what *Thom.* 52 says, and what his redaction of the Synoptics confirms, *Thomas* does not see Jesus' identity as bound up in his fulfillment of the Scriptures and of Israel's destiny. Once again it seems that his decision to write a sayings gospel is not an accident of his social location or proximity to early sayings traditions. *Thomas's* identity as a sayings gospel is connected with its negative attitude to the Hebrew Bible.[46]

Conclusion

The difficulty with some contemporary scholarship on *Thomas* is that it is still working with a kind of evolutionary perspective. It is as if *Thomas* studies are still stuck where Synoptic studies were in the 1920s and 1930s, beginning with the alleged traditional material and then attempting to explain how the Gospel was built up from there, so that passages like the Incipit and *Thom.* 13, far from being the hermeneutical keys to the work, become later accretions, their importance marginalized. The ideal is to use a model like the one used for other early Christian works, and to begin from the top, starting with what the document says about itself, and continuing the exploration from there. The analogy of Luke's Gospel may be helpful. No one seriously sidelines the preface (Luke 1:1-4) if they are trying to understand the Gospel. They begin from the way the work characterizes itself and they do not relegate it to a later layer to be trumped by consideration of the formative materials.

The Gospel of Thomas is proud to present itself as a book of the secret sayings of the living Jesus, secret sayings that point beyond themselves, that invite the hearer to discover the true, Thomasine interpretation that leads to life. Ultimately, though, the modern scholar's search is a frustrating one. Just as Peter, Matthew, and his companions are not allowed to hear the three secret words that Jesus shared with Thomas, so too we can only get hints of the *Gospel of Thomas's* purpose. That some insist on *Thomas's* Gnosticism while others vigorously deny it illustrates the success of *Thomas's* project. *Thomas* reinvents Jesus as the mysterious, enigmatic Living One who sometimes sounds suspiciously like the Synoptic Jesus but who, in the end, is not the same man. He preaches but he does not heal; he speaks in parables but

---

46. Marcion's alternative route, to compile a narrative gospel from which the Old Testament references are extricated, is likewise an attempt to gain legitimacy for his viewpoint by adopting the now familiar genre, while adapting it.

he is not the Son of Man. He uses familiar metaphors but he does not quote the Scriptures; he speaks of the kingdom but he does not expect the end. *Thomas*'s Jesus does not speak about the passion, and his disciples do not witness the resurrection. *The Gospel of Thomas*'s genius is that it conveys its radical difference from the Synoptic Gospels by hiding its theology in words and images it derives from them.

Conclusion: The Fifth Gospel?

Half a century ago, Oscar Cullmann derided the idea that *Thomas* was a "fifth gospel" as a "silly rumor."[1] It is now something boldly claimed in book titles.[2] *The Gospel of Thomas* has come of age, and it has an assured place in a scholars' canon of key texts on Jesus and early Christianity. The appreciation of *Thomas's* value, and its elevation to the highest place in the study of Christian origins, should encourage us to consider *Thomas* among the Gospels, and to pay serious attention to the case for its familiarity with the Synoptics.

I have argued in a series of steps that the *Gospel of Thomas* knew and used the Synoptic Gospels, with special reference to Matthew and Luke. First impressions can instill a sense of prejudice against the idea that *Thomas* knew the Synoptics, but the general arguments in favor of independence turn out to be weaker than we might at first have imagined; and the presence of parallels in *Thomas* to every strand of Synoptic data, including triple tradition, double tradition, special Matthew, special Luke, suggests direct contact between the works (chapter 1 above), a view confirmed by the evidence of verbatim agreement between *Thomas* and the Synoptics (chapter 2), a step in the discussion that is often missed. The Oxyrhynchus fragment of *Thom.* 26 (P.Oxy. 1), which features a thirteen-word verbatim agreement with texts of Luke 6:42 (// Matt. 7:5), is particularly striking.

But verbatim agreement only takes us so far. The diagnostic shards

---

1. Cullmann, "Gospel of Thomas," 419, "the silly rumor has already gone around about a 'fifth gospel'"; cf. Fitzmyer, "Oxyrhynchus Logoi," 419.

2. Patterson et al., *Fifth Gospel*, though the term "fifth Gospel" is not used in the body of the book; cf. Funk and Hoover, *Five Gospels*.

(chapter 3) that are provided by the presence, in *Thomas*, of Matthean redaction (chapter 4) and Lukan redaction (chapters 5–6) are telling. *Thomas* has parallels to places where Matthew and Luke are clearly redacting Markan material, as well as to material that is shot through with the thought and imagery that is characteristic of the evangelists. When *Thomas* uses the Synoptics, its author does not always do so in a coherent fashion, and there is a tendency to reproduce passages with their middles missing (chapter 7).

The burgeoning interest in orality in antiquity might be thought to tell against a case for *Thomas*'s familiarity with the Synoptics, but in chapter 8 I suggested that when studying the interaction between orality and literacy, the role played by literacy in Christian origins should not be underestimated. *Thomas* does not witness to orality as social location but sayings gospel as generic preference. Chapter 9 played the dating game and suggested that the Synoptics make best sense in a post-70 CE context, and that *Thomas* emerges after 135 CE. Chapter 10 explored how and why *Thomas* used the Synoptic Gospels, suggesting that Synoptic material provides the means by which the work authenticates the secret sayings of its living Jesus.

The "Fifth Gospel" tag may ultimately be more of a curse than a blessing. It is a bit like being labeled "the fifth Beatle." However legendary a producer George Martin was, however great a manager Brian Epstein was, neither will ever come close to the recognition earned by John, Paul, George, and Ringo. *Thomas* is worth reading as *Thomas*, as a brilliant attempt to re-create Jesus' words in its own voice, drawing on the Synoptics but transcending them by providing new twists on the old sayings, and adding many more from its own, secret treasure chest. It is not disparaging to characterize *Thomas* as it wishes to be characterized, as an apocryphal work, full of mysteries that tease the interpreter to search for the key to eternal life, by listening to the voice of its living Jesus. This is a text for the inner circle, the enlightened elite, one out of a thousand and two out of ten thousand, those who aspire to see the Living One in a world-renouncing new Eden.

That we want to pull *Thomas* into the first century and to see it as an independent witness to early Jesus tradition may say something about our scholarly anxieties. The ancient historian's task is a thankless one, endlessly grappling with the same, limited source material as we look for hitherto undiscovered insights, desperate for some scrap of new data. We are naturally inclined to pore over a fascinating text like *Thomas*, still a relatively recent discovery, and hope that in it we can find some witness to the topic that interests many of us more than any other, the historical Jesus.

It is a temptation, however, that we will be wise to resist. The privileging of *Thomas* has several damaging effects on the way that we pursue our scholarship. For one thing, the excessive attention given to *Thomas* can detract attention from the many other noncanonical texts of interest. More books seem to be written about *Thomas* than about all the other Nag Hammadi tractates put together. It is a disappointing irony that the charge of canonical bias has often resulted in the attempt to canonize *Thomas* rather than to pay serious attention to the full range of noncanonical works.

Similarly, the search for a first-century parallel for *Thomas* encourages comparisons with the hypothetical text Q, and unnecessarily complicates the already fraught quest of the historical Jesus. *Thomas* is nothing like Q or, rather, Q as it is reconstructed by those who are persuaded that Luke wrote independently of Matthew. As in the study of Q, so too in the study of *Thomas*, paying careful attention to the relationship between literary works helps to dispel certain myths of Christian origins.

Our sources for the study of the historical Jesus and Christian origins are more limited than we would like them to be, but our consciousness of the problem should not give rise to wishful thinking. Where the gaps in our knowledge cannot be filled in by informed speculation, an honest confession of ignorance may have to suffice. If this sounds unduly negative, it is worth bearing in mind that there are certain gains to facing up to the fact that *Thomas* is not, after all, the scholars' holy grail. One of these is that the literary history of early Christianity turns out to be a little more straightforward than we had previously imagined. There is a genealogical relationship among the key works that enables us to map a trajectory that has a greater elegance than those reconstructed by Helmut Koester and James Robinson. *Thomas* is familiar with the Synoptic Gospels just as Luke too is familiar with predecessor Gospels. Matthew knows Mark, who stands at the beginning of the entire process, though preceded by traditions witnessed by Paul, and preached by him in the first generation.[3]

The attempt to elevate *Thomas* to "Fifth Gospel" status in the end only serves to draw attention to its differences from the Synoptic Gospels. Although it has many parallels with them, the *Gospel of Thomas* distinguishes itself from the Synoptics in genre, literary conceit, and antiquity. To grant *Thomas* "Fifth Gospel" status encourages a kind of ahistorical privileging of one noncanonical gospel over many others. In other words, it is time to let *Thomas* be *Thomas*, to hear the gospel as the character of Thomas hears

---

3. This is not to say, of course, that there may not have been other lost texts and traditions but rather to construct our model on the basis of the ones we have.

it within the text (*Thom.* 13), as something secret, something surprising, something other. It may not be the lost, best source for Jesus traditions, a rediscovered voice from a primitive, oral past; but it is a fascinating artifact offering an early, enigmatic portrait of an esoteric Jesus. *Thomas*'s genius is in making his living Jesus sound sufficiently similar to the Synoptic Jesus to give him authority while allowing his new, distinctive voice to emerge. It may not be the "Fifth Gospel," but it deserves the special place it has earned in the scholar's canon.

Bibliography

Aland, Kurt. *Synopsis Quattuor Evangeliorum.* 15th ed. Stuttgart: Deutsche Bibelgesellschaft, 2001.

Attridge, Harold. "The Gospel According to Thomas: Appendix: The Greek Fragments." In Layton, ed. *Nag Hammadi Codex II, 2-7.* 1:95-128.

Aune, David E. "Assessing the Historical Value of the Apocryphal Jesus Traditions: A Critique of Conflicting Methodologies." In J. Schröter and R. Brucker, eds. *Historische Jesus.* BZNW 114. Berlin: de Gruyter, 2002. Pp. 243-72.

———. "Oral Tradition and the Aphorisms of Jesus." In H. Wanbrough, ed. *Jesus and the Oral Gospel Tradition.* JSNTSup 64. Sheffield: JSOT Press. Pp. 211-65.

Baarda, Tjitze. "The Gospel of Thomas." *PIBA* 26 (2003): 46-65.

———. "The Gospel of Thomas and the Old Testament." *PIBA* 26 (2003): 1-28.

———. "Luke 12.13-14: Text and Transmission from Marcion to Augustine." In J. Helderman and S. J. Noorda, eds. *Early Transmission of Words of Jesus: Thomas, Tatian and the Text of the New Testament.* Amsterdam: VU Boekhandel and Uitgeverij, 1983. Pp. 117-72.

Bailey, Kenneth. "Informal Controlled Oral Tradition and the Synoptic Gospels." *AJT* 5 (1991): 34-54 = *Themelios* 20/2 (1995): 4-11.

———. "Middle Eastern Oral Tradition and the Synoptic Gospels." *ExpT* 106 (1995): 363-67.

Bartlett, F. C. *Remembering: A Study in Experimental and Social Psychology.* 1932. Repr. Cambridge: Cambridge University Press, 1995.

Baum, Armin D. "The Anonymity of the New Testament History Books: A Stylistic Device in the Context of Greco-Roman and Ancient Near Eastern Literature." *NovT* 50 (2008): 120-42.

Blomberg, Craig L. "Tradition and Redaction in the Parables of the Gospel of Thomas." In David Wenham, ed. *Gospel Perspectives.* Vol. 5: *The Jesus Tradition Outside the Gospels.* Sheffield: JSOT Press, 1984. Pp. 177-205.

Bock, Darrell L., and Daniel B. Wallace. *Dethroning Jesus: Exposing Popular Culture's Quest to Unseat the Biblical Christ.* Nashville: Nelson, 2007.

Bovon, F. "Sayings Specific to Luke in the *Gospel of Thomas*." In *New Testament and Christian Apocrypha: Collected Studies*. WUNT 2/237. Tübingen: Mohr, 2009. Pp. 161-73.

Bruce, F. F. "The Gospel of Thomas." *Faith and Thought* 92/1 (1961): 3-23.

Bultmann, Rudolf. *History of the Synoptic Tradition*. ET. 2nd ed. Oxford: Blackwell, 1968.

Byrskog, Samuel. "A New Perspective on the Jesus Tradition: Reflections on James D. G. Dunn's *Jesus Remembered*." *JSNT* 26 (2004): 459-71.

Cameron, Ron. "Ancient Myths and Modern Theories of the *Gospel of Thomas* and Christian Origins." In Ron Cameron and Merrill P. Miller, eds. *Redescribing Christian Origins*. SBLSymS 28. Atlanta: Society of Biblical Literature, 2004. Pp. 89-108.

———. "Parable and Interpretation in the Gospel of Thomas." *Foundations & Facets Forum* 2/2 (1986): 3-39.

———. *Sayings Traditions in the Apocryphon of James*. HTS 34. Philadelphia: Fortress, 1984.

———. "Thomas, Gospel of." *ABD* 6:535-40.

Carlson, Stephen. "Thomas and the Twenty-Four Prophets." *Hypotyposeis* blog, http://www.hypotyposeis.org/weblog/2007/05/thomas-and-twenty-four-prophets.html (30 May 2007).

Carlston, Charles E., and Dennis Norlin. "Once More — Statistics and Q." *HTR* 64 (1971): 59-78.

Catchpole, David R. "John the Baptist, Jesus and the Parable of the Tares." *SJT* 31 (1978): 557-70.

Churton, Tobias. *The Gnostics*. London: Weidenfeld & Nicolson, 1987.

Conzelmann, Hans. *The Theology of St Luke*. ET. London: Faber & Faber, 1960.

Crossan, John Dominic. *The Birth of Christianity: Discovering What Happened in the Years Immediately After the Execution of Jesus*. San Francisco: HarperSanFrancisco, 1998.

———. *Four Other Gospels: Shadows on the Contours of Canon*. Minneapolis: Seabury, 1985.

———. *The Historical Jesus: The Life of a Mediterranean Jewish Peasant*. San Francisco: HarperSanFrancisco, 1991.

———. *Sayings Parallels: A Workbook for the Jesus Tradition*. Philadelphia: Fortress, 1986.

Crossley, James G. *The Date of Mark's Gospel: Insight from the Law in Earliest Christianity*. JSNTSup 266. London: T & T Clark International, 2004.

Cullmann, Oscar. "The Gospel of Thomas and the Problem of the Age of the Tradition Contained Therein: A Survey." *Interpretation* 16 (1962): 418-38.

Dart, John, Ray Riegert, and John Dominic Crossan. *Unearthing the Lost Words of Jesus: The Discovery and Text of the Gospel of Thomas*. Berkeley: Seastone, 1998.

Davies, Stevan L. "The Christology and Protology of the Gospel of Thomas." *JBL* 111 (1992): 663-82.

———. *The Gospel of Thomas and Christian Wisdom*. 2nd ed. Oregon House, CA: Bardic Press, 2005.

————. "Mark's Use of the Gospel of Thomas." *Neotestamentica* 30 (1996): 307-34.

————. "Thomas: The Fourth Synoptic Gospel." *BA* 46/1 (1983): 6-9, 12-14.

————. "Thomas, Gospel of." In David Noel Freedman, Allen C. Myers, and Astrid B. Beck, eds. *Eerdmans Dictionary of the Bible*. Grand Rapids: Eerdmans, 2000. Pp. 1303-4.

Davies, W. D., and Dale Allison. *A Critical and Exegetical Commentary on the Gospel According to Saint Matthew*. 3 vols. ICC. Edinburgh: T & T Clark, 1988-97.

DeConick, April D. "The Gospel of Thomas." *ExpT* 118 (2007): 469-79.

————. "Human Memory and the Sayings of Jesus." In Tom Thatcher, ed. *Jesus, the Voice, and the Text: Beyond the Oral and Written Gospel*. Waco: Baylor University Press, 2008. Pp. 135-80.

————. *The Original Gospel of Thomas in Translation: With a Commentary and New English Translation of the Complete Gospel*. LNTS 287. London: T & T Clark, 2006.

————. *Recovering the Original Gospel of Thomas: A History of the Gospel and Its Growth*. LNTS 286. London: T & T Clark, 2005.

Derrenbacker, R. A., Jr. *Ancient Compositional Practices and the Synoptic Problem*. BETL 186. Leuven: Peeters, 2005.

DeSilva, David A. *An Introduction to the New Testament*. Downers Grove, IL: InterVarsity, 2004.

Dewey, Joanna. "From Storytelling to Written Text: The Loss of Early Christian Women's Voices." *BTB* 26 (1996): 71-78.

————, ed. *Orality and Textuality in Early Christian Literature*. Semeia 65. Atlanta: Scholars Press, 1995.

————. "Textuality in an Oral Culture: A Survey of Pauline Traditions." In Dewey, ed. *Orality and Textuality*. Pp. 37-65.

Dibelius, Martin. *From Tradition to Gospel*. ET. London: Ivor Nicholson and Watson, 1934.

Dickerson, Patrick L. "The New Character Narrative in Luke–Acts and the Synoptic Problem." *JBL* 116/2 (1997): 291-312.

Dodd, C. H. *Parables of the Kingdom*. Rev. ed. New York: Scribner, 1961.

Dunderberg, Ismo. "*Thomas* and the Beloved Disciple." In Uro, ed. *Thomas at the Crossroads*. Pp. 65-88.

Dunn, James D. G. "Altering the Default Setting: Re-envisaging the Early Transmission of the Jesus Tradition." *NTS* 49/2 (2003): 139-75.

————. "Jesus and Ritual Purity: A Study of the Tradition-History of Mark 7.15." In F. Refoulé, ed. *À cause de l'Évangile: Études sur les Synoptiques et les Actes, offertes au P. Jacques Dupont*. LD 123. Paris: Cerf, 1985. Pp. 251-76. Repr. in James D. G. Dunn, *Jesus, Paul and the Law: Studies in Mark and Galatians*. London: SPCK, 1990. Pp. 37-60.

————. "Jesus in Oral Memory: The Initial Stages of the Jesus Tradition." In D. Donnelly, ed. *Jesus: A Colloquium in the Holy Land*. London: Continuum, 2001. Pp. 84-145.

————. *Jesus, Paul, and the Gospels*. Grand Rapids: Eerdmans, 2011.

———. *Jesus Remembered*. Christianity in the Making 1. Grand Rapids: Eerdmans, 2003.

———. "Kenneth Bailey's Theory of Oral Tradition: Critiquing Theodore Weeden's Critique." *JSHJ* 7 (2009): 44-62.

Ehrman, Bart D. *Jesus: Apocalyptic Prophet of the New Millennium*. Oxford: Oxford University Press, 1999.

———. *Lost Christianities: The Battle for Scripture and the Faiths We Never Knew*. Oxford: Oxford University Press, 2003.

Esler, Philip. *New Testament Theology: Communion and Community*. Minneapolis: Fortress, 2005.

Evans, Craig A. *Ancient Texts for New Testament Studies: A Guide to the Background Literature*. Peabody, MA: Hendrickson, 2005.

———. *Fabricating Jesus: How Modern Scholars Distort the Gospels*. Downers Grove, IL: InterVarsity Press, 2006.

———. "Predictions of the Destruction of the Herodian Temple in the Pseudepigrapha, Qumran Scrolls and Related Texts." *JSP* 10 (1992): 89-147.

Fee, Gordon. "Modern Textual Criticism and the Synoptic Problem: On the Problem of Harmonization in the Gospels." In Eldon Jay Epp and Gordon D. Fee, *Studies in the Theory and Method of New Testament Textual Criticism*. Grand Rapids: Eerdmans, 1993. Pp. 174-82.

Fieger, Michael. *Das Thomasevangelium: Einleitung, Kommentar und Systematik*. Neutestamentliche Abhandlungen N.F. 22. Münster: Aschendorff, 1991.

Fitzmyer, Joseph A. *The Gospel According to Luke: Introduction, Translation, and Notes*. 2 vols. AB. Garden City, NY: Doubleday, 1981-85.

———. "The Oxyrhynchus Logoi of Jesus and the Coptic Gospel According to Thomas." *Theological Studies* 20 (1959): 505-60. Repr. in *Essays on the Semitic Background of the New Testament*. London: Geoffrey Chapman, 1971. Pp. 355-433.

Foster, Robert. "Why on Earth Use 'Kingdom of Heaven'? Matthew's Terminology Revisited." *NTS* 48 (2002): 487-99.

Fowler, Robert. "How the Secondary Orality of the Electronic Age Can Awaken Us to the Primary Orality of Antiquity, or What Hypertext Can Teach Us About the Bible, with Reflections on the Ethical and Political Issues of the Electronic Frontier." Paper presented to the Semiotics and Exegesis Section, Society of Biblical Literature Annual Meeting, Chicago, IL, November 19, 1994, reproduced at http://homepages .bw.edu/~rfowler/pubs/secondoral/index.html. Accessed 15 June 2011.

Fredriksen, Paula. "Judaism, the Circumcision of Gentiles and Apocalyptic Hope: Another Look at Galatians 1 and 2." *JTS* 42 (1991): 532-64.

Funk, Robert W. *Honest to Jesus: Jesus for a New Millennium*. San Francisco: HarperSanFrancisco, 1996.

———. "Rules of Oral Evidence: Determining the Authentic Sayings of Jesus." *The Fourth R* 4/2 (1991): 8-10. Repr. in Bernard Brandon Scott, ed. *Finding the Historical Jesus: Rules of Evidence*. Jesus Seminar Guides. Sonoma, CA: Polebridge, 2008. Pp. 25-29.

————, Roy Hoover, and the Jesus Seminar. *The Five Gospels: The Search for the Authentic Words of Jesus.* New York: Macmillan, 1993.

Gamble, Harry Y. *Books and Readers in the Early Church: A History of Early Christian Texts.* New Haven: Yale University Press, 1995.

Gathercole, Simon. "Luke in the *Gospel of Thomas.*" *NTS* 57 (2010): 114-44.

Gerhardsson, Birger. *Memory and Manuscript: Oral Tradition and Written Transmission in Rabbinic Judaism and Early Christianity*; with *Tradition and Transmission in Early Christianity.* Combined edition; The Biblical Resource Series; Grand Rapids: Eerdmans, 1998.

————. "The Secret of the Transmission of the Unwritten Jesus Tradition." *NTS* 51 (2005): 1-18.

Goodacre, Mark. *The Case Against Q: Studies in Markan Priority and the Synoptic Problem.* Harrisburg: Trinity Press International, 2002.

————. "Fatigue in the Synoptics." *NTS* 44 (1998): 45-58.

————. *Goulder and the Gospels: An Examination of a New Paradigm.* JSNTSup 133. Sheffield: Sheffield Academic Press, 1996.

————. Review of Jeffrey Tucket, *Example Stories: Perspectives on Four Parables in the Gospel of Luke. RRT* 6 (1999): 387-88.

————. *The Synoptic Problem: A Way Through the Maze.* Biblical Seminar 80. Sheffield: Sheffield Academic Press, 2001.

————. "When Is a Text Not a Text? The Quasi-Text-Critical Approach of the International Q Project." In Mark Goodacre and Nicholas Perrin, eds. *Questioning Q.* London: SPCK, 2004; Downers Grove, IL: InterVarsity Press, 2005. Pp. 115-26.

Goulder, Michael. "Is Q a Juggernaut?" *JBL* 115 (1996): 667-81.

————. *Luke: A New Paradigm.* 2 vols. JSNTSup 20. Sheffield: Sheffield Academic Press, 1989.

————. "Luke's Knowledge of Matthew." In Georg Strecker, ed. *Minor Agreements: Symposium Göttingen 1991.* Göttinger theologische Arbeiten 50. Göttingen: Vandenhoeck & Ruprecht, 1993. Pp. 143-60.

————. *Midrash and Lection in Matthew.* London: SPCK, 1974.

Gowler, David. Review of James Crossley, *Why Christianity Happened. CBQ* 69 (2007): 815-16.

Grant, Robert M., David Noel Freedman, and William R. Schoedel. *The Secret Sayings of Jesus: The Gnostic Gospel of Thomas.* London: Collins, 1960.

Gregory, Andrew. "Prior or Posterior? The *Gospel of the Ebionites* and the Gospel of Luke." *NTS* 51 (2005): 344-60.

————. *The Reception of Luke-Acts in the Period before Irenaeus: Looking for Luke in the Second Century.* WUNT 2/169. Tübingen: Mohr, 2003.

————, and Christopher M. Tuckett. "Reflections on Method: What Constitutes the Use of the Writings That Later Formed the New Testament in the Apostolic Fathers?" In Andrew F. Gregory and Christopher M. Tuckett, eds. *The Reception of the New Testament in the Apostolic Fathers.* Oxford: Oxford University Press, 2005. Pp. 61-82.

Bibliography

Grenfell, Bernard P. "The Oldest Record of Christ's Life." *McClure's Magazine*, Oct. 1897, 1022-30.

———, and Arthur S. Hunt. *ΛΟΓΙΑ ΙΗΣΟΥ: Sayings of Our Lord from an Early Greek Papyrus Discovered and Edited, with Translation and Commentary*. Egypt Exploration Fund. London: H. Frowde, 1897.

———, and Arthur S. Hunt. *New Sayings of Jesus and Fragment of a Lost Gospel from Oxyrhynchus*. Egypt Exploration Fund; London: H. Frowde, 1904.

———, and Arthur S. Hunt. *The Oxyrhynchus Papyri*. Vols. 1 and 4. London: Egypt Exploration Fund, 1893, 1904.

Guillaumont, A., H.-Ch. Puech, G. Quispel, W. Till, and Yassah 'Abd al Masih, eds. *The Gospel According to Thomas: Coptic Text Established and Translated*. Leiden: Brill, 1959.

Gundry, R. H. *Matthew: A Commentary on His Handbook for a Mixed Church Under Persecution*. Grand Rapids: Eerdmans, 1994.

Guthrie, Donald. *New Testament Introduction*. Downers Grove, IL: InterVarsity Press, 1971.

Haenchen, E. "Literatur zum Thomasevangelium." *Theologische Rundschau* 27 (1961): 147-78.

Haines-Eitzen, Kim. *Guardians of Letters: Literacy, Power, and the Transmitters of Early Christian Literature*. Oxford: Oxford University Press, 2009.

Hatina, Thomas R. "The Focus of Mark 13:24-27 — The Parousia, or the Destruction of the Temple?" *BBR* 6 (1996): 43-66.

Hawkins, John. *Horae Synopticae: Contributions to the Study of the Synoptic Problem*. 2nd ed. Oxford: Clarendon, 1909.

Hearon, Holly E. "The Implications of 'Orality' for Studies of the Biblical Text." *Oral Tradition* 19/1 (2004): 96-107.

Hedrick, Charles W. "Thomas and the Synoptics: Aiming at a Consensus." *Second Century* 7/1 (1989/1990): 39-56.

Herzog, William. *Jesus, Justice and the Reign of God: A Ministry of Liberation*. Louisville: Westminster John Knox, 2000.

Holtzmann, H. J. *Handkommentar zum Neuen Testament*. 3rd ed. Tübingen: Mohr, 1901.

Huck, Albert. *Synopsis of the First Three Gospels*. 13th ed., fundamentally revised by Heinrich Greeven. Tübingen: Mohr (Siebeck), 1981.

Hurtado, Larry W. "The Greek Fragments of the *Gospel of Thomas* as Artefacts: Papyrological Observations on Papyrus Oxyrhynchus 1, Papyrus Oxyrhynchus 654 and Papyrus Oxyrhynchus 655." In Jörg Frey, Enno Edzard Popkes and Jens Schröter, eds. *Das Thomasevangelium: Entstehung – Rezeption – Theologie*. Berlin: de Gruyter, 2008. Pp. 19-32.

———. *Lord Jesus Christ: Devotion to Jesus in Earliest Christianity*. Grand Rapids: Eerdmans, 2003.

Incigneri, Brian J. *The Gospel to the Romans: The Setting and Rhetoric of Mark's Gospel*. Biblical Interpretation Series 65. Leiden: Brill, 2003.

Ingolfsland, Dennis. "The Gospel of Thomas and the Synoptic Gospels." on-line article, http://dennis-ingolfsland.blogspot.com/2009/04/gospel-of-thomas-and-synoptic-gospels.html. Accessed 15 June 2011.

Instone Brewer, David. Review of James Crossley, *Date of Mark's Gospel. JTS* 57/2 (2006): 647-50.

Iverson, Kelly R. "Orality and the Gospels: A Survey of Recent Research." *Currents in Biblical Research* 8 (2009): 71-106.

James, M. R. "The New Sayings of Christ." *Contemporary Review* 72 (July-December 1897): 153-60.

Jaschik, Scott. "Technology Gap." *Inside Higher Ed*, November 5 2009, http://www.in sidehighered.com/news/2009/11/05/survey.

Jones, F. Stanley. *Which Mary? The Marys of Early Christian Tradition.* SBLSymS 19. Atlanta: Society of Biblical Literature, 2002.

Juel, Donald H. *A Master of Surprise: Mark Interpreted.* Minneapolis: Fortress, 1994.

Jülicher, Adolf. *Die Gleichnisreden Jesu.* 2nd ed. 2 vols. Tübingen: Mohr (Siebeck), 1910.

Kaestli, J.-D. "L'utilisation de l'Évangile de Thomas dans la recherche actuelle sur les paroles de Jésus." In D. Marguerat, E. Norelli, and J.-M. Poffet, eds. *Jésus de Nazareth: Nouvelles approches d'une énigme.* Monde de la Bible 38. Geneva: Labor et Fides, 1998. Pp. 373-95.

Kelber, Werner H. "Gnosis and the Origins of Christianity." In Kenneth Keulman, ed. *Critical Moments in Religious History.* Macon, GA: Mercer University Press, 1983. Pp. 41-58.

———. *The Oral and the Written Gospel: The Hermeneutics of Speaking and Writing in the Synoptic Tradition, Mark, Paul, and Q.* Philadelphia: Fortress, 1983.

———. "Orality and Biblical Studies: A Review Essay." *RBL* 12/2007, http://www.bookre views.org/pdf/2120_6744.pdf.

———. "Oral Tradition in Bible and New Testament Studies." *Oral Tradition* 18/1 (2003): 40-42.

———. "Sayings Collection and Sayings Gospel: A Study in the Clustering Management of Knowledge." *Language & Communication* 9 (1989): 213-24.

———, and Samuel Byrskog, eds. *Jesus in Memory: Traditions in Oral and Scribal Perspectives.* Waco: Baylor University Press, 2009.

Khatry, Ramesh. "The Authenticity of the Parable of the Wheat and the Tares and Its Interpretation." PhD diss., Westminster College, 1991.

Kirk, Alan. "Memory." In Kelber and Byrskog, eds. *Jesus in Memory.* Pp. 155-72.

Kloppenborg, John S. "*Evocatio Deorum* and the Date of Mark." *JBL* 124/3 (2005): 419-50.

———. *Excavating Q: The History and Setting of the Sayings Gospel.* Minneapolis: Fortress, 2000.

———. *The Formation of Q: Trajectories in Ancient Wisdom Collections.* Studies in Antiquity and Christianity. Philadelphia: Fortress, 1987.

———. "The Life and Sayings of Jesus." In Mark Allan Powell, ed. *The New Testament Today.* Louisville: Westminster John Knox, 1999. Pp. 10-30.

———. "Variation in the Reproduction of the Double Tradition and an Oral Q?" *ETL* 83/1 (2007): 53-80.

Knox, John. *Chapters in a Life of Paul*. Rev. ed. London: SCM, 1989.

Koester, Helmut. *Ancient Christian Gospels: Their History and Development*. Harrisburg: Trinity Press International, 1990.

———. "*GNOMAI DIAPHOROI*: The Origin and Nature of Diversification in the History of Early Christianity." *HTR* 58 (1965): 279-318. Repr. in Robinson and Koester, *Trajectories*. Pp. 114-57.

———. "The Gospel According to Thomas: Introduction." In Layton, ed. *Nag Hammadi Codex II, 2-7*. Pp. 38-49.

———. *Introduction to the New Testament*. Vol. 2: *History and Literature of Early Christianity*. 2nd ed. Berlin: de Gruyter, 2000.

———. *Synoptische Überlieferung bei den Apostolischen Vätern*. TU 65. Berlin: Akademie, 1957.

———. "Written Gospels or Oral Tradition?" *JBL* 113 (1994): 293-97.

Lapham, Fred. *Introduction to the New Testament Apocrypha*. London: T & T Clark, 2003.

Layton, Bentley, et al. "The Gospel According to Thomas." In Layton, ed. *Nag Hammadi Codex II, 2-7*. 2 vols. NHS 20-21. Coptic Gnostic Library. Leiden: Brill, 1989. 1:38-130.

Le Donne, Anthony. *The Historiographical Jesus: Memory, Typology and the Son of David*. Waco: Baylor University Press, 2009.

Lincoln, Bruce. "Thomas-Gospel and Thomas-Community: A New Approach to a Familiar Text." *NovT* 19 (1977): 65-76.

Linnemann, Eta. *Is There a Synoptic Problem? Rethinking the Literary Dependence of the First Three Gospels*. Grand Rapids: Baker, 1992.

Loisy, A. *L'Evangile selon Luc*. Paris: E. Nourry, 1924.

Lord, Albert Bates. "The Gospels as Oral Traditional Literature." In William O. Walker Jr., ed. *The Relationships among the Gospels: An Interdisciplinary Dialogue*. San Antonio: Trinity University Press, 1978. Pp. 33-91.

———. *The Singer of Tales*. Cambridge: Harvard University Press, 1960.

Lüdemann, Gerd. *Jesus after Two Thousand Years: What He Really Said and Did*; with contributions by Frank Schleritt and Martina Janssen. London: SCM, 2000.

Lyons, W. J. "A Prophet Is Rejected in His Home Town (Mark 6.4 and Parallels): A Study in the Methodological (In)Consistency of the Jesus Seminar." *JSHJ* 6 (2008): 59-84.

Mack, Burton L. *Who Wrote the New Testament? The Making of the Christian Myth*. San Francisco: HarperSanFrancisco, 1995.

Marcovich, M. "Textual Criticism on the Gospel of Thomas." *JTS* 20 (1969): 53-74.

Marshall, John W. *The Five Gospel Parallels* (1996-2001). http://www.utoronto.ca/religion/synopsis/. Accessed 15 June 2011.

———. "The *Gospel of Thomas* and the Cynic Jesus." In William E. Arnal and Michel

Desjardins, eds. *Whose Historical Jesus?* Studies in Christianity and Judaism 7. Waterloo, Ont.: Wilfrid Laurier University Press, 1997. Pp. 37-60.

Massaux, Edouard. *The Influence of the Gospel of Saint Matthew on Christian Literature Before Saint Irenaeus.* Vol. 3: *The Apologists and the Didache.* ET. New Gospel Studies 5/3. Macon, GA: Mercer University Press, 1993.

McArthur, Harvey K. "The Dependence of the Gospel of Thomas on the Synoptics." *ExpT* 71 (1959-60): 286-87.

———. "The Gospel According to Thomas." In Harvey K. McArthur, ed. *New Testament Sidelights: Essays in Honor of Alexander Converse Purdy.* Hartford: Hartford Seminary Foundation Press, 1960. Pp. 43-77.

Meier, John P. *A Marginal Jew: Rethinking the Historical Jesus.* 4 vols. New York: Doubleday, 1991-2009.

Ménard, J.-É. *L'Évangile selon Thomas.* NHS 5. Leiden: Brill, 1975.

Meyer, Marvin. *The Gnostic Discoveries: The Impact of the Nag Hammadi Library.* San Francisco: HarperSanFrancisco, 2006.

———, ed. *The Nag Hammadi Scriptures.* New York: HarperCollins, 2007.

Montefiore, Hugh. "A Comparison of the Parables of the Gospel According to Thomas and of the Synoptic Gospels." In H. E. W. Turner and H. Montefiore. *Thomas and the Evangelists.* Studies in Biblical Theology 35. London: SCM Press, 1962. Pp. 40-78.

Moreland, Milton. "The Twenty-Four Prophets of Israel Are Dead: Gospel of Thomas 52 as a Critique of Early Christian Hermeneutics." In Jon Ma. Asgeirsson, April D. DeConick, and Risto Uro, eds. *Thomasine Traditions in Antiquity: The Social and Cultural World of the Gospel of Thomas.* Leiden: Brill, 2006. Pp. 75-91.

Moule, C. F. D. *An Idiom Book of New Testament Greek.* 2nd ed. Cambridge: Cambridge University Press, 1960.

Mournet, Terence. *Oral Tradition and Literary Dependency: Variability and Stability in the Synoptic Tradition and Q.* WUNT 2/195. Tübingen: Mohr Siebeck, 2005.

Nestle, Eberhard, Barbara Aland, et al. *Novum Testamentum Graece.* 27th ed. Stuttgart: Deutsche Bibelgesellschaft, 1993.

Nordsieck, Reinhard. *Das Thomas-Evangelium: Einleitung; Zur Frage des historischen Jesus; Kommentierung aller 114 Logien.* 3rd ed. Neukirchen-Vluyn: Neukirchener Verlag, 2006.

Ong, Walter. *Orality and Literacy: The Technologizing of the Word.* London: Methuen, 1982.

———. *Rhetoric, Romance, and Technology: Studies in the Interaction of Expression and Culture.* Ithaca: Cornell University Press, 1971.

Pagels, Elaine. *Beyond Belief: The Secret Gospel of Thomas.* New York: Random House, 2003.

———. "Exegesis of Genesis 1 in the Gospels of Thomas and John." *JBL* 118 (1999): 477-96.

———. *The Gnostic Gospels.* New York: Random House, 1979.

Bibliography

Painter, John. *Just James: The Brother of Jesus in History and Tradition*. Edinburgh: T & T Clark, 1999.

Parker, David. *The Living Text of the Gospels*. Cambridge: Cambridge University Press, 1997.

Patterson, Stephen J. *The Gospel of Thomas and Jesus*. Foundations and Facets. Sonoma, CA: Polebridge, 1993.

Patterson, Stephen J., James M. Robinson, and Hans-Gebhard Bethge. *The Fifth Gospel: The Gospel of Thomas Comes of Age*. Harrisburg: Trinity Press International, 1998.

Pennington, Jonathan T. *Heaven and Earth in the Gospel of Matthew*. NovTSup 126. Leiden: Brill, 2007.

Perkins, Pheme. "The Rejected Jesus and the Kingdom Sayings." In Charles W. Hedrick, ed. *The Historical Jesus and the Rejected Gospels*. Semeia 44. Atlanta: Society of Biblical Literature, 1988. Pp. 79-94.

Perrin, Nicholas. *Thomas and Tatian: The Relationship between the Gospel of Thomas and the Diatessaron*. Academia Biblica 5. Atlanta: Society of Biblical Literature, 2002.

———. *Thomas: The Other Gospel*. Louisville: Westminster John Knox, 2007.

"Plagiarism FAQs." *Plagiarism dot org*, http://www.plagiarism.org/plag_article_plagiarism_faq.html. Accessed 15 June 2011.

Plisch, Uwe-Karsten. *The Gospel of Thomas: Original Text with Commentary*. Stuttgart: Deutsche Bibelgesellschaft, 2008.

Poirier, John C. "Memory, Written Sources, and the Synoptic Problem: A Response to Robert K. McIver and Marie Carroll." *JBL* 123 (2004): 315-22.

———. "The Roll, the Codex, the Wax Tablet, and the Synoptic Problem." *JSNT* 35 (2012): 3-30.

Popkes, Enno Edzard. *Das Menschenbild des Thomasevangeliums*. WUNT 206. Tübingen: Mohr Siebeck, 2007.

Prensky, Marc. "Digital Natives, Digital Immigrants." *On the Horizon* 9/5 (October 2001) and "Digital Natives, Digital Immigrants, Part 2: Do They Really *Think* Differently?" *On the Horizon* 9/6 (December 2001), reproduced at Marc Prensky, http://www.marcprensky.com/ Accessed 23 August 2011.

Puech, H.-Ch. "Un logion de Jésus sur bandelette funéraire." *RHR* 147 (1955): 126-29.

Quarles, Charles L. "The Use of the Gospel of Thomas in the Research on the Historical Jesus of John Dominic Crossan." *CBQ* 69 (2007): 517-36.

Quispel, Gilles. "L'Evangile selon Thomas et le Diatessaron." *VC* 13 (1959): 87-117.

———. "L'Evangile selon Thomas et le 'Texte Occidental' du Nouveau Testament." *VC* 14 (1960): 204-15.

———. "The Gospel of Thomas and the New Testament." *VC* 11 (1957): 189-207.

———. "Some Remarks on the Gospel of Thomas." *NTS* 5 (1958-59): 276-90.

———. "Das Thomasevangelium und das Alte Testament." In W. C. van Unnik, ed. *Neotestamentica et Patristica: Eine Freundesgabe, Herrn Professor Dr. Oscar Cullmann zu seinem 60. Geburtstag überreicht*. NovTSup 6. Leiden: Brill, 1962. Pp. 243-48.

Reed, Jonathan. *The HarperCollins Visual Guide to the New Testament: What Archaeology Reveals about the First Christians*. New York: HarperCollins, 2007.

Riley, Gregory J. "Influence of Thomas Christianity on Luke 12:14 and 5:39." *HTR* 88/2 (April 1995): 229-35.

Robbins, Vernon K. "Interfaces of Orality and Literature in the Gospel of Mark." In R. Horsley, J. Draper and J. Foley, eds. *Performing the Gospel: Orality, Memory, and Mark: Essays Dedicated to Werner Kelber*. Minneapolis: Fortress, 2006. Pp. 125-46.

————. "Oral, Rhetorical, and Literary Cultures: A Response." In J. Dewey, ed. *Orality and Textuality*. Pp. 75-92.

————. "Rhetorical Composition and Sources in the *Gospel of Thomas*." In *1997 Society of Biblical Literature Seminar Papers*. Atlanta: Scholars Press, 1997. Pp. 86-114. Reproduced at http://www.religion.emory.edu/faculty/robbins/Pdfs/RhetCompTho mas.pdf.

Robinson, James M. "The Discovery of the Nag Hammadi Codices." *BA* 42/4 (1979): 206-24.

————, ed. *The Facsimile Edition of the Nag Hammadi Codices: Introduction*. Published under the auspices of the Department of Antiquities of the Arab Republic of Egypt. In conjunction with the United Nations Educational, Scientific and Cultural Organization; Leiden: Brill, 1984.

————. "From Cliff to Cairo: The Story of the Discoverers and the Middlemen of the Nag Hammadi Codices." In Bernard Barc, *Colloque international sur les textes de Nag Hammadi: Québec, 22-25 août 1978*. Bibliothèque copte de Nag Hammadi 1. Québec: Presses de l'Université Laval, 1981. Pp. 21-58.

————. "LOGOI SOPHON: On the Gattung of Q." In Robinson and Koester. *Trajectories*. Pp. 71-113.

————, ed. *The Nag Hammadi Library in English*. 3rd ed. Leiden: Brill, 1988.

————. *The Sayings Gospel Q: Collected Essays*. Ed. Christoph Heil and Joseph Verheyden. BETL 189. Leuven: Leuven University Press, 2005.

————, Paul Hoffmann, and John S. Kloppenborg. *The Critical Edition of Q: Synopsis including the Gospels of Matthew and Luke, Mark and Thomas with English, German, and French Translations of Q and Thomas*. Hermeneia. Minneapolis: Fortress, 2000.

————, and Helmut Koester. *Trajectories through Early Christianity*. Philadelphia: Fortress, 1971.

Robinson, John A. T. *Redating the New Testament*. London: SCM, 1976.

Rodriguez, Rafael. "Reading and Hearing in Ancient Contexts." *JSNT* 32 (2009): 151-78.

————. *Structuring Early Christian Memory: Jesus in Tradition, Performance, and Text*. LNTS 407. London: T & T Clark, 2009.

Roskam, H. N. *The Purpose of the Gospel of Mark in Its Historical and Social Context*. NovTSup 114. Leiden: Brill, 2004.

Sanders, E. P. *Jewish Law from Jesus to the Mishnah*. Philadelphia: Trinity Press International, 1990.

————. *The Tendencies of the Synoptic Tradition*. Cambridge: Cambridge University Press, 1969.

————, and Margaret Davies. *Studying the Synoptic Gospels*. Philadelphia: Trinity Press International, 1989.

Schenke, Hans-Martin. "Bemerkungen zu #71 des Thomas-Evangeliums." *Enchoria: Zeitschrift für Demostistik und Koptologie* 27 (2001): 120-26.

————. "On the Compositional History of the Gospel of Thomas." *Foundations and Facets Forum* 10/1-2 (1994): 9-30.

Schoedel, William R. "Naassene Themes in the Coptic Gospel of Thomas." *VC* 14 (1960): 225-34.

Schrage, Wolfgang. "Evangelienzitate in den Oxyrhynchus-Logien und im koptischen Thomas-Evangelium." In W. Eltester and F. H. Kettler, eds. *Apophoreta: Festschrift für Ernst Haenchen*. BZNW 30. Berlin: Töpelmann, 1964. Pp. 251-68.

————. *Das Verhältnis des Thomas-Evangeliums zur synoptischen Tradition und zu den koptischen Evangelien-übersetzungen: Zugleich ein Beitrag zur gnostischen Synoptikerdeutung*. BZNW 29. Berlin: Töpelmann, 1964.

Schröter, Jens. "Die Herausforderung einer theologischen Interpretation des *Thomasevangeliums*." In Jörg Frey, Enno Ezard Popkes, and Jens Schröter, *Das Thomasevangelium: Entstehung — Rezeption — Theologie*. BZNW 157. Berlin: de Gruyter, 2008. Pp. 435-59.

Schürmann, H. "Das Thomasevangelium und das lukanische Sondergut." *BZ* 7 (1963): 236-60. Repr. in H. Schürmann, *Traditionsgeschichtliche Untersuchungen zu den synoptischen Evangelien*. Düsseldorf: Patmos-Verlag, 1968. Pp. 228-47.

Scott, B. B. *Hear Then the Parable: A Commentary on the Parables of Jesus*. Minneapolis: Fortress, 1989.

Sellew, Philip. "Interior Monologue as a Narrative Device in the Parables of Luke." *JBL* 111 (1992): 239-53.

Senior, Donald. *Matthew*. Abingdon New Testament Commentaries. Nashville: Abingdon, 1998.

Sieber, John. "A Redactional Analysis of the Synoptic Gospels with regard to the Question of the Sources of the Gospel according to Thomas." PhD diss., Claremont Graduate School, 1966. Ann Arbor: University Microfilms International, 1976.

Smith, Charles W. F. "The Mixed State of the Church in Matthew's Gospel." *JBL* 82 (1963): 149-68.

Smith, D. Moody. *John Among the Gospels*. 2nd ed. Columbia, SC: University of South Carolina Press, 2001.

Snodgrass, Klyne R. "The Gospel of Thomas: A Secondary Gospel." *Second Century* 7/1 (1989-90): 19-38. Repr. in Craig A. Evans, ed. *The Historical Jesus*. Vol. 4: *Lives of Jesus and Jesus Outside the Bible*. London: Routledge, 2004. Pp. 291-310.

————. *Stories with Intent: A Comprehensive Guide to the Parables of Jesus*. Grand Rapids: Eerdmans, 2008.

Spielmann, Ruth. "Secondary Orality." *TIC Talk* 53 (2002): 1-4.

Streeter, Burnett Hillman. *The Four Gospels: A Study of Origins Treating of the Manuscript Tradition, Sources, Authorship and Dates.* London: Macmillan, 1924.

Swete, Henry Barclay. "The Oxyrhynchus Fragment." *ExpT* 8 (1897): 540-50, 568.

Talbert, Charles. Review of James Crossley, *Date of Mark's Gospel. Perspectives in Religious Studies* 33/4 (2006): 524-27.

Taylor, Charles. *The Oxyrhynchus Logia and the Apocryphal Gospels.* Oxford: Clarendon, 1899.

Taylor, Vincent. *The Formation of the Gospel Tradition.* London: Macmillan, 1933.

Thatcher, Tom. "Beyond Texts and Traditions: Werner Kelber's Media History of Christian Origins." In Tom Thatcher, ed. *Jesus, the Voice, and the Text: Beyond the Oral and Written Gospel.* Waco: Baylor University Press, 2008. Pp. 1-26.

Theissen, Gerd. *The Gospels in Context: Social and Political History in the Synoptic Tradition.* Minneapolis: Fortress, 1991.

———, and Annette Merz. *The Historical Jesus: A Comprehensive Guide.* ET. Minneapolis: Fortress, 1998.

Thrall, Margaret E. *Greek Particles in the New Testament: Linguistic and Exegetical Studies.* New Testament Tools and Studies 3. Leiden: Brill, 1962.

Tucker, Jeffrey T. *Example Stories: Perspectives on Four Parables in the Gospel of Luke.* JSNTSup 162. Sheffield: Sheffield Academic Press, 1998.

Tuckett, Christopher M. "The *Beatitudes*: A Source-Critical Study." With a reply by M. D. Goulder. *NovT* 25/3 (1983): 193-216.

———. "Form Criticism." In Kelber and Byrskog, eds. *Jesus in Memory.* Pp. 20-38.

———. "Q and Thomas: Evidence of a Primitive 'Wisdom Gospel'?" A Response to H. Koester." *ETL* 67 (1991): 346-60.

———. Review of Uwe-Karsten Plisch, *The Gospel of Thomas: Original Text with Commentary. RBL* [http://www.bookreviews.org] (2009).

———. "Thomas and the Synoptics." *NovT* 30/2 (1988): 132-57.

Uro, Risto. "Asceticism and Anti-Familial Language in the Gospel of Thomas." In Halvor Moxnes, ed. *Constructing Early Christian Families: Family as Social Reality and Metaphor.* London: Routledge, 1997. Pp. 216-34.

———. "Is Thomas an Encratite Gospel?" In Uro, ed. *Thomas at the Crossroads.* Pp. 140-62.

———. "'Secondary Orality' in the Gospel of Thomas? Logion 14 as a Test Case." *Forum* 9/3-4 (1993): 305-29. Repr. as "*Thomas* and the Oral Gospel Tradition." In Uro, ed. *Thomas at the Crossroads.* Pp. 8-32.

———, ed. *Thomas at the Crossroads: Essays on the Gospel of Thomas.* Studies of the New Testament and Its World. Edinburgh: T & T Clark, 1998.

———. *Thomas: Seeking the Historical Context of the Gospel of Thomas.* London: T & T Clark, 2003.

Valantasis, Richard. *The Gospel of Thomas.* London: Routledge, 1997.

Van Voorst, Robert E. *Jesus Outside the New Testament.* Grand Rapids: Eerdmans, 2000.

Bibliography

Watson, Francis. "The Fourfold Gospel." In Stephen C. Barton, ed. *The Cambridge Companion to the Gospels*. Cambridge: Cambridge University Press, 2000. Pp. 34-52.

Weeden, Theodore, J. "Kenneth Bailey's Theory of Oral Tradition: A Theory Contested by Its Evidence." *JSHJ* 7 (2009): 3-43.

Wendling, Emil. *Die Entstehung des Marcus-Evangeliums: Philologische Untersuchungen*. Tübingen: Mohr, 1908.

Williams, Francis E. "The Apocryphon of James (I,2)." In James M. Robinson, ed. *Nag Hammadi Library in English*. Pp. 29-37.

Williams, P. J. "Alleged Syriac Catchwords in the Gospel of Thomas." *VC* 63/1 (2009): 71-82.

Wilson, R. McL. *Studies in the Gospel of Thomas*. London: Mowbray, 1960.

Winn, Adam. *The Purpose of Mark's Gospel: An Early Response to Roman Imperial Propaganda*. WUNT 245. Tübingen: Mohr Siebeck, 2008.

Wood, John Halsey, Jr. "The New Testament Gospels and the *Gospel of Thomas*: A New Direction." *NTS* 51 (2005): 579-95.

Wright, N. T. *Jesus and the Victory of God*. Christian Origins and the Question of God 2. London: SPCK, 1996.

Wrong, N. T. "The Relative Unimportance of Oral Culture for Interpreting Biblical Books." The N. T. Wrong Blog, 14 November 2008, http://ntwrong.wordpress.com/2008/11/15/the-relative-unimportance-of-oral-culture-for-interpreting-biblical-books/.

Zöckler, Thomas. *Jesu Lehren im Thomasevangelium*. Nag Hammadi and Manichaean Studies 47. Leiden: Brill, 1999.

Index of Authors

Index of Subjects

Index of Subjects

Papias, 139-40

Parables, 73-80, 87-96, 109-12, 115, 126, 130, 146, 147, 148, 181, 185, 186, 190, 191

Passion narrative, lack of in *Thomas*, 2, 10, 12-13

Pedagogy, 149, 154-55

Peter, 178, 191; connection with Mark, 178

Pistis Sophia, 159n.13

Plagiarist's charter, 36, 38, 45-46, 54-56, 84

Prayer, 95

Protevangelium of James, 134, 175

Protology, 185

Pseudo-Clementines, 69

Ptolemaeus, *Letter to Flora*, 179n.17

Q (hypothetical source), 2, 9-14, 117n.16, 146; analogy with *Thomas*, 9-14, 17, 144n.52, 159-60, 195; scribal error in, 60; singly attested sayings in, 95, 99n.4; literary stratigraphy of, 160; skepticism about, *see* Farrer theory

Redaction criticism, 54, 100, 115, 122, 146, 172-73, 178

Salome, 159

Sayings Gospels, *see* Genre

Scissors and paste, 129, 150

Second Apocalypse of James, 10n.36, 145

Secondary orality, 135-37; in New Testament scholarship, 137-40, 153

Secrecy, 102, 172-92

Singularity, 92, 181, 185

Soliloquy, *see* Interior monologue

Solitary, 182-84, 185

Sophia of Jesus Christ, 10n.36

Special Mark, 21, 78n.42

Spread of traditions, argument from, 20-24, 193

Synopsis, *Thomas* and the Synoptics, lack of, 64-65

Synoptic Problem, vii-viii, 19, 31, 33, 45, 49, 52, 53, 58n.29, 59n.30, 150, 161; ignorance of, 131n.11, 149n.70, 152, 154; modeling Synoptic relations, 58

Tatian's *Diatessaron*, 157n.5

Temple, destruction of, 162-71; in *Thomas*, 95, 167-71

Textual assimilation, 57-63

Thomas (Gospel character), 159, 174, 178-79, 191, 195-96

Thomas, enigmatic nature of, 16, 17, 18, 20, 145, 153, 160, 191, 196; genius of, 192; as "Fifth Gospel," 193-96; as Holy Grail, 195

Tradents, literacy of, 140-42

Trajectories model of Christian origins, 2-3, 86n.20, 127, 159, 195

Triple tradition, 20-24, 45, 82, 86, 96, 115, 146n.63, 193

Two-Source Theory, 9, 19n.56, 53n.13, 67n.4, 67n.5, 152n.80, 161

Verbatim agreement, 26-48, 59-60, 83, 84, 96, 99, 114n.7, 119n.20, 124, 150, 193

Wealth, hostility to, 89, 91, 93, 94; connection with death, 94

Word of God, hearing, 104-7

Words of Jesus, hearing, 12-13, 106-7, 194

Index of Ancient Texts

Printed and bound by CPI Group (UK) Ltd, Croydon, CR0 4YY

13/04/2025

14656472-0004